"In Search of Organs"

"In Search of Organs"

Andrew Freeman: Priest, Photographer, and Scholar

edited by
Katharine Pardee

The British Institute of Organ Studies
2016

BIOS
The British Institute of Organ Studies

Ashcroft,
10 Ridgegate Close,
Reigate
RH2 0HT

www.bios.org.uk

BIOS is a Registered Charity: 283936

The Freeman collection is part of the British Organ Archive, owned by BIOS and housed in the Cadbury Research Library, University of Birmingham.

www.birmingham.ac.uk/facilities/cadbury

"In Search of Organs"
Andrew Freeman: Priest, Photographer, and Scholar

First published 2016

ISBN: 978-0-9955419-0-0

Designed and typeset in Garamond Premier Pro by Julian Littlewood

Printed by Biddles Books Ltd, Norfolk

Contents:

ANDREW

FREEMAN

Preface

On a bright spring afternoon some one hundred years ago, an affable-looking clergyman of middling years pulled up on his bicycle in front of a country church somewhere in England, unloaded his awkward cases, and ventured in. When his eyes had adjusted to the darkened interior, he peered around carefully for a long while, taking in architectural features and details of angles, windows, and light. At last he unpacked his bags, removing his equipment: a large camera, two lenses, tripod, and a small wooden box. Choosing his location carefully, he began setting up. The tripod was first: he perched it on a pew, wedging the legs under the seat to get a firm purchase. Next came the camera: he took it out of its case, unfolded it and screwed it on the tripod head. Which lens should he use – normal or wide angle? This could be a time-consuming decision as he peered at the ground glass screen at the back of the camera, his eyes straining to set focus in the dim light. Finally, the glass plate: using his light-tight 'changing bag', he loaded it carefully into its holder, which he then fitted into the back of the camera. The length of exposure was his last and perhaps most important decision, but fortunately he was helped by tables issued by Kodak, the plate manufacturer. Sometimes he needed to leave the shutter open for only five minutes, but other times the exposure was as long as a half-hour or even more. Deciding that in spite of the bright day, a longer exposure would be necessary in this dark church, our photographer took one last look at his set-up, opened the shutter, put his hat back on, and went out in search of a cup of tea.

Thus might have gone the taking of another in the extraordinary series of photographs of organ cases that now make up the Andrew Freeman photographic collection in the British Organ Archive (BOA). Housed in the Cadbury Research Library of the University of Birmingham, the BOA is a repository of organ building records, manuscripts, journals, and other papers related to (mostly) British organs and organ building. The Freeman collection, which includes not only his photographic plates but also diaries, article proofs, cuttings, and other organ-related miscellanea, represents the core tenets of the British Institute of Organ Studies: recognition of the beauty, significance, and value of the pipe organ, and particularly the British pipe organ. In his study of organs and organ cases, affection for them, and recognition of their aesthetic importance, Freeman himself was one of BIOS' most important forerunners. His precious gifts of observation, documentation and illumination, and his commitment to the aesthetic value of the organ led directly to the foundation and scholarly aims of BIOS.

Fitting, then, that this book has been assembled with the fortieth anniversary of BIOS (2016) in mind. As the work of BIOS over the years has moved increasingly toward playing an advisory role in the preservation of pipe organs, the photographs and writings of Andrew Freeman confirm the importance of this work, providing a window on the past and allowing us to celebrate what we still have and mourn what has been lost. As a purely utilitarian tool, the photographs have been invaluable in recent restorations of organs, where injudicious and inappropriate alterations have been reversed. At St James, Clerkenwell (1792) for example, the 1912 Freeman photograph (Freeman/282 in the CRL) was of great help in reversing a later crude enlargement, during the fine restoration of 1978. At St Andrew, Shifnal (1811), with its gentle gothick mahogany case, Freeman's 1938 image (Freeman/1250) records a location within the transept (to which it was sent from the west gallery), but with the inappropriate swell box that a previous generation thought necessary, now removed. His photographic labours alone represent a nationally important collection of many choice instruments at the end of the nineteenth and the first half of the twentieth century.

The Freeman photographic archive contains more than 1,400 glass plate negatives. The approximately 250 images in this book were chosen to display a wide range of organ cases from across the country and other parts of Europe, as well as a range of sizes from the smallest to the largest; from organs in halls to churches to school-rooms to homes; from ideal photographic conditions to very difficult; from designs that Freeman regarded as exemplary to designs that he would have condemned as appalling (though he rarely spoke in such strong terms; nevertheless, he often made his views clear). A special effort has been made to include instruments destroyed in the second World War. When possible, Freeman's comments are included in the captions. These comments are drawn from his articles in *Musical Opinion* and *The Organ*, as well as from his published books; but some are drawn directly from his diaries and original sketch-books. (It should be mentioned here that a complete bibliography of Freeman's published writings would take a volume of its own, and would place it well outside the scope of this project). It is hoped that the reader will enjoy assessing the pictures which do not have captions as well, since reading what Freeman has written about organ case design is a fascinating education in what to look for when walking into a church for the first time and viewing the entire space and the organ case within it: what might Freeman have thought, for example, of Plate 80, St Mark's, Swindon? Or what might he have said about the way the two nearly identical organ cases in Plate 92 and Plate 234 (St Rose's Convent, Stroud and St George, King Stanley) fit into their two respective churches?

In perusing the plates and reading the journals, the reader cannot help but ask who Freeman had in mind as recipients of his compiled material. Freeman gives us some insight into the question himself, in a note in *The Organ*: 'I took up photography just over forty years ago, chiefly that I might photograph noteworthy organ cases. Organ pictures were then difficult to obtain unless one took them oneself; and I often cycled eighty or a hundred miles in order to photograph some organ I had never seen but which I had heard or read about as possessing a "case". The fruits of many journeyings and no little toil gave pleasure to a small group of friends as well as to myself; and it is a real satisfaction to find that the privilege of having many of my efforts reproduced in the pages of *The Organ* and *Musical Opinion* has been the means of affording a similar pleasure to a much larger circle.'[1]

Freeman's largely unsung concern for the study, careful thought and preservation of historic

Parkend Church, Gloucestershire (BOA, Freeman Collection, Box 83, SBN 9)
Freeman's photograph of this organ can be seen at Plate 127, p.197

1 *The Organ* 15, no. 59 (Jan. 1936): 166 n. 1.

instruments, places him in the pantheon of industry with giants such as Nikolaus Pevsner, Howard Colvin and other British architectural historians. He had a passion for good design and the importance of preserving it from past times, even while adapting it for the future. He would feel at home in this digital age, with note-taking, editing and storage that does not occupy shelf-space, allied to tailored data-bases, easy indexing, cross referencing, instant searches and links to digitised documents. We would do well to ensure that our work matches his standards and be thankful for his often-lonely mission to demand improvement to the quality of British organ-case design.

In reproducing a small number of his photographs and drawings here, one can hope that visitors to churches both in Britain and on the continent do not fail to notice the organ, which as Freeman pointed out in his annotated Austrian tourist guide (Gedye, *A Wayfarer in Austria*; see Chapter 5), are 'amongst the finest of the fittings' in a church, and also that the organ case is never again dismissed as an unnecessary expense. In one of his last contributions to *The Organ*, Freeman wrote:

> 'Let us treasure and preserve intact those [cases] that remain until this utilitarian age be overpast. If we insist on looking at organs as well as listening to them, even the ashes of those that have perished may be renewed unto beauty.'[2]

The five initial chapters in this book attempt to provide a context for the photographs. Chapter One explores Freeman's life and activities as far as they can be known (Nicholas Thistlethwaite); Chapter Two discusses the noble and long-lived history of organ description and documentation, beginning with the earliest continental examples by Virdung in 1511 and stretching up through the nineteenth century in Britain (Christopher Kent); Chapter Three provides an assessment of Freeman as a critic and designer of organ cases, and his activities as a consultant and writer (James Berrow); Chapter Four describes photographic techniques and equipment in Freeman's day (Andrew Hayden); and Chapter Five provides an overview of his journals from his six trips to the continent in the period around the second World War (Katharine Pardee).

Nicholas Thistlethwaite is a former Chairman of the British Institute of Organ Studies. He is author of *The Making of the Victorian Organ* (1990) and co-editor of *The Cambridge Companion to the Organ* (1999) besides many other monographs, articles and reviews relating to the organ and church music. As an organ consultant he has advised on a number of major projects in England including Birmingham Town Hall, Eton College Chapel, St John's College, Cambridge, Buckingham Palace, St Edmundsbury Cathedral and Christ Church, Spitalfields; he served on the Cathedrals Fabric Commission for England, and is currently a member of advisory bodies at Westminster Abbey, Canterbury Cathedral and Norwich Cathedral.

Christopher Kent, a founder member and former Secretary of BIOS, read music at The University of Manchester and musicology at King's College London. After completing a Ph.D. on Elgar's sketches he continued organ and harpsichord studies with Susi Jeans and Gustav Leonhardt, eventually joining the Department of Music at The University of Reading, where he established a postgraduate course in Organ Historiography. His publications include chapters in the *Cambridge Composer Guide to Elgar*, 'The Organ' in the *Cambridge Musical Instrument Guides* and articles for *The New Grove Dictionary of Music and Musicians, Die Musik in Geschichte und Gegenwart* and *The New Dictionary of National Biography*. In 2015 he received the C. B. Oldman Prize of the I.A.M.L. for his 'Elgar Thematic Catalogue and Research Guide.'

Dr James Berrow was an executive producer of music, arts and religious programmes with a major broadcaster, producing programmes for ITV, Channel 4, US PBS, Polyphon/WDR Cologne and the Arts Council. After retirement he became an independent researcher and has been involved in music, architectural history and conservation matters. He was the third Secretary of BIOS and now advises the Dioceses of Lichfield and Birmingham on historic pipe organ issues and is a member of Chester Cathedral's Fabric Advisory

2 *The Organ* 26, no. 103 (Jan. 1947): 128.

Committee. He is also an Honorary Research Fellow in the University of Birmingham and a Fellow of the Royal Historical Society.

ANDREW HAYDEN studied Music with Applied Physics at Surrey University, during which time he studied organ with Richard Hickox and Robert Munns. He subsequently spent some years in sound engineering in Germany and as a postgraduate researcher, documenting the history of radio drama recording technique at Hessischer Rundfunk, Frankfurt. He contributes historical feature articles to *The Organ* and *Choir & Organ* magazines, and collaborated on the BIOS East Anglian Historic Organ Sound Archive project. He is currently working on a history of the organs and organists of Great Yarmouth Parish Church. A keen photographer, he originates the 'Star Organs of Britain' photo archive. He has served as co-editor of the *Reporter*, the BIOS newsletter, and is currently Casework Officer.

KATHARINE PARDEE, Publications Officer for BIOS, is Betts Fellow in Organ Studies, Lecturer in Music at Corpus Christi College, and Director of Chapel Music at Wadham College, University of Oxford. She earned master's and doctoral degrees in organ performance and literature at the Eastman School, and a DPhil in musicology from Oxford. Before moving to England in 2001, she served on the music faculties of Syracuse University and the Eastman School of Music. Active as a teacher and performer, she has performed widely in the United States and in Europe, and has recorded twice on the Pro Organo label.

~

Thanks are due to many people in the assembling of this book: First, to the Cadbury Research Library and its staff, for their unending help, expertise, and generosity in making the Collection available to visitors in such comfortable and helpful surroundings. Second, but no less important, thanks must go to Chris Kearl, archivist, whose careful curation of the British Organ Archive and the Freeman collection is of inestimable value to a volunteer-run society such as BIOS. Together with David Wickens, they have helped organise and catalogue the Freeman collection, and made the initial selection of photographs for this volume. Third, again equally important, thanks must go to the family of Andrew Freeman, whose grandsons graciously assented to this book and provided material for it. Finally, in addition to the other contributors to this volume, special thanks are due to Nicholas Thistlethwaite and James Berrow, who have helped immeasurably and continually with details and decisions both minute and monumental.

Katharine Pardee
Oxford, 2016

Opposite:
Wadham College, Oxford (1908)
Freeman/104; plate 244

Case designed by T. G. Jackson: 'A very successful example of a flat front.' (Freeman, *English Organ Cases*, (London: Geo. Aug. Mate & Son, 1921), 73).
Note the 'ghost' under the case.

Notes on the text:

Freeman numbers and Plate numbers under the organ illustrations refer to the identification numbers given by the Cadbury Research Library.

All the plates can be found online in the Special Collections section of the CRL website: calmview.bham.ac.uk

More information can be found about many of the British organs listed in this book from the National Pipe Organ Register of BIOS: npor.org.uk

Andrew Freeman with grandson Peter Freeman (1937–2006)

Freeman's daughter Greta and son Denys

ANDREW FREEMAN

'a record of remarkable achievement and work well done'

Andrew James Freeman was born in Newbury, Berkshire on 27 March 1876. His father, Benson Fletcher Freeman (1847–1916), was in business in the town, and also served as a rate-collector and overseer. In politics he was a Liberal, and in religion, a Wesleyan Methodist. An obituary paid tribute to his lifelong commitment to his chapel: he had held 'almost every office open to a layman'.[1] More significantly for his son's creative development, 'the services of Mr. Benson Freeman and his family in musical matters connected with the church had been an outstanding feature for many years'.[2]

There were four other surviving children: Benson, Blanche, Sarah ('Daisy') and Margaret. Their mother, Sarah Anne Joyce, had been born in Faccombe, Hampshire, a few miles outside Newbury. The family mounted 'Penny' and 'Two-penny' concerts for the entertainment of their fellow-townspeople – perhaps to promote the temperance movement – but they were also the mainstay of the chapel music. The services were accompanied on a small organ supplied in 1861 by T. Hughes & Co. of Albany Street, London [see illustration below left and Plate 1, p.71] and it is likely that this was the instrument on which Andrew Freeman learned the rudiments of organ technique.[3]

Manual (C–f^3)	
Open Diapason	8
Stopped Diapason Bass, C–B8 (enclosed)	
Claribel, c	8
Dulciana, c	8 (enclosed)
Principal	4
Flute	4
Fifteenth	2
Sesquialtera	III

Pedal (C–c^1)	
Bourdon	16

Great to Pedal
3 composition pedals

Freeman later claimed to have served as the chapel organist between 1892 and 1900. This cannot have been strictly true because his education took him away from Newbury for some of this period, but it can be taken as confirmation that by the age of fifteen or sixteen he was a competent player.

Left: Wesleyan Church, Newbury, Berkshire
Freeman/9; plate 62 (1897)
A different photograph of this organ is at Plate 1, p.71.

1 *Reading Mercury*, 9 September 1916, 6.
2 Obituary of Benson Freeman; unidentified newspaper cutting in possession of Richard Freeman.
3 National Pipe Organ Register (www.npor.org.uk), N09894.

Freeman's childhood home with pedal piano in Newbury.

As a youngster, his life would have revolved around the Wesleyan Chapel and music-making at home: musical scores now in the possession of his grandchildren are evidence that he was developing his piano repertoire, and he also learned to play the double bass.

It is possible that Andrew Freeman attended the local grammar school (St Bartholomew's Boys' Grammar School, founded 1466), but what is certain is that in 1893 he went up to Cambridge University. He did not, however, become a member of one of the older colleges. In 1869, the University had established a non-collegiate students board for undergraduates from less privileged backgrounds; they lived in lodgings around the town, but by 1874 had a quasi-collegiate base in a house in Trumpington Street, opposite the Fitzwilliam Museum; in Freeman's day, this was known as 'Fitzwilliam Hall'.[4] Economy may not have been the only reason for Freeman's father choosing non-collegiate status. As a good Wesleyan, he was perhaps anxious about entrusting his son to one of the older colleges, most of which were still strongly Anglican in character. Yet there can be little doubt that Cambridge enlarged Andrew Freeman's horizons in a number of ways. For someone with a burgeoning interest in organs, the college chapels and town churches had much to offer. Although for the time being he remained loyal to his Methodist upbringing, it was probably in Cambridge that Freeman first experienced the choral service of the Church of England in the hands of some of its leading practitioners. Alan Gray (1855–1935) had just succeeded Stanford as Organist of Trinity College; George Mursell Garrett (1834–97), a former pupil of S. S. Wesley, was Organist of St John's College. Meanwhile at King's College [see Plate 28, p.98] Dr Arthur Henry Mann (1850–1929) had created a choir that was already renowned as one of the finest in England. Years later, Freeman paid tribute to Mann's skill in accompanying the King's choir in the psalms:

> For surely no one except Dr. Mann – and he nowhere, probably, save in King's – has that wonderful art of adding beauty to a thing already beautiful and conveying the effect of atmosphere by a pencil-line of tone that seems "just right." Those who have memories of the Twenty-eighth evening of the month, with *By the waters of Babylon* sung to a plaintive chant of Dr. Garrett, will not easily forget the way a few notes, now of the orchestral oboe and now of the 16ft cormorne, floated in and hovered for a moment before melting away into thin air; while the pedal, felt rather than heard, moved on like that great river, the Euphrates ...[5]

Although written in the 1920s, Freeman's words convey clearly the impression that Mann's psalm accompaniments had made on him in the 1890s, and provide testimony to the hold that the instrument already exerted over his imagination.

He graduated in 1896 as a Bachelor of Arts and returned to Newbury, presumably to resume his post at the Wesleyan Chapel. According to B. B. Edmonds, he had considered becoming an organ-builder, but nothing came of this, and for the next nineteen years, he was to describe himself as 'Organist and Teacher of Music'.[6] He continued to

King's College Chapel, Cambridge
see Plate 28, p.98

4 *A History of the County of Cambridge and the Isle of Ely*: vol. 3, *The City and University of Cambridge* (London: Victoria County History, 1959), 497–9; the author is grateful to James Berrow for this reference.

5 Andrew Freeman, 'The Organs at King's College, Cambridge', *The Organ* 8, no. 31 (January 1929): 137.

6 B.B.Edmonds, 'Andrew Freeman', *BIOS Reporter* 3, no. 3 (1979): 13. Freeman described his occupation as 'Organist and Teacher of Music' in the census returns of 1901 (Newbury) and 1911 (Streatham).

participate in musical performances in Newbury, acting, for example, as organ accompanist for the Choral Society in Mackenzie's *The Rose of Sharon* at the Town Hall in 1899, and he was still appearing as a member of the Newbury Amateur Orchestral Union as late as the 1905–6 season, playing double bass. The musical resources of the Wesleyan Chapel improved significantly in 1898 when a two-manual organ by Alfred Hunter and Son of Clapham, with tubular-pneumatic action and twenty-five stops, replaced the Hughes instrument [see Plate 12, p.82]. Freeman may have had a voice in its tonal design, and it may also have been on his initiative that part of the case front and several ranks of pipes were retained from the old organ.[7]

Wesleyan Chapel
see Plate 12, p.82

Inevitably, he had begun to form friendships with other enthusiasts. One of the earliest was Sidney W. Harvey (1873–1944). They met by chance in the organ loft at the Crystal Palace in 1891 when both had been taking part in a choral performance, and 'a few words sufficed to show that we had much the same interest in organs'.[8] Harvey was a native of Canterbury and a great admirer of the Willis organ in the Cathedral there; he was also an avid collector of organ specifications. A letter of 1897 reveals that he and Freeman were in the habit of sending one another details of the instruments they had visited and also copies of organ photographs.[9] There were similar friendships with others, among them Ernest Adcock from Norwich and Henry T. Lilley, who drew many illustrations of organ cases for Freeman's organ publications.

Freeman was about fifteen years old when he met Harvey. Many years later, he confirmed that he was already visiting churches to seek out organs:

> Although the organ is not always the first thing one sees on entering a church, it is one of the first things I look for when I go inside an unfamiliar building. That is the outcome of a habit that was begun in schooldays and has persisted ever since. One of the pleasures of a visit to a new neighbourhood, then as now, was the opportunity it afforded of seeing fresh organs. The possession of a bicycle extended the radius of one's explorations considerably; and the delight of a cycle trip was always fuller when it included the sight of a fresh instrument, especially if its specification could be captured and included in an ever-growing collection.[10]

During the 1890s, Freeman laid the foundations of the collection of organ materials which was eventually to blossom into the voluminous archive now in Birmingham. Initially, the process was fairly random, but he rapidly brought to it his formidable powers of organisation and a preoccupation (verging on the obsessive) with detail. The two main series of note-books did not commence until 1906 and 1909.[11] They include lengthy transcriptions from books and articles about organs (British and foreign), stop-lists, drawings of cases, and comprehensive indexes. The detail is astonishing: Freeman carefully recorded the stop layout of the console, and often the combination settings of the organs he visited; many of the entries also include a sketch of the organ front or at least a note of the pipe arrangement. However, he seldom passed critical comment: 'a fine instrument' (Cirencester Parish Church, visited in 1908 and 1931) is unusually forthcoming.[12] Then there are the scrap-books into which he pasted methodically cuttings of his published articles – sometimes with later corrections – and another series with illustrations collected from a variety of printed sources. Yet more note-books included transcriptions from the Public Record Office and British Library

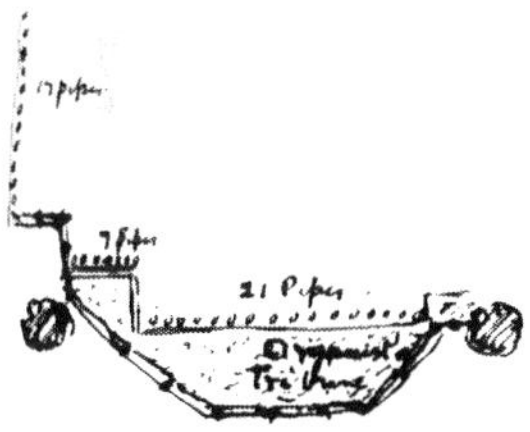

Diagram of case front, from SBN vol. 2, 241.

7 National Pipe Organ Register (www.npor.org.uk), N09895.

8 Andrew Freeman, 'Sidney William Harvey', *The Organ* 24, no. 95 (January 1945): 144.

9 BOA, Freeman Collection, Box 092; S.W.Harvey to Andrew Freeman, 20 May 1897. Sidney Harvey was one of the founders and first secretary of the Organ Club (1926); although he and Freeman continued to be friends and correspondents until Harvey's death, Freeman appears not to have been involved with the Organ Club which, in its early years, was held somewhat in thrall by Henry Willis III. (I am grateful to Colin Menzies for this insight.)

10 Andrew Freeman, 'Some Gothic Organ Cases of a Hundred Years Ago', *The Organ* 18, no. 69 (July 1938): 39.

11 'Small Black Notebooks', 14 vols. with 2384 organ specifications, commenced 1906 (BOA, Box 83/0672); 'Blue Notebooks', 16 vols, including transcriptions and specifications, commenced 1909 (BOA, Box 81/0602).

12 BOA, Freeman collection, Box 8300673. SBN 1, p.128, spec. number 86.

which Freeman used as a source for his 'Records of British Organ Builders' series.[13]

Unlike earlier organ collectors, such as Leffler or Sperling, Freeman was able to photograph the instruments he visited. How he acquired the skill is not known. The earliest surviving negative dates from 1897: it is the one showing the Hughes organ in Newbury Wesleyan Chapel [see Plate 1, p.71]. Already, Freeman had gained a creditable technique. Over the next fifty years, he created the unique photographic archive that now resides at Birmingham. According to Bernard Edmonds who came to know him during the 1930s, Freeman was 'very modest' about his photography; he once told Edmonds that with a single exception ('a charming Swiss view') he had only ever photographed organs.[14] This cannot have been entirely true because he certainly took family photographs, some of which survive, but otherwise his photographic activities seem to have been almost exclusively devoted to recording organs.

13 The hand-list of the Freeman Collection in the British Organ Archive can be consulted via www.bios.org.uk (resources/Andrew Freeman Photographic Collection).
14 B.B.Edmonds, Letter to the Editor, *The Organ* 27, no. 108 (April 1948): 185.

Ethel Freeman at the console, with Sam Harris, Sacristan or Verger at the organ of St Nicholas, Standish.
Freeman/1354; plate 1627

By 1900, organs had become an absorbing pastime for Freeman, but they had also to serve as the means of earning a living. During the time that he held posts at Congregational chapels in Guildford (1900–1902) and Newbury (1903–1909), Freeman applied himself to acquire additional qualifications: he graduated as a Bachelor of Music at Cambridge in 1903 and as a Fellow of the Royal College of Organists in 1905. He found time to act as an occasional assistant to Dr George Huntley on the Lewis organ at St Peter's, Eaton Square, London, and gave a series of recitals at St Clement Danes in the Strand [see Plate 36, p.106].[15] Freeman also began to contribute articles and reviews to musical journals, sometimes using a nom de plume. One of his earliest was a letter in *Musical Opinion* in November 1897 concerning organs in Cambridge, signed 'Lethe';[16] he was to publish occasional pieces and regular series of articles in this journal for the rest of his life. The *Musical Times* also included pieces by Freeman from time to time: one of the earliest was probably, 'Some notes on former organs at St George's Chapel, Windsor', in June 1910.[17]

On 4 August 1904, Andrew Freeman and Ethel Mary Male were married at Hills Road Wesleyan Church, Cambridge. Perhaps they met through the chapel when Freeman was an undergraduate. As an organist and freelance music teacher, his uncertain prospects may have left them no alternative to a long courtship. A family tradition claims that they met first 'on the organ stool'; Ethel was herself an organist and was described in the 1901 Census as a 'Teacher of Music'; in later years she played for the services at Standish when Freeman was Vicar [see illustration left]. There were to be two surviving children of the marriage: Margaret ('Greta') and Denys, born respectively in 1907 and 1909; a third child, Harold, lived only a few days.

Family responsibilities may have encouraged Freeman to strike out in a new direction. Leaving Newbury and Wesleyan Methodism behind, he moved in 1909 to South London to become

15 Edmonds, 'Andrew Freeman', 13.
16 *Musical Opinion* 21, no. 242 (November 1897): 95.
17 *Musical Times* 51, no. 809 (June 1910): 379–80.

organist of Immanuel Church, Streatham. This was an Anglican parish church with a 3-manual Hill organ of 1865, slightly modified in 1890; a correspondent in *The Organ* later recalled Freeman's 'great ability', and his 'splendid performance ... at one of the Streatham Church Choir Festivals'.[18] The Freemans lived at 57 Buckleigh Road, Streatham. This meant that he could take advantage of the proximity of the British Museum and the Public Record Office to pursue his researches, but it must have been a precarious existence.

Whether it was cause or effect is not known, but Freeman's move to employment in the Church of England seems to have coincided with a change of religious affiliation. He became an Anglican (as presumably did his wife). In due course, he felt a call to ordination and was accepted for training; in 1915, he was made deacon in Southwark Cathedral with a title (curacy) at St Margaret's, Lee. Ordination to the priesthood followed in 1916.

At the age of thirty-nine, Freeman was a mature ordinand for those days. The impact of the change of routine on his family must have been considerable. Curates were expected to study and prepare sermons in the mornings, visit parishioners in the afternoons and attend meetings of church groups in the evenings, as well as being present at the daily services and officiating at the numerous baptisms, weddings and funerals demanded by a busy parish. For Freeman, there would have been less time for trips to the British Museum.

In 1918, he moved to a second curacy at St Mary's, Lambeth, the ancient parish church that stands beside the Archbishop's Palace. The population of nearly ten thousand included many who lived in abject poverty, and the Rector and three curates must have had their work cut out providing pastoral support and practical relief. Freeman's particular duties included a ministry as 'priest-organist'; it is not clear what this entailed, but he certainly played the organ for some services. After his death, a correspondent in *Musical Opinion* wrote,

18 E.G.Osborn, letter to the editor, *The Organ* 27, no. 107 (January 1948): 141–2.

> my mind goes back to 1922, the days when St Mary's had a mighty evensong congregation and dear old Rev. Andrew [Freeman] used to be worked to death reading absolution, moving quickly to the console to play on the old tracker and two octaves of pedals, back for the first lesson, another race back to the console, Magnificat, another race for second lesson and Nunc Dimittis. I closed my eyes and ears to the lesson but no living person with a soul could close his ears to the Rev. Andrew's magnificent playing ...

St Mary's, Lambeth
see Plate 40, p.110

(Presumably the other clergy were engaged in duties elsewhere.) The organ had been built originally by Renatus Harris (1701); some pipework survived, but the three-tower case had been emasculated when the instrument was moved from the west gallery to the north side of the chancel during the nineteenth century [see Plate 40, p.110]. J. W. Walker & Sons had undertaken work in 1852 and 1879, and the console at which Freeman presided was much as they had left it. With its old-fashioned mechanical key and stop actions, it must have been a somewhat intractable instrument.

The console of St Mary's, Lambeth in 1923, about the time Freeman moved to Standish.
Freeman/542; plate 788

Amidst his parochial duties Freeman still found time for writing and research. Harvey and Lilley were both in London, and they were involved, with him, in an important initiative in 1921 when it was decided to launch a new journal devoted entirely to the organ. The first issue of *The Organ, a quarterly review for its makers, its players & its lovers* appeared in July of that year. It included six articles, of which Freeman and Ernest Adcock each contributed two. Freeman's opening article, 'The organs and organists of St Martin-in-the-Fields', established the pattern for his many contributions over the next twenty-six years; eventually, they numbered around one hundred-and-twenty, and hardly an issue appeared without a piece by Freeman. His role was critical; as Dr W. L. Sumner noted in an obituary, 'it is no secret that but for him *The Organ* would not have been published when it was, if ever'.[19] It was all the more remarkable that, in the same year that *The Organ* saw the light of day, Freeman's book, *English Organ-Cases*, was published.[20] Although based on an article he had written for *The Dictionary of Organs and Organists* in 1912, it represented a substantial and original piece of work, illustrated with Freeman's own photographs and drawings by Lilley.

Working as a priest in Lambeth must have been demanding in the years immediately following the Great War, with men returning from the Front and families having to adjust; in any case, after two curacies, Freeman could reasonably expect a living of his own. He expressed an interest in a minor canonry (probably the one linked to the post of precentor) at Bristol Cathedral in 1921, writing confidentially to the organist Hubert Hunt (1865–1945) for advice; Hunt told him that there were thirty-five candidates and Freeman seems not to have pursued the matter.[21] Then, on 14 April 1923, it was announced that the King had approved the appointment of the Reverend Andrew James Freeman, 'curate of St Mary Lambeth', to the vicarage of Standish-with-Hardwicke in Gloucestershire.[22]

The circumstances of Freeman's preferment are obscure. The family tradition is that he was found the living by Archbishop Randall Davidson whom he had come to know during his years in Lambeth. On the face of it, this seems improbable because the right of presentation belonged to the Bishop of Gloucester. However, in April 1923 there was an episcopal interregnum at Gloucester, and in those days patronage reverted to the Crown during a vacancy. Perhaps this gave Davidson an opportunity to pull some strings. Whatever the truth of the matter, the newly-enthroned Bishop of Gloucester, Dr A. C. Headlam, instituted Freeman as Vicar of Standish-with-Hardwicke on 19 July.[23]

Standish is some six miles south of Gloucester. To the east is the Cotswold escarpment and to the west Hardwicke and the main road to Bristol. The two settlements had been linked for ecclesiastical purposes since at least the twelfth century: Hardwicke was technically a chapel-of-ease and still, throughout Freeman's incumbency, had its own curate-in-charge. As Standish's population in 1921 was 353 and Hardwicke's 575, the vicar was in the fortunate position of being able to pursue scholarly interests without being guilty of neglecting his parochial duties. The income was fairly modest – £470 per annum: probably not very different from the national minimum stipend for an incumbent today – but there was a fine vicarage at Little Haresfield dating back in part to the fourteenth century, albeit (in 1923) without the benefit of electricity, and relying on a pump to draw water from a well.[24] Both churches were mediaeval (although Hardwicke had been substantially altered in the nineteenth century), and there were manor houses in both settlements – Standish Court, and Hardwicke Court with its park bordering the Bristol road.

Freeman's predecessor, Canon Alexander Nash, had served as vicar for thirty-three years (1889–

19 W.L.Sumner, 'Andrew Freeman: an Appreciation', *The Organ* 27, no. 105 (July 1947): 3.
20 Andrew Freeman, *English Organ-Cases* (London: G.A.Mate & Son, 1921).
21 Hubert W. Hunt to the Rev'd Andrew Freeman, 13 July 1921; BOA, Freeman Collection, Box 092.
22 *Gloucester Journal*, 14 April 1923, 1.
23 Ibid., 21 July 1923, 12.
24 C.R.Elrington and N.M.Herbert (eds), *Victoria History of the Counties of England: Gloucestershire*, vol. 10 (Institute of Historical Research, 1972), 187, 230–40. *Crockford's Clerical Directory* (London: Oxford University Press, 1940), 472.

1923) and for a further eight years as curate before that (1868–76). His retirement was hastened by a bicycle accident from which 'he had never fully recovered'; Freeman conducted his funeral in September 1924.[25]

Nash seems to have been a much-loved and conscientious parish priest but there was work waiting to be done. In 1927, some £300 was spent on the restoration of the tower at Hardwicke; a similar sum was raised to re-hang the bells and augment the ring with a new one.[26] Electric light and a new heating system were installed at Standish around the same time, and in 1935, substantial repairs to the tower were completed in time for the bells to be rung to celebrate the King's Golden Jubilee; 'cider, beer, perry or lemonade' were served from a wagon in the churchyard, and Mrs Freeman and forty ladies provided tea for two hundred and fifty people in the school room.[27]

For other works, Freeman turned to a young architect whose maternal grandfather, Archdeacon Sheringham, had been Vicar of Standish in the 1860s. The dating of the improvements is problematic, but Stephen Dykes Bower (1903–94) designed a high altar and lych-gate for Standish;[28] he also designed an organ case for Hardwicke (1938), and another for Standish (c.1940), which, however, was only installed after the war as a memorial to Freeman (1950). The creative relationship between the two men is further explored below in Chapter 3.

The usual round of parish activities – sales of work ('in the spacious grounds of the vicarage'),[29] national thanksgivings, summer fetes, harvest festivals, weekly choir rehearsals (Standish had a surpliced choir), Girls' Friendly Society exhibitions, a rummage sale ('the splendid result was due in the main to the untiring and energetic work put in by the Vicar'),[30] weddings and funerals – must have occupied much of Freeman's working day. He would also have played his part in the rural deanery and diocese, amongst other responsibilities serving on the Diocesan Advisory Committee for the Care of Churches, newly established following the recommendations of the Dibdin Committee.[31]

Meanwhile, Freeman's collection of organ materials continued to grow. His move to Gloucestershire opened up a new field of enquiry, and the organ stop-lists and photographs reveal him exploring the Cotswolds, Wiltshire and Somerset, as well as towns such as Cheltenham, Tewkesbury and the city of Gloucester. During his early years in Standish most of these journeys were

25 *Gloucester Journal*, 6 September 1924, 17.
26 Ibid., 22 October 1927, 23.
27 Ibid., 11 May 1935, 17.
28 David Verey and Alan Brooks (eds.), *The Buildings of England – Gloucestershire 2: The Vale and the Forest of Dean* (Yale University Press, 3rd ed. 2002), 682; Anthony Symondson, *Stephen Dykes Bower* (London: RIBA Publishing, 2011), 7, 9. Verey and Brooks give 1930 and 1932 as the dates of the altar and gate respectively; Symondson gives both as 1935.
29 *Gloucester Journal*, 22 June 1935, 6.
30 Ibid., 19 October 1935, 6.

31 Donald Findlay, *The Protection of our English Churches* (London: Council for the Care of Churches, 1996), 8–12.

Drawing of the Standish case; cf. photo on p.31.
Freeman/1356, plate 1629

probably made by bicycle or public transport – no mean feat when weighty photographic equipment had to be transported – so the proximity of railway stations at Standish Junction and Stonehouse, with connections to Swindon, Bristol and Birmingham must have been a boon. Back in the vicarage, the work of making fair copies, cataloguing, cross-referencing, developing, printing and mounting was carried on, often (surely) into the early hours of the morning. Freeman also compiled scrap-books in simple bindings of his own making in which he arranged categories of materials. Some contained cuttings of his own published articles from *Musical Opinion* and *The Organ*; others were devoted to notes on the work of particular organ-builders or accounts of organs in particular places; yet others were compilations of photographs illustrating a specific theme – consoles, cases, or a companion to the stop-lists in Hopkins & Rimbault.[32] Freeman's application to the task is little short of astonishing. At the same time, he was producing a steady stream of articles for publication, and, in 1926 another book: *Father Smith, otherwise Bernard Schmidt, being an account of a seventeenth century organ maker.*[33] It was the earliest substantial publication devoted to the work of a single English organ-builder, and the prologue was contributed by M. R. James, who was then Provost of Eton.

There was a new development in 1927 when the Freemans made the first of several summer trips to the continent. They travelled by train and bicycle, and Freeman's exhaustive research ensured that the itinerary was arranged around visits to historic French organs. (What his family thought of this is not recorded.) These were photographed and in due course accompanied published accounts of the instruments (it is probably needless to add that Freeman produced his own bound and illustrated record of the journey). The foreign tours are described in greater detail below. In July 1933, a car ('Matilda Freeman') was acquired, and after this the journeys became more adventurous and, presumably, more comfortable for all concerned.

Detail of pipe mouth,
from SBN 10
(BOA, Freeman Collection, Box 83)

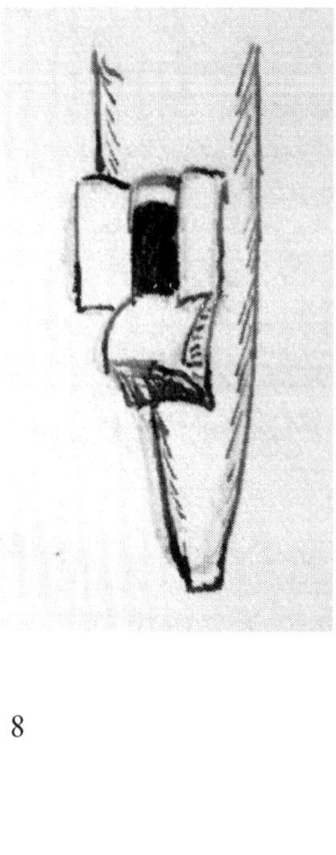

32 E.J.Hopkins and E.F.Rimbault, *The Organ, its History and Construction* (London, (i) 1855, (ii) 1870, (iii) 1877).

33 Andrew Freeman, *Father Smith, otherwise Bernard Schmidt, being an Account of a Seventeenth Century Organ Maker* (London: Musical Opinion, 1926).

Characteristically, Freeman maintained a log book in which he recorded details of every outing, including the destination, route, exact mileage, and (sometimes) the passengers and purpose of the journey. By January 1937, when Freeman parted with her, 'Matilda' had clocked up 49,610 miles.

Freeman seldom said much about the tonal design of organs in his writings, though as a more than competent player he must have had his views. As a member of the Gloucester Diocesan Advisory Committee, he would have been called upon to advise parishes on organ work. If his reconstructions of the organs at Chalford (1926) and Hardwicke (1938) are anything to go by, his priority was to provide a chorus on the Great to accompany the congregation and a Swell with a selection of strings, diapasons and reeds to offer colour and varying dynamics. The two stop-lists are very similar. Hardwicke (rebuilt by Percy Daniel and Co.) was as follows.[34]

Great Organ (C–g^3)	
Open Diapason	8
Stopped Diapason	8
Dulciana	8
Principal	4
Flute	4
Fifteenth	2 *

Swell Organ (C–g^3)	
Lieblich Bourdon	16 †
Open Diapason	8
Echo Dulciana	8 *
Vox Angelica (c)	8 *
Principal	4
Nazard	2⅔*
Tierce	1⅗*
Oboe	8

Pedal Organ (C–f^1)	
Bourdon	16
Echo Bass (Swell)	16 *
Flute (extension)	8 *

3 couplers
2 composition pedals

* *new* † *adapted*

The wind pressure was lowered to 2½ inches.

34 Andrew Freeman, 'The Organs at Standish and Hardwicke, Gloucestershire', *The Organ* 19 (July 1939): 33–6.

The design was mildly forward-looking (as was the accompanying reordering, which included the removal of the organ and choir from the small chancel area to the west end), and its introduction of mutations and a 2' stop on the Great reflected changes of emphasis that can be found elsewhere at the period. Stephen Dykes Bower's new case front ensured that the instrument made an architectural as well as a musical contribution to the church interior [see p.11]. Freeman later summarised his views on the placing of organs and the design of organ cases in a practical little booklet published by SPCK in 1942, *Church organs and organ cases*.[35] Much of his advice remains relevant today for those considering the re-ordering of churches and the appearance of the organ.

By the end of the 1930s, Freeman was in occasional correspondence with the next generation of organ writers. As a young man he had corresponded with writers and musicians who were his elders: J. H. Burn, C. W. Pearce and A. H. Mann; now letters were exchanged with W. L. Sumner (1904–73) – who had contributed articles to *The Organ* in the mid-1930s on organs in Germany, Holland and France, and on the organ-builders Schnitger and Silbermann – and Cecil Clutton (1909–91) – who wrote to Freeman in 1939 about relocating the Renatus Harris organ from All Hallows, Lombard Street to Twickenham, and extolling the virtues of mechanical action, low wind-pressures and classical casework. Then there was Bernard Edmonds (1910–2003), like Freeman an Anglican priest and photographer with an interest in organs, who would inherit his mantle. He also corresponded with organ-builders. Jess Davison tried (unsuccessfully) to persuade Freeman to become her business partner in Gray & Davison (1924), Arthur Harrison wrote to him several times in 1926 about old organs in Abingdon and Jesus College, Cambridge, and in 1935 Roger Yates consulted Freeman about a Snetzler organ that he had restored for Arnold Dolmetsch at Haslemere.[36]

The war years brought the same privations to Standish and Hardwicke as were experienced by countless rural communities up and down the country. Freeman, the conscientious parish priest, would have had many calls on his time and played a key role in the local war effort. More controversially, he also found himself engaged in a battle with the Royal Air Force. A nearby airfield had been extended and brought into service as 'RAF Moreton Valence'. The decree went forth that any structures that might endanger the planes should be reduced in height, and a request was made for the demolition of the mediaeval stone spire of St Nicholas, Standish. Freeman took great exception this, and was fortunately able to enlist the assistance of his son, Denys, who was Principal Private Secretary to Sir Archibald Sinclair, the Secretary of State for Air. Possibly to the bemusement of the RAF, the spire survived.

Freeman experienced a personal loss in June 1943 when his wife died; they had been married almost thirty-nine years.[37] He himself now faced problems with his health; a prolonged illness had left him with a weakened heart, and although he continued to visit churches and organs, and even resumed his continental trips with a tour in Switzerland in 1946, he confessed to his friend Ernest Adcock 'how tired' it had left him.[38] The end came the following year. During the early months of 1947, England endured one of the most severe winters of the century. Freeman's failing health, coupled with the detrimental effects of living in a large unheated vicarage, left him ill-equipped to cope with these conditions, and he died 'after a short illness' on 24 March at the age of seventy.[39] The funeral took place at Standish on Friday 28 March, and he was buried in the churchyard beside his wife.

In the tributes that followed in the musical press, those who had known and worked with Freeman described his essential qualities. Ernest Adcock, one of his oldest friends, acknowledged 'a truly kind-hearted Christian gentleman', whilst Stephen Dykes Bower referred to 'a faithful and conscientious country parson', who had experienced difficulties and discouragements, but whose 'interest never flagged, and as a result he

St Nicholas, Hardwicke
see p.11 for full-size plate

The Freeman headstone, Standish

35 Andrew Freeman, *Church Organs and Organ Cases* (London: SPCK, 1945).
36 All the letters are collected in BOA Box 92.

37 *Gloucester Citizen*, 16 June 1943, 6.
38 Ernest E. Adcock, 'Andrew Freeman: in Appreciation', *The Organ* 27, no. 105 (July 1947): 4.
39 *Gloucester Journal*, 29 March 1947, 5.

was happy in his work'.[40] W. L. Sumner captured his unique contribution to the study and appreciation of the organ:

> The passing of Andrew Freeman has left a gap in the organ world which cannot be filled. A first-class musician and organist, he had made the study of organ cases his own. He envisaged the organ as an instrument of music which should look as beautiful as it sounded. For him the organ must express in visible as well as in audible terms, the highest aspirations of man in Divine service. As a priest, he saw the organ in relation to Christian worship throughout the centuries. He left it to others to discuss the minutiae of voicing, action and pipe scales, so beloved by many enthusiasts. He saw the organ clearly and he saw it whole, and he preferred to think of it in its ecclesiastical setting. In an age which produced so much which was unlovely in church furnishings, his missionary work is gradually leading us back to an appreciation of the factors which make a good organ case ...[41]

In the next generation, many English organ-builders would follow Freeman in rediscovering the aesthetic and musical value of a fine organ case, and many organists would find themselves treading in his footsteps as they made the pilgrimage to see and hear the surviving baroque and classical organs of France, Germany and Austria.

Freeman's family – his son, Denys, and his daughter, Greta – had the unenviable task of emptying the vicarage at Standish within a few weeks of his death. One of the most pressing questions was what to do with the organ materials. Initially, Greta took charge of them in her cottage in Minchinhampton. When, twenty years later, she moved house, it fell to Bernard Edmonds to act (at her request) as temporary custodian. Freeman had never expressed a firm view about what should happen to his notebooks and photographs but the family had a sense that he hoped they would be preserved in a public collection. So when the British Institute of Organ Studies was founded in 1976, and the English (later, British) Organ Archive was established, an ideal solution presented itself. Edmonds continued to make use of the material for his own research and writing, but gradually handed items to the Archive. Eventually, following his death in 2003, the remaining materials were reunited with the rest of the collection, then in Birmingham Central Library. A few years later, it moved to The Cadbury Research Library at the University of Birmingham where another generation can appreciate that 'record of remarkable achievement and work well done'[42] which is the Andrew Freeman collection.

40 Stephen Dykes Bower, W.L.Sumner, Ernest E. Adcock, 'Andrew Freeman: in Appreciation', *The Organ* 27, no. 105 (July 1947): 4, 2.

41 Ibid., 3.

42 Ibid., 2.

Opposite:
St Nicholas, Hardwicke, Gloucestershire (1938)
Freeman/1273; plate 1546

'The case ... was designed by Mr. Stephen E. Dykes-Bower, M.A., F.R.I.B.A ... Mr. Dykes-Bower used all the front pipes of the old organ in his scheme. These are of plain metal of excellent quality, for they have retained their polish after sixty years exposure to Gloucestershire air. The pipe shades, of an intricate and pleasing pattern, are lavishly gilded with gold leaf: which gives a rich appearance to this beautiful front. The case was made by the organ builders, Messrs. Percy Daniel & Co.' (*The Organ* 19, no. 73 (July 1939): 36).

Overleaf: Sketches from SBN 7
(BOA, Freeman Collection, Box 83)

1184

Organ b. by Bishop, 1883
East end of S. aisle of
chancel, facing West.
Varnished case.
Decorated pipes, leaf lips.

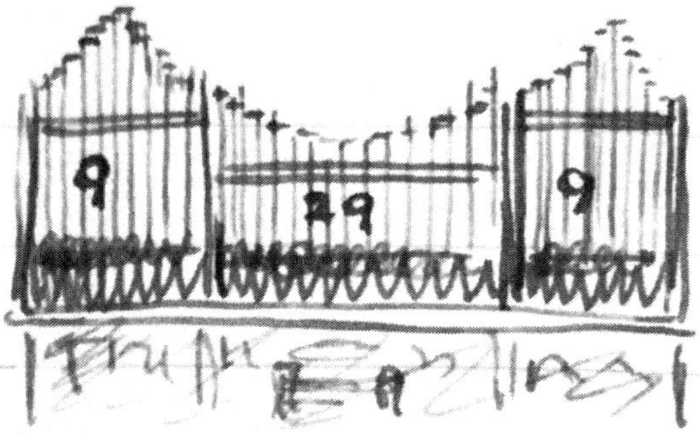

[10.8.21

893 Wonersh – S. John the Baptist.

Built by Lewis & Co. Placed on a platform against the East wall of the South Chapel.

Lged 4
Ob 8
V Cel^s 8
Voix angelique 8
Rohr fl. 8
G Pr. 8
Sw P.
Gt Pdls

CC to A.
CCC to F (c + 11).

Fl H^arm 4
Lged 8
Dul 8
OD 8
Fl Bass 8
Sw Bass 16
Super on Sw
Sw Gt.

+ G Pr Ob Lg
V.A RFl
Gt to Pdls
Lg Dul
Full Gt.

Oak case, impost high only.
Spotted metal pipes, with
(rounded lips) – effectively
grouped.

(10.9.21)

894. Sheet – S. Mary's Ch (nr Petersfield).

orman & Beard 1913. S. side of Chancel.

[Swell]

Salicet 4

Gamba 8

SD 8

[Choir] 8

Sw Sub 8 Octave Super Sw P

Gt P.

Pedal CCC to F (c & r).

[Great]

Fl Trav 4

OD 8

Cl Fl 8

[Pedal]

Bourdon 16

Full Sw

Gamba

Cl Fl

Full Gt

Oak case, impost high (no uprights): zinc front pipes (leaf lips). ase bracketed over keys. Chancel has no aisles. [11. 8. 21]

895 Purbrook – S. John the Baptist.

Trem

Ob 8

Gem 4

VCel 8

Gamba 8

SD 8

OD 8

Sw Sub Oct

Sw Gt

Sw P

Gt P

No builder's name attached.

N. side of Chancel.

Oak case with two uprights and cross-piece.

34 decorated front pipes in one flat. (leaf lips).

Pedal CCC to F (c & r).

Piccolo 2

Flute 4

Dul 8

Claribel 8

OD 8

Bdn 16

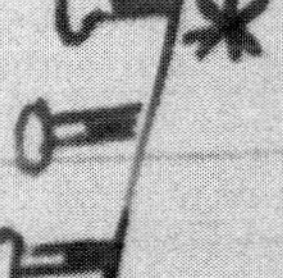

\+ OD Gem Ob

Gamba SD

Dul Claribel

\+ OD Fl.

Stop-jambs placed on the slope as at *

[11. 8. 21]

COLLECTORS AND ENTHUSIASTS

Some aspects of organography before Andrew Freeman

Andrew Freeman's precursors in the study and chronicling of organs in Britain were numerous, whether as antiquaries, encyclopaedists, organ-builders, scholars, or enthusiasts who collected stop lists. Freeman's own invaluable work as a pioneer in documentary research helped to establish new standards with the invaluable aid of photography. Although the foundation of the Public Record Office in 1838 was followed in the twentieth century by the establishment of County Record Offices, much of Freeman's documentary research from the 1890s onwards still relied on materials held by churches and cathedrals. The nineteenth century had seen other advances that assisted researchers, including an expanding railway network and the proliferation of music periodicals and local newspapers. A further important development was the foundation of the Royal College of Organists, which from its inception in 1864 included the provision of library and research facilities amongst its aspirations. Yet it was not until 1978 that the 'Parochial Registers and Records Measure' enforced the obligation of churches to deposit their archives in county record offices. Had Andrew Freeman's active life extended into the later decades of the twentieth century he would have experienced the post-war growth in historical musicology in which organ studies would become a sector of organology, the former being energised by the foundation of The British Institute of Organ Studies in 1976.

Where do we find the beginnings of the study and chronicling of organs? The first European book to include vernacular information on the instrument and its related tablature notations was Sebastian Virdung's *Musica getutscht* (Basel, 1511). This publication was followed by Martin Agricola's *Musica instrumentalis deudsch* (Wittenburg, 1529). It was not until Praetorius' *Syntagma musicum II: De organographia* (Wolfenbüttel, 1619) however that each part of the organ received extensive description, including every species of pipe with directions for tuning, and histories and stoplists of the foremost organs in Germany.

Apart from lists of materials and accounts of organ-builders, the first document of English provenance is the Talbot Manuscript (c.1695),[1] which contains material apparently taken, if not always clearly, from Marin Mersenne's *Harmonie universelle* (Paris, 1636), as well as information

1 Oxford, Christ Church, archives: Talbot MS., Mus.MS 1187.

Opposite:
St Stephen's Church, Old Radnor, Radnorshire (1912)
Freeman/330; plate 533
This case, from the early 16th century, is the oldest organ case in the British Isles. It is the model for the BIOS logo.

Woodcut prints of Church and Positive Organs and a Bible Regal from Virdung's *Musica getuscht* (1511)

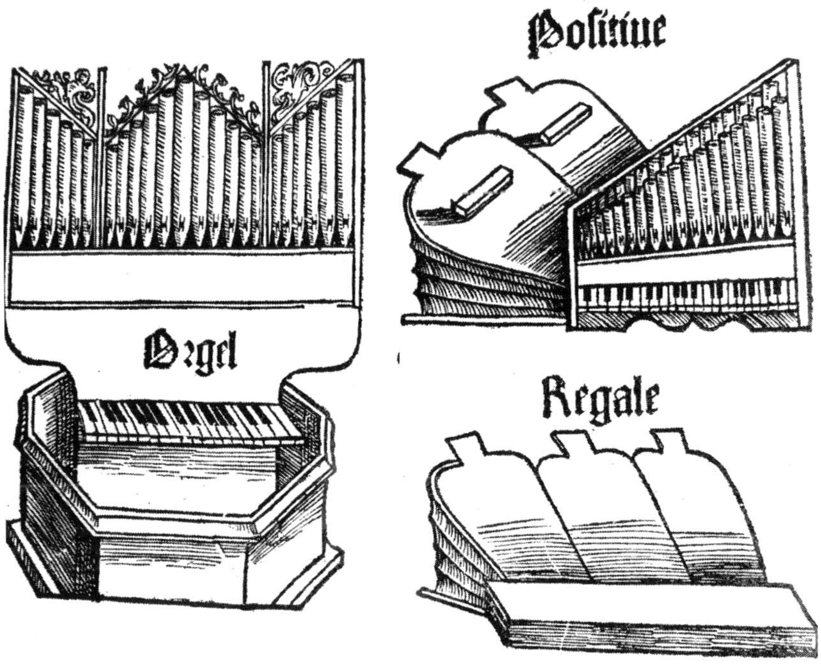

about organs the author knew first-hand. As Stephen Bicknell suggested there is scope for more extensive study of this document, in view of its early descriptions of pipe metals, scalings, and voicing.[2]

The leading English musical historians of the eighteenth century were Charles Burney (1726–1814) and John Hawkins (1719–1789).[3] Hawkins – very much the gentleman amateur – was descended from the Elizabethan naval commander of the same name, and was well connected to London's music life, being acquainted with Handel and John Stanley. Burney was apprenticed early on to Thomas Arne, and developed his gifts as a linguist and astronomer, eventually becoming similarly well connected musically in the metropolis.

In his music publications, Burney included overviews of organs he had seen in the course of his travels in Germany, Holland, France and Italy.[4] In Germany, he visited (among others) J. G. Hildebrandt's impressive organ in the Michaeliskirche, Hamburg, where his host was C. P. E. Bach. According to Burney, the instrument was 'the largest and most complete in Europe', with four keyboards and sixty-four stops; it had a 'noble chorus', but Burney was critical of the small and ineffective swell.[5] In Berlin he commented on the Garnisonkirche organ (J. Wagner, 1725), with its 50-note keyboard compasses, and a splendid case with moving statuary.[6] In France, Burney noted the wide range of styles in the organ verses of alternatim singing. In Italy, however, he was critical of the intrusive use of the strident timbres of the organs in choir accompaniments: his preference was for gentle 8' 'character stops', like the sounds of the Baarpijp and Vox Humana he had encountered at Haarlem. Similarly he found the South German and Swiss *Suabe Flöten* reminiscent of the tone of Snetzler's dulcianas. It was on Snetzler's advice that he visited the organ in the Michaeliskirche in Vienna with its divided cases, and also other instruments in Frankfurt and Prague.

Hawkins' book, *A General History of the Science and Practice of Music*, reveals the author's familiarity with the activities of organ builders in England, particularly on movements and partnerships between builders. In contrast to Burney, he considered Renatus Harris's work superior to 'Father' Smith's, and took a particular interest in Harris's career, noting, among other things, his retirement to Bristol.[7]

The diaries and journals of the lawyer-musician John Marsh (1752–1828) give us a singular overview of English organ culture in the late Georgian and Regency periods.[8] As a performer, composer, and observant critic of organ-builders, organists, clergy and their idiosyncrasies, Marsh was an avid chronicler of organs and organ-builders from a multitude of perspectives. This extended to the exposure of the dishonest Salisbury builder, 'Mr. Diapason Green', who was not beyond removing reed pipes from the Harris organ of the Cathedral and selling them to the Dean and Chapter of Wells.[9] His extensive knowledge of the organs and organ-builders of London and the Home Counties, East Anglia and the Midlands was such that his opinions were sought after and held in high regard.

From the mid-nineteenth century we have a flood of publications relating to many aspects of the organ (some of which achieved several editions), which reflect a burgeoning interest in the instrument. Joshua Done (died 1848) included a short history of the organ in his *Complete Treatise on the Organ* (c.1837) with

2 Stephen Bicknell, *The History of the English organ* (Cambridge: Cambridge University Press, 1996), 142–3.

3 Both were authors of important early histories of music: Charles Burney, *A General History of Music, from the Earliest Ages to the Present Period,* 4 vols. (London: 1776–89); Sir John Hawkins, *A General History of the Science and History of Music*, 5 vols. (London: 1776).

4 Besides his *General History* and other works, Burney wrote *The Present State of Music in France and Italy* (London: 1771); and *The Present State of Music in Germany, the Netherlands, and the United Provinces* (London: 1773).

5 *The Present State of Music in Germany, the Netherlands, and the United Provinces*, 274–5.

6 Ibid., 104–5.

7 Hawkins, *General History*, 356.

8 John Marsh, *The John Marsh Journals: the Life and Times of a Gentleman Composer (1752–1828)*, ed. Brian Robins (Stuyvesant, NY: Pendragon Press, 1998). Further information on John Marsh can be found at John Marsh, *A Most Elegant and Beautiful Instrument, the Organ,* ed. Martin Renshaw (Chichester: Martin Renshaw 2002); and Christopher Kent, 'John Marsh and the Organ: Introducing an RCO Manuscript', *RCO Journal* 1 (1993), 24–45.

9 Marsh, *Journals*, 229.

some references to earlier English builders.[10] Shortly afterwards (c.1838), the first edition of Alexander Hamilton's *Catechism of the Organ* appeared, followed by a second edition edited by Joseph Warren in 1842. It included a list of foreign publications on the organ, and stop-lists of English and foreign organs. A third edition appeared in 1851, and concluded with a valuable bibliography on music theory, solo organ music and cathedral and church music.[11]

Sir John Sutton (1820–73) was an ecclesiologist and antiquarian whose *Short Account of Organs built in England* (1847) reflected a growing concern about the destruction of surviving organs from the seventeenth and eighteenth centuries, and a personal dislike for the 'music mills' of contemporary builders. His clerical brother, Fredrick Heathcote Sutton (1833–88), had similar interests and published *Some Account of the Mediaeval Organ Case still standing at Old Radnor, South Wales* in 1866; in 1872, this was succeeded by *Church Organs: their Position and Construction*, which incorporated the earlier publication in an appendix.[12] Other clergy among the Sutton brothers' contemporaries who took an interest in old organs and cases included John Gibson (c.1818–92), Osmond Fisher (1817–1913), and Canon William Edward Dickson (c.1826–1910) whose *Practical Organ Building* was first published in 1881 and went into three editions.[13]

The publication of *The Organ, its History and Construction* (1855) by Edward J. Hopkins (1818–1901) and Edward F. Rimbault (1816–76) was a landmark in English organ studies; subsequent editions appeared in 1870 and 1877.[14] Rimbault's introductory history included a chronological survey of organ-building in England, with accounts of the work of particular builders and lists of their known instruments; he also printed transcriptions of documents for the first time, such as the accounts for Thomas Dallam's organ in King's College, Cambridge (1605) and John Loosemore's proposal to Sir George Trevilyan for an organ at Nettlecombe Court (1665/6).[15] The second part of the book comprised Hopkins's detailed technical description of the organ, and concluded with more than 250 pages of stop-lists, British and foreign, old and new. 'Hopkins & Rimbault' became the foundation on which many subsequent writers were to rely.

Rimbault's history almost certainly drew on a number of related manuscript collections of specifications that were in circulation during this period. These important sources have been discussed in an article by Nicholas Thistlethwaite.[16] The best known is the Leffler manuscript compiled mainly in the first decade of the nineteenth century by a member of the Leffler family; it was acquired by BIOS in 2007 and published in a limited facsimile edition with the generous financial assistance of the Mercers' Company of the City of London. The other related sources include the Flackton folio, *Organographia*, the 'G. P. England' notebook (copied by F. G. Edwards from the original), and the Russell Manuscript. The Sperling Notebooks (compiled by the Reverend John Henry Sperling, c.1850–1855) make extensive use of this common material but add to it considerably with details of organs built in the period up to c.1855.

A further, lesser-known manuscript source from the second half of the nineteenth century is the notebook of the Reverend Leighton G Hayne.[17] In addition to his clerical duties, Hayne was also active as a consultant and designer of organs, working with large and small manufacturers, and sometimes adding critical observations to his record of stop-lists. The organ

10 Joshua Done, *A Complete Treatise on the Organ* (London: *c.*1837).

11 Joseph Warren, *Hamilton's Catechism of the Organ*, 2nd edition (London: 1842); 3rd edition (London: 1851).

12 [John Sutton], *A Short Account Of Organs Built in England* (London: 1847); Fredrick Heathcote Sutton, *Some Account of the Mediaeval Organ Case Still Standing at Old Radnor, South Wales* (London: 1866); *Church Organs: their Position and Construction* (London: 1872, 1883).

13 W.E.Dickson, *Practical Organ Building* (London, 1881). The second edition of 1882 has been reprinted in Oxford (Positif Press, 1983).

14 Edward John Hopkins, and Edward Francis Rimbault, *The Organ, its History and Construction* (London: 1855, 1870, 1877).

15 Hopkins and Rimbault, *The Organ*, 2nd edition (1870), 62–6; 1st edition (1855), 52.

16 Nicholas Thistlethwaite, 'Source Materials for the Early-Nineteenth Century', *JBIOS* 1 (1977): 75- 100.

17 See: Christopher Kent, 'Tenbury MS. 1467: the Notebook of the Revd. Leighton G. Hayne', *JBIOS* 11 (1987): 82–8.

in Bath Abbey by Smith of Bristol, for example, was 'very unsatisfactory', whilst Willis's organ at St Matthias, Stoke Newington had tone that was 'very bright, especially the Great Trumpet which is a little too loudly voiced' (1856).[18] In 1869 he wrote approvingly of the new organ by Lewis in St Mary's R.C. Cathedral in Newcastle-upon-Tyne: 'This is in many respects a remarkably fine organ, full of character and variety'.[19]

Like the Reverend Sir Frederick Arthur Gore Ouseley (1825–89), founder of St Michael's College, Tenbury (1856), Professor Music at Oxford, and an enormously influential figure in church music circles, Hayne visited European organs, particularly in Holland. He was not without reservations concerning Müller's organ at Haarlem, finding the tone of the oboe to be 'execrable' and the Pedal open 32' 'a perfect failure'; on the other hand, the vox humana was 'fair' and the 32' bazuin 'good'. He was, however, unreserved in his praise for the organ by Batz in Utrect Cathedral: 'A very fine organ. Vox Humana the best I have met with & the flue work is excellent.'[20]

Frederick Rothwell's transcriptions of the various pitch engravings from the pipes of Bernard Smith's Great Organ Principal rank at The Temple Church

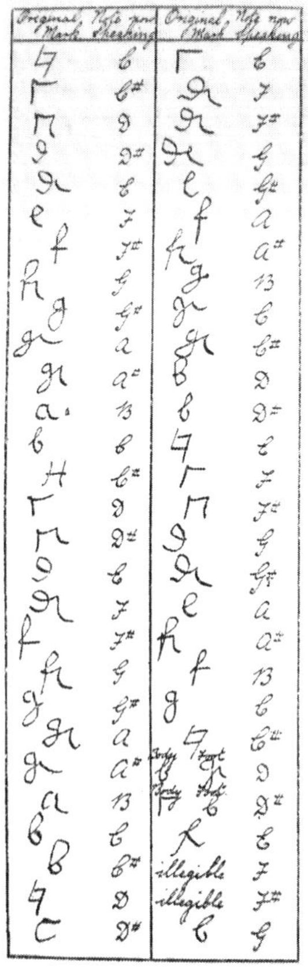

Among the subscribers to the first edition of Hopkins & Rimbault in 1855 was Edmund Macrory (1831–1904), the author of *A Few Notes on the Temple Organ* (1859).[21] It was the prototype of many monographs published later in the century about particular instruments and their histories. A third edition, revised and enlarged by M. Muir Mackenzie (1847–1919), appeared many years later in 1911, and included an appendix researched and written by the organ-builder Frederick Rothwell (1853–1944). This comprises extensive descriptions and precise transcriptions of the pitch markings on all of the then-surviving pipes from the famous 'Father' Smith organ of 1683. Rothwell produced detailed commentaries on each rank noting how some had been transposed, renamed or redeployed. His was a pioneering attempt to record the 'archaeology' of an instrument, and it was to be almost seventy years before something similar was appeared in print, following the foundation of BIOS in 1976.[22] Meanwhile, Andrew Freeman wrote his monograph on Smith (1926) with references to the work of Macrory and Rothwell.[23]

In marked contrast to the magisterial authority of Hopkins & Rimbault, the later decades of the nineteenth century witnessed the publication of modest books on organs and organ-building that were more accessible to all sorts and conditions of reader. Canon W. E. Dickson's Practical organ building has already been mentioned. In a revised edition (1882), Dickson added a chapter on village church organs. His emphasis was on simplicity of construction, simple cases devoid of ornamentation, and excellent materials. A village organ 'should admit of no experiments or eccentricities' or contain mechanisms 'liable to sudden derangement'. 'It should stand well in tune', notwithstanding fluctuations of ambient temperature and humidity. All were sentiments with which Andrew Freeman would have agreed, and which he put into practice in his own advisory work a generation later.

Dickson also expressed strong sentiments over the conservation of historic organs and deplored their destruction:

> The eighteenth century witnessed the erection in churches of many country towns, of noble organs, honestly constructed by true artists, men who disdained the use of inferior timber or of base metal. A great number of these costly and beautiful instruments remain unaltered, or at least uninjured, within the recollection of the present writer, but demolition rather than restoration has been at work during the last thirty or more years, and the plea we would put forward for the reverent preservation of the works of the old masters may now be opportune in but few and isolated cases.[24]

He concluded by exhorting anyone who discovered organs by Snetzler or the Englands in remote locations to treat them with respect, and

18 Oxford, Bodleian Library: Tenbury MS. 1467, f.5v and f.25v.
19 Ibid., f.79.
20 Ibid., f.62 and 62v.
21 Edmund Macrory, *A Few Notes on the Temple Organ* (London: 1859); 2nd ed, 1861.
22 See, for instance: Nicholas Thistlethwaite, 'Organo Pneumatico: the Construction and Design of Bernard Smith's Organ for the University Church, Cambridge, 1698', *JBIOS* 2 (1978): 31–62.
23 Andrew Freeman, *Father Smith* (London: Musical Opinion, 1926), 4, 75–7.
24 Dickson, *Practical Organ Building*, 178–79.

berated organ-builders who scrapped or melted down the high-content tin pipes of the former on the pretence that these instruments were 'screamy'. Instead he encouraged balancing shrill mutations against modern pipework at the same wind pressure, as well as conserving old casework and keyboards where possible. He was responsible for retrieving a Cornet by Bernard Smith during the rebuilding of the Cambridge University organ in 1893.[25]

Finally, mention should be made of two older contemporaries of Freeman:

Charles William Pearce (1856–1928) spent most of his working life as a teacher and practical musician. He was organist successively of St Luke, Old Street (1874–85) and St Clement, Eastcheap (1885–1919), and from 1882 until his retirement in the 1920s, served as Professor of Organ and Composition at Trinity College, London. For almost quarter of a century, he was joint editor of *The Organist and Choirmaster*. Pearce's publications are extensive and include many articles of antiquarian interest. He is particularly remembered today for publishing transcriptions of the stop-lists recorded in the Leffler note-book; these appeared in two neat pocket-sized books as *Notes on Old London City Churches, their Organs, Organists, and Musical Associations* (1909), and *Notes on English Organs of the Period 1800–1810* (c.1912).[26] He lived long enough to become an early contributor to *The Organ* when it began publication in 1921; an article of 'Reminiscences of organ enthusiasts of the past' (1926) is particularly relevant here.[27]

The second figure was Canon Francis William Galpin (1858–1945) whose influence and interests extended to an all-embracing study of historic European and non-European instruments. Galpin was an organ pupil of William Sterndale Bennett (1816–75) at the Royal Academy of Music before undertaking theological studies at Cambridge where he also played the clarinet in the University Music Society Orchestra, conducted by Stanford. The first edition of his *Old English Instruments of Music* was published whilst he was incumbent of Hatfield Regis, Harlow (1891–1915). Galpin's closing remark in his 1910 preface remains pertinent to those working in the field of historical musicology today: 'That further research will reveal new facts is certain, and no one will welcome more gladly than myself all contributions toward a better knowledge and appreciation of the old English instruments of music.'[28] It is a view with which Andrew Freeman and his forebears in the field of studying, recording and playing historic English organs would surely heartily agree.

25 Nicholas Thistlethwaite, *The Making of the Victorian Organ* (Cambridge: Cambridge University Press, 1990), 327.

26 Charles William Pearce, *Notes on Old London City Churches, their Organs, Organists, and Musical Associations* (London: Vincent Music Co.,1909); *Notes on English Organs of the Period 1800–1810* (London: Vincent Music Co. c.1912).

27 Charles William Pearce, 'Reminiscences of Organ Enthusiasts of the Past', *The Organ* 19 (January 1926):138–49.

28 Francis William Galpin, *Old English Instruments of Music* (London: Methuen and Co., 1910), xi.

Overleaf left:
Sketch from SBN 5
(BOA, Freeman Collection, Box 83)
Freeman's photograph of this organ, St Mary's, Cheshunt, Hertfordshire, can be seen in the CRL online catalogue at Freeman/723, plate 983.

Overleaf right:
Sketch from SBN 11
(BOA, Freeman Collection, Box 83)
Freeman's photograph of this organ is at Plate 159, p.229

designed by G. F. Bodley)   x = largest pipe

Kinnersley Ch. (Heref.) See no 1686 page 1995

Case designed by G. F. Bodley, (who is buried in the Churchyard here)

Case painted red, with brown, white & gold decorations, also a few texts on scrolls.

Plain metal pipes; the centre one is embossed: all the others have a nail-head punch above the upper lip.

[22. 5. 35]

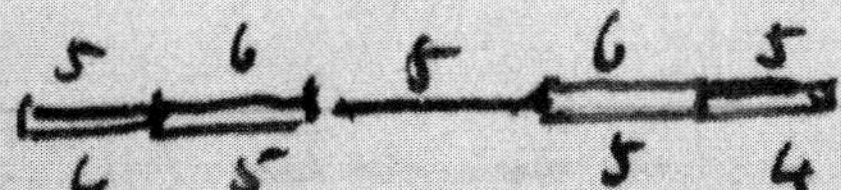

AΩ
OF THE
LORD ARE

Andrew Freeman
A Case History

> When the west door was thrown open, Mr Davidson could not repress an exclamation of pleased surprise at the completeness and richness of the interior. Screen-work, pulpit, seating, and glass – all were of the same period; and as he advanced into the nave and sighted the organ-case with its gold embossed pipes in the western gallery, his cup of satisfaction was filled. The glass in the nave windows was chiefly armorial; in the chancel were figure-subjects, of the kind that may be seen at Abbey Dore, of Lord Scudamore's work. But this is not an archaeological Review.[1]

And this was not Andrew Freeman, though it could have been.[2] The happy investigator is one of M. R. James' church-crawling characters, eager for new architectural experience and about to find one surprise too many. He makes his appearance in 'The Uncommon Prayer-book', published in 1925. In the following year Freeman sent a proof copy of his own second book, *Father Smith,* to James soliciting a foreword.[3] In return came James' approval:

> Many thanks for your very interesting letter. I have written what occurs to me for you. The reading of the sheets you sent was a great pleasure. Do with it as you will, but please don't, if you can help it, call it a Foreword, for I don't hold with that expression.[4]

Following publication, James wrote again:

> I have just received your delicious book, and turned over the delicious pictures and feel a thrill of pleasure at being associated with it. Thank you very much.
>
> I hope you will ere long take a look at our latest acquisition here.[5]

This was a Snetzler chamber organ, newly installed in the Election Hall of Eton College, where James was now Provost [see plate 100, p.170].[6] In the *Father Smith* prologue he expressed trenchant views about the loss of the 'ancient organs, and, in particular, the organ *cases* of what is here rightly called the Golden Age.'[7] Unlike Freeman, whose emotions were under tighter control, he railed against the destructive forces of the gothic revival and the demolished galleries, organs, cases and in particular the lost screens and organs of Durham, Salisbury and Hereford. Some of his feelings are conveyed through the character of an old verger, in conversation with Mr Lake, a visitor:

> It was in 1840 that the wave of the Gothic revival smote the Cathedral of Southminster. 'There was a lot of lovely stuff went then, sir',

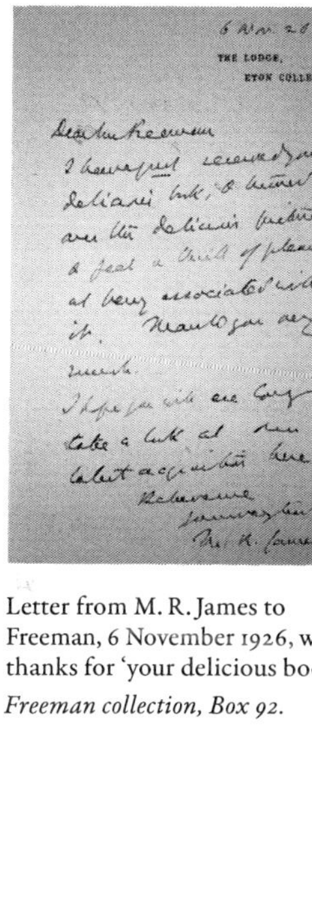
6 Nov 26
THE LODGE,
ETON COLLEGE.
Dear Mr Freeman
I have just received your delicious book, & turned over the delicious pictures, & feel a thrill of pleasure at being associated with it. Thank you very much.
I hope you will ere long take a look at our latest acquisition here.
Believe me
Sincerely yours
M. R. James

Letter from M. R. James to Freeman, 6 November 1926, with thanks for 'your delicious book'.
Freeman collection, Box 92.

Opposite: St John's, Hampstead, London (1913)
Freeman/381; plate 606
Case by T. G. Jackson. 'A bold and pleasing front in perfect accord with its surroundings. The three pendants beneath the towers, the *campanili* (or lanterns) above them and scroll carving between them are features to be noted.' (from 'A lecture on English organ cases', given in the Theatre of the Royal College of Music (Saturday, 20 October 1934), *The calendar of the Royal College of Organists* (1935–6), 126–45.

1 M.R.James, 'The Uncommon Prayer-book', *A Thin Ghost*, accessed June 24, 2015, www.thin-ghost.org/items/show/161. Originally published in *Atlantic Monthly* 127, no. 6 (1921), reprinted in *A Warning to the Curious and Other Ghost Stories* (1925).

2 Subsequent to selecting this quotation, the author discovered another antiquarian candidate for the inspiration of Mr Davidson: that of F.C.Eeles, the first secretary of the Central Council for the Care of Churches and an early member of the Gloucester DAC, this suggested by Donald Findlay, *The protection of our English churches* (1996), xi.

3 Andrew Freeman, *Father Smith otherwise Bernard Schmidt, being an Account of a Seventeenth-Century Organ Maker* (London: At the office of 'Musical Opinion', 1926).

4 BOA Freeman collection, box 92, file of three letters from James to Freeman, 7 September 1926 and a short obituary cutting, dated 19 June 1936.

5 Ibid., 6 November 1926.

6 Formerly in St Decuman, Watchet, West Somerset. See Henry T. Gilberthorpe, 'A notable chamber organ by John Snetzler', *The Organ* 5, no. 20 (April 1926): 235–6.

7 Freeman, *Father Smith,* n.p.

said Worby, with a sigh. 'My father couldn't hardly believe it when he got his orders to clear out the choir. There was a new dean just come in – Dean Burscough it was – and my father had been 'prenticed to a good firm of joiners in the city, and knew what good work was when he saw it. Crool it was, he used to say: all that beautiful wainscot oak, as good as the day it was put up, and garlands-like of foliage and fruit, and lovely old gilding work on the coats of arms and the organ pipes. All went to the timber yard – every bit except some little pieces worked up in the Lady Chapel, and 'ere in this overmantel. Well – I may be mistook, but I say our choir never looked as well since. Still there was a lot found out about the history of the church, and no doubt but what it did stand in need of repair. There were very few winters passed but what we'd lose a pinnicle.' Mr. Lake expressed his concurrence with Worby's views of restoration ...[8]

A James McBryde illustration from 'Canon Alberic's Scrapbook', showing the then-empty case at St Bertrand de Comminges.

THE ENGLISHMAN WAS TOO DEEP IN HIS NOTE-BOOK TO GIVE MORE THAN AN OCCASIONAL GLANCE TO THE SACRISTAN

M. R. James' earlier collection, *Ghost Stories of an Antiquary*, appeared in 1905 and James McBryde[9] contributed an illustration of the then-dilapidated screen organ in St Bertrand de Comminges (south-west France), at that time devoid of most of its pipes and a perfect specimen for Freeman's scrutiny (though he does not appear to have visited the town).[10] Again, it is not far-fetched to assume that James had someone such as Freeman in mind, for

> our Englishman had come early on the day in question, and proposed to himself to fill a note-book and to use several dozens of plates in the process of describing and photographing every corner of the wonderful church ...[11]

Among James' many college and university appointments were the assistant directorship and then directorship of the Fitzwilliam Museum, located opposite Fitzwilliam Hall (to which Freeman was allegedly attached as a non-collegiate student). One biographer of James records:

> happy were the generations of undergraduates which succeeded each other during that period. To a very large number of them, and by no means of Kingsmen only, he was the centre of their Cambridge life. It is safe to say that not one of them ever found him

8 M.R.James, 'An Episode of Cathedral History', *A Thin Ghost* (1925), accessed June 24, 2015, www.thin-ghost.org/items/show/138.

9 James McBryde arrived in Cambridge in 1893 and frequently travelled with James between 1899 and 1901. He died prematurely in 1904.

10 A.G.Hill attempted a reconstruction of the Comminges case and took 'the liberty to draw them [the front pipes] as they originally existed.' The attempt fails, with too many small-scaled pipes crowded to stair-rod proportions. See Arthur George Hill, *Organ-Cases and Organs of the Middle Ages and Renaissance: a Comprehensive Essay on the Art Archæology of the organ ... Illustrated, etc.* (1883–91, 1883), 80–1.

11 M.R.James, 'Canon Alberic's Scrap-book', *Ghost-Stories of an Antiquary* (London: Edward Arnold, 1904). Includes four illustrations by James McBryde.

too busy to talk to them, play games with them, make music with them on that very clangy piano, and entertain them with his vast stores of knowledge, his inexhaustible humour, and his unique power of mimicry.[12]

During his Cambridge years, Freeman surely fell under the spell of Montague Rhodes James (1862–1936), respected for cataloguing early manuscript collections and famous for his tales of the supernatural. Was it with James' encouragement that Freeman honed his careful disciplined note-taking and transcribing abilities? Whether Freeman imbibed his antiquarian skills from James or no, his gifts were built on firm foundations, much needed in the field of organ scholarship (then and now) and the depth and scope of his work is easily under-estimated. As an example, it may come as a surprise to find that long before other more recent claimants, he identified Pugin's authorship of the case in Jesus College Chapel, Cambridge [see plate 7, p.77].[13]

Prior to Freeman, F. H. Sutton, John Norbury and A. G. Hill had already awakened wider interest in ancient organ cases, though to a narrow readership.[14] But Freeman, who did not have their social advantages, must have felt frustration when he tried to bridge his comfortable Cambridge *milieu* with the world of trade organ-builders, indifferent to his aesthetic tastes. Perhaps he understood that greater understanding might be brought about through publishing and, especially, the world of journal production – there he made significant progress. The scope of Freeman's reading and the transcriptions from manuscript sources, church guides, county archaeological and architectural transactions and other specialist texts was phenomenal, only matched by his writings and note-taking. While his notebooks might suggest a little of George Eliot's Mr Casaubon,[15] one cannot help but be impressed by the meticulous recording and indexing that, of itself, must have taken much thought and, certainly, much time and care to devise. An attempt to define his particular interests through an analysis of his photographic pilgrimages is probably doomed to failure, because he took in anything on the long road to a destination only limited by time and budget, and (perhaps) the patience of his family. But his notes and publications, especially when he did eventually underline the design faults and errors of those who should know better, do offer a guide of sorts and it is some comfort to know that Freeman suffered frustration in distilling his own thoughts on organ cases:

> In 1925 the writer [Freeman] was commissioned to compile a brief article on this subject for a new edition of a well-known Dictionary of Music [it was *Grove*]. When completed it turned out to be double the length required. Three successive revisions, spread over several months, lopped off about six hundred words, but a fourth attempt was less successful; the thing began to grow. It was evidently time to write finis and send it in to the Editor. It was not really a surprise to find that it was too late for inclusion since the greater part of the Dictionary was already in type.[16]

Jesus College Chapel, Cambridge, the chancel organ case designed by A.W.N. Pugin.
see Plate 7, p.77

12 S.G.Lubbock, *A Memoir of Montague Rhodes James* (Cambridge: Cambridge University Press, 1939). The book includes a list of his writings by A.F.Scholfield (pages 16–17). Page 34 suggest an enthusiasm for the organ and recounts a story of James and his party travelling in France, when they were 'allotted a fine sitting room containing a piano, which was tuned with the help of a bicycle spanner, there was no surprise when Monty produced from his valise a volume of Handel's Organ Concertos.'

13 Andrew Freeman, 'Organ Cases of the Gothic Renaissance', *The Organ* 18, no. 71 (January 1939): 143. The late Dr Clive Wainwright of the Victoria and Albert Museum was to rediscover this attribution at a later date and bring it to wider notice.

14 In the eighteenth and early-nineteenth century, there were relevant publications, but essentially in the form of pattern books, *e.g.* Thomas Faulkner, *Designs for Organs ... In twenty ... plates*, second edition (1838). In the later nineteenth century, several privately printed volumes circulated, touching on the scholarship of organ cases, among the most influential: the Rev. Frederick Heathcote Sutton, *Some Account of the Medieval Organ Case Still Existing at Old Radnor, South Wales, with an Appendix Containing Fifteen Etchings of Gothic Organs...* (various editions from 1866). John Norbury, *The Box of Whistles. An Illustrated Book on Organ Cases; with Notes on Organs at Home and Abroad* (1877) and Hill, *Organ-cases and Organs.* The Sutton and Hill volumes have been reproduced in facsimile and in more recent times interest in the form was rekindled through the efforts of Austin Niland and Michael Gillingham.

15 The Rev. Mr Casaubon, the desiccated pedant of Eliot's *Middlemarch* (1871–2).

16 Andrew Freeman, 'The Organ Case', *The Organ* 21, no.81 (July 1941): 18.

An attempt to categorise some simple and complex case-front plans (at impost level).
Freeman collection, box 81, vol. 1, 218-19.

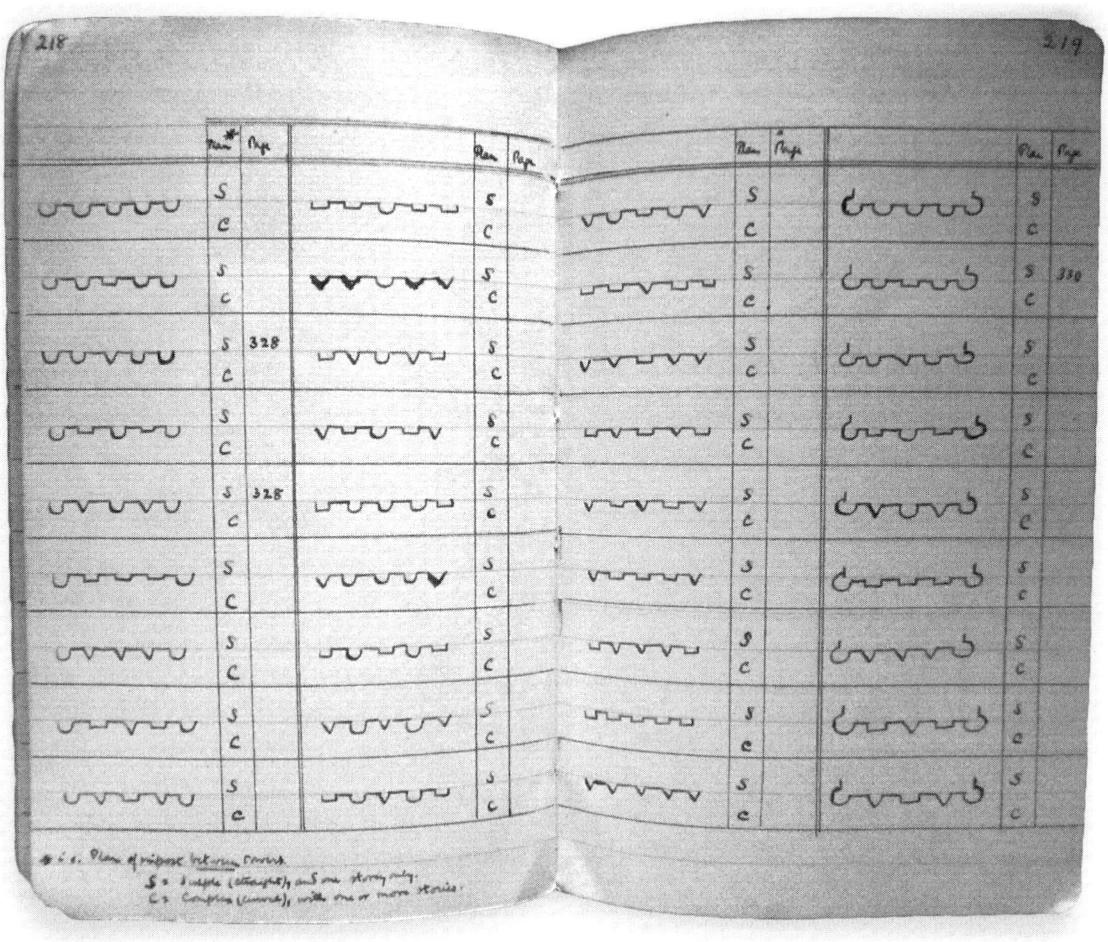

Surely this is a warning to those who might try to summarise him! Rather than attempt an all-encompassing digest, given the wealth of plates reproduced here, it is therefore best to offer a selection of Freeman's opinions on case design, drawn from his published writings and some modest projects that were close to him.

English Organ Cases, Freeman's first brave book (1921),[17] was presented in a rather old-fashioned style, with a history of the evolution of the form, and a critique of largely extant examples. It was more concerned with *categorising* styles, something that appeared to be a life-long ambition. John Norbury had attempted the task in his *Box of Whistles*, but with little influence. Freeman's more confident notes of guidance would come later, but he hoped for a renaissance in good design and the desire to see every instrument properly clothed, even at the cost of a stop or two.

> If there is such a thing as Beauty, surely an organ that appeals to the eye as well as to the ear has a double value; for the same reason, an admittedly ugly organ should never be allowed to disfigure a beautiful church.[18]

The notebooks offer measured comment on what he found around him, but give away little in personal preferences, though that might be seen positively as the result of an open mind. Even 'pipe-rack' fronts are carefully recorded and sketched in detail.

In passing, this writer will not be the first to consider the intended readership of the bound archive material. The carefully compiled notebooks contain a universally useful list of specifications, console layout and case details. The collected volumes of cuttings (mostly of his own writings, cut and pasted from galley proofs),

17 The foreword by Alan Gray, Trinity College, Cambridge.

18 Andrew Freeman, 'Some Gothic Organ Cases of a Hundred Years Ago', *The Organ* 18, no. 69 (July 1938): 39.

with additional photographs and hand-written notes, appear to offer a convenient consolidated source on topics that he might want as reference – the three organ-building Fathers (Howe, Smith and Willis), the Dallams and so on. But why, in addition to the organ information, did he transcribe so much from easily available volumes that touched on appearance and probably sat on his own shelves? G. A. Audsley, Frederick Bligh Bond, Thomas Faulkner, A. G. Hill, Hopkins and Rimbault, John Norbury, the Suttons,[19] and so on are all quoted. Why copy out well-known architectural terms, or the dimensions of famous churches that did not appear to be of particular significance to his immediate work in hand?[20] A careful, compact definition of an 'ogee' is understandable,[21] when it might surface (as it did) in some article or other, but why write out the definition of an 'arch'? Why did he feel the need to sign off comments and little explanations in his own notebooks as 'AF'? Such an attribution could only be intended for others – for example a sketch labelled 'The mouths (lips) of the pipes ...'[22] – which of his organophile friends would not know what a 'mouth' was? Who were the readers he had in mind?

If his undeclared motive were to document every organ in the country and as many as he could on the continent, his further intentions remain unclear, but there are possible clues in his methods and the subsequent development of that parallel discipline, architectural history. Until the publication of the first volume of Nikolaus Pevsner's *Buildings of England* series (from 1951) and Howard Colvin's *Biographical Dictionary of British Architects* (1954), specialists and the interested traveller could not conveniently obtain reliable topographical information on a county in general, or a building and its designer in particular. It was necessary to consult scattered, uneven (in the case of Arthur Mee, very uneven)[23] and generally bulky sources such as the *Victoria County Histories*, the publications of the National Monuments Record, the Royal Commission on the Historical Monuments of England, the London Survey, the *Shell Guides*, *Murray's Architectural Guides*, the volumes of Francis Bumpus and so on. (Even M. R. James entered this field with *Abbeys* (1925), published by and for the Great Western Railway Company.) Nothing comparable to Pevsner's county series was available as a composite record of the organs of the country. A number of important manuscript sources existed, but these were not accessible to the general reader, though Frederick Thornsby's *Dictionary of Organs and Organists* (1912 and 1921)[24] was a short-hand attempt to document some instruments of interest, and Batsford, early publisher of the *Shell Guides*, was later to produce *The British Organ*, with a short county gazetteer by Austin Niland (1963).[25]

Freeman may well have been aware of the new scholarship brought to these shores by Pevsner and others who settled here in the 1930s. Like Pevsner (1902–83) he enjoyed categories, patterns, and crisp distillation, and would surely admire his endeavours to bring to the British academy discipline and rigour in art and architectural topics. Did Freeman foresee the possibility of an *Organs of England* series, whether on a national, regional or county basis, complemented with details of relevant dimensions, building materials and a glossary of architectural terms? (The internal dimensions and the acoustic properties of buildings that contain organs are still statistics omitted from most organ literature, yet of interest to Freeman. A short dictionary of architectural terms is thought essential to every volume of the Pevsner *Buildings of England* series.) It is possible that such a project was in his mind, yet

19 All were authors familiar to the organ world with, perhaps, the exception of Frederick Bligh Bond (1864–1945), architect and writer on many (sometimes unusual) topics.

20 BOA Freeman collection, SBN 1: 189–83 or volume 2: 416–23 and 428–9.

21 BOA Freeman collection, box 81, notebook, 'Notes on Organs and Organ Builders', (cutting of *Musical Opinion*, December 1927), 199–203.

22 BOA Freeman collection, box 81, Notebook volume III: 490–1.

23 For instance, *The King's England*, a guide to the counties of England, with an overly patriotic perspective of the role of church and state.

24 Frederick W. Thornsby, *Dictionary of Organs and Organists* (Bournemouth, two editions, 1912 and 1921).

25 Clutton, Cecil and Austin Niland, *The British Organ* (1963), 280–304, expanded in the second edition (1982), with smaller print (265–95). Niland's gazetteer led directly, through the work of Nicholas Plumley and Michael Sayer, to the British Institute of Organ Studies' National Pipe Organ Register.

St Mary the Virgin, Wotton-under-Edge, a detail from one of Freeman's case analyses. *Freeman collection, box 83, vol. 9.* Freeman's photograph of this organ is at Plate 193, p.263.

was thought too daring to be directly expressed. Without the template of Pevsner's popular *Buildings* series, Freeman, working to a standard then unmatched by most British organ scholars, might find the task to compile and publish such a daring venture a step too far. We still do.

~

An attempt to explore Freeman's specific case interests might start with an image that graces most of his volumes. His bookplate [see p.vi] portrays a small, quirky organ of the Italian renaissance. The image is derived from a fruit bowl from Deruta, Umbria (*circa* 1520–25)[26] and perhaps attracted Freeman's attention when it was acquired by the Victoria and Albert Museum in 1899. Its catalogue entry describes 'a monk playing an organ, a tonsured boy standing by singing from a book, a dog or a sheep howling to the left, and to the right, a man in a cap blowing the organ-bellows.'[27] The organ is inscribed with an early-Italian text, 'Adi celo el mio lameto' ('Heaven, hear my lament')[28] and we can only imagine the cause of the dog's unhappiness. At first glance its asymmetry alone (more so than in the original) might make it an odd choice but, writes Freeman,

> absolute symmetry is not an essential of a good design. There are some extremely beautiful cases more especially in Spain, Italy and Austria where the front pipes display their natural speaking lengths, and where the carving has been cut so as to accentuate this fact and to make the most of it with charming effect.[29]

Deruta's rectilinear form, with a simple scroll flourish as pediment, indicates a stylistic preference that occurs elsewhere, especially in the case at St Nicholas, Standish (one of Freeman's two Gloucestershire parish churches which he

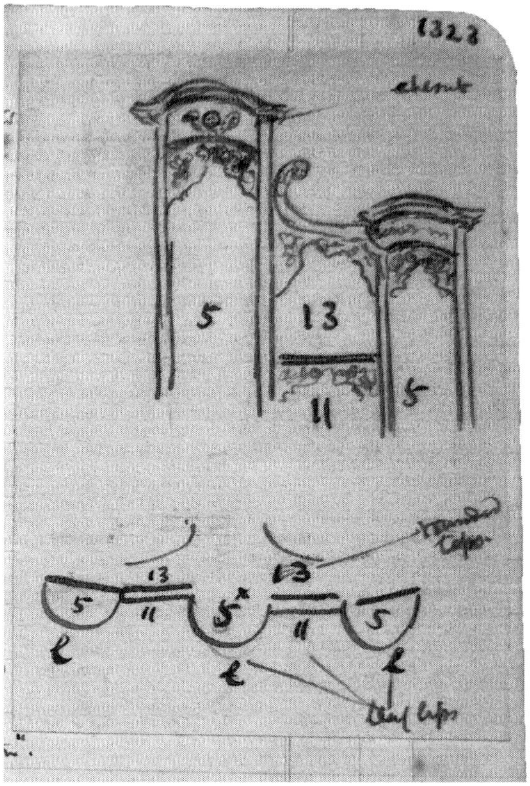

served from 1923–47) [see drawing of Standish case, p.7].

We know of the family connections at Standish with Stephen Dykes Bower, (1903–94, see Chapter 1, above) and his early commissions for the parish. Dykes Bower (hereafter SDB) is rightly held in high standing in the field of twentieth-century case design and his imagination and touch transformed much church furnishing and many modest instruments. But apart from parochial business between SDB and Freeman over (non-organ) furnishing matters, no other correspondence appears to survive in the Freeman files. Again, given Freeman's passion for architecturally literate cases, though as discrete objects rather than as part of overall furnishing schemes, one of the archival surprises is the absence of relevant correspondence with other architects. A notable exception is a letter from T. G. Jackson, the distinguished and prolific architect who did so much to change the face of Oxford. On the 28 December 1912 (the year before his baronetcy) he wrote from Eagle House, Wimbledon:

> I am much interested by your letter & thank you for the photographs. Like you I am a

26 The birthplace of Girolamo Diruta, organist and composer. Freeman does not appear to have visited the area.

27 Museum number C.2183–1910; collections.vam.ac.uk/item/O161967/fruit-dish/, accessed 15 August 2015.

28 I am indebted to Dr David Dunn for translation and thus establishing the source.

29 Andrew Freeman, *Church Organs and Organ Cases* (Society for Promoting Christian Knowledge (SPCK), 32 pages, paper covers, 1942), 11–12.

fanatic about organ cases, and am never happier than when I get one to design.

> Of the 12 you mention one is not mine, that of Pembroke College Oxford.
>
> The old organ case of the little organ in the Sheldonian on which according to tradition Handel played at the first performance of Athaliah, lay for some time in the crypt of the Sheldonian Theatre. I once tried to get it for some place I was concerned with, I forget where, but the University would not part with it then. A few years ago I went into Pembroke Chapel and recognised it in [*sic*] the organ there, of which you have a photograph.
>
> You ask what other cases I have done. The only others I can think of are one in my new chapel for Giggleswick School, Yorkshire, given with the chapel by Mr. Walter Morrison, at the cost of nearly £30,000, and one in Rye Church, Sussex.
>
> But the last is not altogether as I should like it, owing to an alteration in the organ after the case had been designed.
>
> By the way there is another in the Church I built at Stratton Hants for Ld. Northbrook.
>
> I agree with you in liking to clothe the tops of the pipes & not let them stick out nakedly above the case. But some people will have it so, & I am forced to do it in the new organ cases in the Speech-Room I built for Rugby school. I have made the best I can of it there. If you think of going to see it, wait till I have the little trumpeting boys put up which will not be for a month or two hence.
>
> The Oriel organ I was told came from Eton chapel, but I doubt it – I quite forget how much of the case is mine. I fancy not much – I cannot remember when [*sic*] I found it.
>
> The Cathedral organ case at Oxford is not mine. The Bilton organ case is very pretty. That at Winchcombe seems all of Chippendale work, & so would be 18-century. It is very curious. Could it have been a chamber organ? I have in hand an organ & organ loft for Bath Abbey. Yours very truly TG Jackson[30]

Freeman valued this contact and in a lecture given to the Royal College of Organists (1934), the final lantern slides, demonstrating 'The modern renaissance', were of Jackson's cases at the Sheldonian Theatre, Oxford, the two fronts of Brasenose College Chapel, Oxford and the elaborate case in Hampstead Parish Church, 'A bold and pleasing front in perfect accord with its surroundings. The three pendants beneath the towers, the *campanili* (or lanterns) above them and scroll carving between them are features to be noted.'[31]

Hampstead Parish Church
see p.22 for full-size plate

Also in 1934 SDB wrote a mammoth paper on 'Organs and Organ Cases' for the *Journal of the Royal Institute of Architects*. (Given the year, see above, was this in some way competition with Freeman? Surprisingly, Freeman is only acknowledged for the loan of some of Henry Lilley's drawings for the article and the lecture that preceded it.)[32] In turn, in 1942, Freeman refined his views and became much more prescriptive when he wrote a 32-page booklet, probably encouraged by the then Council for the Care of Churches, a support body for Diocesan Advisory Committees. He advised on greater care with proportions and stated that 'so many of our churches are crammed with rubbishy fittings ... one of the reasons why the organ is relegated to a wall or a corner'. As ever, he pleaded that no pipes should protrude over the cornice and that light must not be allowed to show through pipes or carving.[33] As well as the woodwork of the case structure, prospect pipes were a major concern and much space was given over to their visual treatment, materials, finish, layout and general presentation. Probably with architects in mind, in 1927 he set out more original thoughts:

> Now a row of organ pipes offers an architect three lines of which he may avail himself in

30 BOA Freeman collection, box 87: 'Old organ cases' volume I, contains a headed notelet from Thomas George Jackson to Freeman.

31 Andrew Freeman, 'A lecture on English organ cases', given in the Theatre of the Royal College of Music (Saturday, 20 October 1934), *The calendar of the Royal College of Organists* (1935–6), 126–45.

32 Bower, Stephen Dykes, 'Organs and organ Cases', *Journal of the Royal Institute of Architects*, third series, 41, no. 18 (August 1934): 945–65, based on a paper (of almost 11,000 words) read to the St Paul's Ecclesiastical Society. 'The drawings by Mr H.T.Lilley have been lent for reproduction by kind permission of the owner, the Rev. Andrew Freeman, *of* Standish, Glos.' Other drawings were reproduced from Hill, *Organ Cases and Organs*. Henry Thomas Lilley was an artist, friend, and frequent collaborator with Freeman.

33 Freeman, *Church Organs and Organ Cases*.

St Andreas, Kitzbühel.
Freeman/1217; plate 1490

A photograph taken by Mr T. P. Garnish, of Lambeth and copied by Freeman, the inspiration for the Standish case.

> his design, namely, the line of their feet, the line of their mouths, and the line of their tops. Any one, or any two, of these lines may be horizontal, *but not all three.* If he desires their tops to be level, he should obtain this result by giving longer feet to the shorter pipes – a perfectly natural way, and one which brings an unobtrusive, but pleasant, curve into the scheme, through the medium of the mouths and lips of the pipes.[34]

The documentary evidence for the inspiration of SDB's case at Standish, planned with Freeman though posthumously installed (1950),[35] suggests the source was the gallery organ in St Andreas, Kitzbühel, in the Austrian Tirol. Stylistically this is a descendant of the Annenkirche, Augsburg, whose case had itself evolved to fit around a rose-window [see Plate 145, p.215]. Two outer towers and an inverted, semi-circular, central section produce a simple and visually satisfying result. The decorated case doors (not a feature that found much favour in England, despite the encouragement of the Suttons and the occasional adoption by Ninian Comper)[36] follow the shape of the diminishing central flat and the doors could therefore be beneficially hinged on their longest and strongest side, with the panels lightest at their extremity. Kitzbühel is a more complex expression of the formula and the mannerist case is framed by two fluted Corinthian columns. The outer towers are surmounted with large scrolls, cherubs and deep carved shades that descend towards the centre. The central flat is compressed, suggesting that the Oberwerk is an organ in the gallery of another building inferred by the lower case (incidentally, a perfect solution to hide an English swell box), but the monochrome plate does not show the lavish gilt decoration to advantage. Freeman was initially sent a small photograph of this organ by a friend and wrote, 'Directly I set eyes on it I felt a desire for the Standish organ to be modelled upon it. In this Mr S. E. Dykes Bower has concurred.'[37]

SDB was a deft designer and it is difficult to know who the dominant partner was in the Standish and Hardwicke projects – Freeman or the younger (by a generation) SDB? The outcomes suggest that the architect was his own man though, as with the near-contemporary Norwich Cathedral case, the designs were not without fault, perhaps caused by economy and the need to provide a screen (rather than an integral case) to an existing instrument. At Standish SDB produced a very free interpretation of Kitzbühel – the towers and swan-necked scrolls are quoted, but the two columns have become four, flat, fluted pilasters, separating towers and

34 BOA Freeman collection, box 81 ('Notes on organs and organ builders') contains Andrew Freeman, 'The organ case in British concert halls', *The complete organ recitalist*, Herbert Westerby, ed. (published by *Musical Opinion* and the *Organ*, 1927). This quotation from Freeman's proof copy of the chapter, pasted into a cuttings book.

35 Gloucestershire Archives, P305 CW 3/24, Standish faculty, 4 September 1940. *NB* the faculty preparations are meticulous.

36 See Comper's examples in the crypt of St Mary Magdalene, Paddington (1895) (Plate 89, p.XXX) and Our Lady of Egmanton, Egmanton, Nottinghamshire (1896).

37 BOA Freeman collection, box 40A, 'Notes of a car tour in France, Belgium, Germany, Austria and Switzerland during July & August 1935: 248–9. The photograph was taken by Mr. T.P.Garnish, of Lambeth.

St Nicholas, Standish, the west-gallery case designed by Stephen Dykes Bower. The console on the south side.

flats. The central section becomes two small flats with rather mean carving and a small three-pipe central tower. SDB's pipe mouths do not follow the horizontal prototype and, uncomfortably, do not move in contrary motion to the carved flats, leaving the smallest pipes over-length. More successfully, the complex superstructure of the Kitzbühel prototype becomes a much simpler garlanded cartouche, Austrian mannerism giving way to a rectilinear, English, eighteenth-century feel, with bold, carved corbels suggesting Father Smith. Whatever the relationship, SDB and Freeman shared an eye for simplicity, and they understood that less is more.

In fact SDB was surely influenced by other cases developed from the Augsburg model, notably Freiburg Cathedral (which Freeman did not photograph) and the Franziskanerkirche, Innsbruck, Austria. Hardwicke follows the latter example: 'surely' wrote Freeman 'one of the most perfect cases in the whole world'.

> The man who designed this case knew his business and loved his task – of that there can be no possible doubt – while the men who made it must have shared to the full its creator's delight as the work gradually took shape under their hands.[38]

At Hardwicke, possibly because of economies in the re-use of existing pipework, the effect is

38 Andrew Freeman, 'Essays in Case Design', *The Organ* 8, no. 32 (April 1929): 224.

Left: St Nicholas, Hardwicke, unexecuted proposal for an organ case, cf with the less expensive result opposite.
Freeman/875; plate 1136, photographed in 1932.

Right: St Nicholas, Standish, unexecuted proposal for a west-end organ case by Stephen Dykes Bower (this confirmed from the framed original, in the care of the Diocese of Europe and identified by Canon Adrian Mumford).
Freeman/962; plate 1227, photographed 1932.

slightly spoiled, as the feet of the smaller pipes in the central flat are reduced in length, shorter than the pipes of the outer towers.

One mystery surrounds designs for the organs in Freeman's own parish churches. Two of his plates, both unattributed and dated 1932, show highly original treatments and Hardwicke is the most striking. The organ is shown at the west end of the north aisle (where it now stands) and contains gothic and renaissance elements. There is no provision for a central console and some side panelling suggests that, as with the present arrangement, the console would project from the bass side. There are three towers, the central containing a single, over-length pipe, capped with an urn. The hand of Henry Lilley is suggested in its design.[39] At Standish, the unrealised drawing omits the present SDB gallery in favour of a three-tower renaissance structure, without lower panelling, standing on Tuscan columns above the west tower-door (a detached console would have been essential!). There is rich carving, trumpeting cherubs, pendants and Flemish panelling, but a design attribution is not as obvious as Hardwicke.

~

Freeman was to become a respected member of the influential Gloucester Diocesan Advisory Committee for the Care of Churches (the DAC) and was formally invited to join around 1939,[40]

39 *Cf* with the un-executed design for Christ Church, Chalford, p.34.

40 Jonathan MacKechnie-Jarvis, *A History of the Gloucester Diocesan Advisory Committee 1919–92* (Stroud, 1992), 82. The DACs are statutory bodies and there can be conflict between them, parishes and diocesan authorities when controversial proposals are mooted. This was

Left: St Nicholas, Hardwicke, the case designed by Stephen Dykes Bower and located at the west-end of the north aisle. *See p.11.*

Right: Franziskanerkirche, Innsbruck, Austria.

Plate 170, p.240

when DACs were put on a statutory basis. Until then, any organ advice sought and given must have taken place directly with the parish concerned, or informally behind the DAC scenes. He served as its organs adviser until his death and his parish experience must have been valued when liturgical re-orderings were being considered.

In its early years the Committee included many of the movers and shakers (though not necessarily Committee attenders) of the Arts and Crafts movement: Sidney Barnsley, Detmar Blow, Arthur Gaskin, Charles Gere, Norman Jewson and the photographer, Sidney Pitcher. The first Chair was the architect, engineer and political activist, Sir Philip Sidney Stott, Bart[41] and Freeman's first minuted involvement occurred in November 1925. It concerned a drawn-out scheme for rebuilding the organ, with a new case and organ-gallery, at Christ Church, Chalford, Gloucestershire:

> The Committee wish to endorse the substance of a letter from the Rev A. Freeman Vicar of Standish, who has made a special study of organs & especially of their cases & for whose opinion they asked. They thoroughly agree with his criticisms & suggestions. Messrs. Liddiatt's specification for the organ itself is quite satisfactory &

certainly true of the Gloucester DAC and page 18 notes the illegal installation of a memorial tablet without permission, 'what might be tolerated under protest at Pitchcombe was not necessarily tolerable at all in the case of Standish'. (Though this was in 1920, predating Freeman's arrival.)

41 Gloucestershire Archives, GDR/A17/15/1/1, Gloucester DAC minute book 1924–28, a list of members and others, inside the front cover, as at 31 October 1924. It includes F.C.Eeles (see above), first Secretary of the Central Council for the Care of Churches. Also MacKechnie-Jarvis, *A History*, 80–4.

Christ Church, Chalford, unexecuted design for an organ case by H.T. Lilley, dated May 1925, inspired at Freeman's suggestion on the Hofkapelle, Innsbruck.

Freeman/745; plate 1011, photographed 1929.

they are quite of opinion [*sic*] that a Faculty should be issued for the whole.[42]

Eventually, the distinguished designers and woodworkers of the Sapperton Arts and Crafts tradition were to provide a distinctive but unsatisfactorily contrived case, with poorly scaled pipes, as part of a major furnishing scheme[43] [see Plate 99, p.169]. Freeman's own note offers background information that, in the circumstances, is very restrained:

I got H. T. Lilley to design a case, simple and inexpensive, after the lines of that in the Hofkapelle at Innsbruck, but this was turned down in favour of one by the Vicar's brother (Mr. A. A. Canter) who made a very effective design, marred only by one or two idiosyncrasies. Chief of these was the stopping short of the pipes in the side flats some inches below the shades whilst letting those in the central compartment run up behind the carved work. This destroys the unity of the design. A bar of wood across the front of the pipes dividing them into two parts is also an unnecessary and mistaken feature [see Lilley drawing, opposite].[44]

However, Freeman was invited to give the opening recital.[45]

It would be interesting to know whether Freeman was able to enthuse and turn to action any of the architects who were his fellow members of the Gloucester Committee. Some comments suggest not:

Unhappily, the half-century that has witnessed the accession of so many fine modem cases – Gothic, Renaissance and Classical – has also seen the wanton destruction of some extremely good ones of earlier times. Advisory boards and diocesan chancellors seem far more interested and successful in securing the right lettering for a modern memorial than they are in securing the preservation of an organ case of a past age, frequently beautiful, sometimes extremely so, and always, on account of its associations, priceless.[46]

At least one project ended well, again with some influence from that strand of the Arts and Crafts movement that developed in the Cotswolds. At Holy Trinity, Wickwar (1929), Freeman was involved in the substantial rebuild and

Christ Church, Chalford, 'a distinctive but unsatisfactorily contrived case, with poorly scaled pipes'

see Plate 99, p.169

42 Gloucester DAC minute book (November 1925), Chalford, P39, 27.

43 Gloucester Archives, P73, Chalford, Christ Church, parish Council minute book, 1920–53: 161 and 163. Also, www.britishlistedbuildings.co.uk/en-132860, accessed 6 July 2015. The western arch of the organ chamber was eventually filled with beautiful, but sound-blocking panelling designed by Norman Jewson and executed by Peter Waals.

44 BOA Freeman collection, box 83, volume 9: 1,471–3, the case made by Moffatt of Gloucester. Also see *Freeman, 'Essays in Case Design'*, 224, taking 'as his model the very lovely organ case in the Presbyterium, or Quire, of the Franziskaner Hofkirche at Innsbruck.'

45 BOA Freeman collection, box 83, volume 9: 1,473, on Thursday April 22, 1926.

46 BOA Freeman collection, box 81, 'Notes on Organs and Organ Builders', Andrew Freeman, 'Fifty Years of the Organ World: a Retrospect', *Musical Opinion* (October 1927); cuttings book: 170–7. Such criticism emerges from Freeman's own difficulties with some matters at Standish and Hardwicke.

handsome encasement of the organ, designed by L. W. Barnard & Partners of Cheltenham. He wrote in the third person, 'on lines suggested by A. F. & H. T. Lilley, and made by Wake & Dean of Yatton. Cost £200. Light oak, well carved: zinc pipes in front, with bright tin lips, rounded.'[47] [See Plate 124, p.194.]

~

On one occasion he sought to offer practical advice to organ builders in a very direct way and the line between a genuine case study and (in part?) the fictionalisation of one of his own churches is blurred. In 1929 he claims to have come across a project to move an organ to a western aisle location under a low roof. The early Victorian case (five compartments and gilded pipes) was to be abandoned, 'No one could call it a "good" case; but, in that it provided proper frames for all its displayed pipe-work and enclosed the instrument on all four sides, it was a "case" in the true sense of the word.' He talked to the organ builder and was shown the new approved replacement. (See figure 1, below.) Again he takes a swipe at 'ecclesiastical authorities who can take a lot of trouble over almost every other object within and without their church [but] should be so ignorant and so callous as to pass a thing like THAT!' After a conversation with the rector, he offers to have 'a friend of mine'[48] design an alternative that would cost little more. (See figure 2, below.)

> The problem was to clothe the tops of the pipes without altering their arrangement – except as to the correction of the very obvious blunder on the part of the draughtsman[49] – and to do it in such a manner that it should not add more than (say) £10 to the cost.... To save expense, the decorations on the pipe shades (not shown here) and on the cresting were to be painted, though the idea was that these were eventually to be carved.[50]

Holy Trinity, Wickwar, designed, 'on lines suggested by A.F. & H.T. Lilley'
see Plate 124, p.194

47 BOA Freeman collection, box 83, volume 9: 1,613–17, entry number 1,312.

48 H.T.Lilley

49 The right-hand tower pipes were not reversed symmetrically

50 Freeman, '*Essays in Case Design*', 220–3.

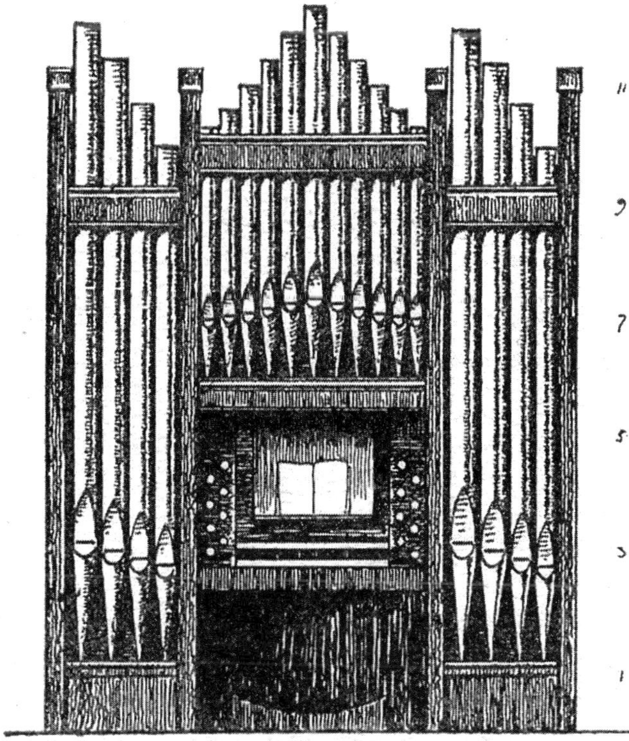

Fig. 1

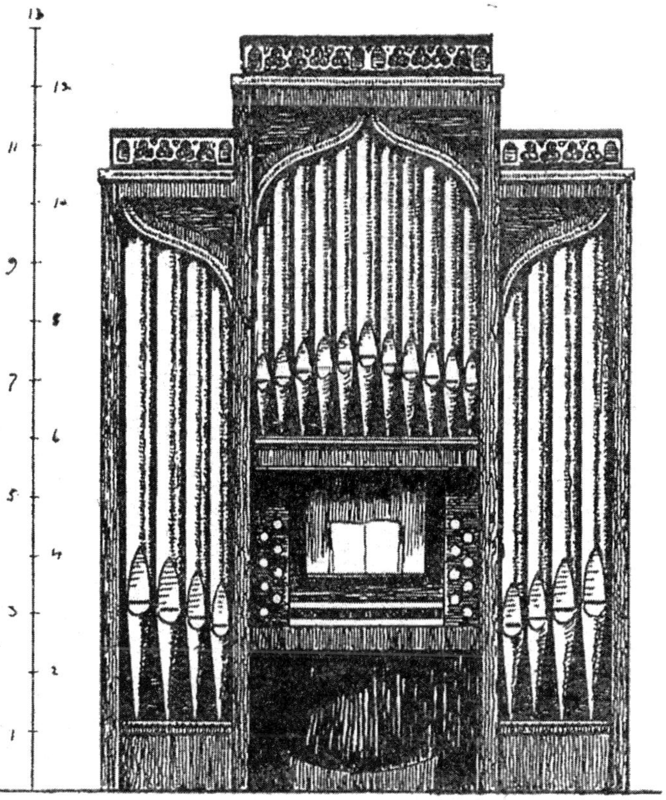

Fig. 2

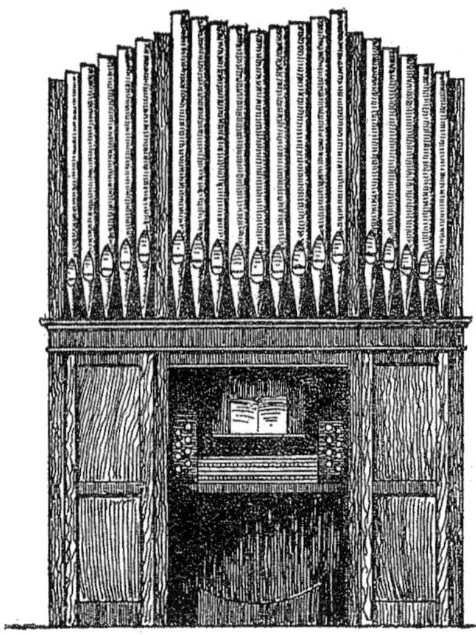

Fig. 3

Fig. 4

In the event this suggestion was not found acceptable because of an unforeseen change in the location. He was sent another even worse 'disfigurement' by the organ builder (see figure 3, above), and another solution was attempted. (See figure 4, above.) 'There can be no doubt that his design was an enormous improvement upon the builder's, but the scales were too heavily weighted this time to get an entirely satisfactory result', but he hoped

> that the drawings will convince the Goth and the unbeliever – if such a one is to be found amongst readers of *The Organ* – that two very ugly and (alas!) very typical "Designs for Church Organs" could have been made rather more than presentable at what would have proved to be a very slight additional cost, – too slight for expense to be used as a reason for rejection.
>
> *It is not so much lack of money that makes organs ugly, but apathy and ignorance.*[51]

Surprisingly, he had a soft spot for the early nineteenth-century designer-builders, trying to do their best, who probably used Thomas Faulkner's *Designs for Organs*,[52] a key resource for the trade at that time. He wrote of the simple but charming instrument in St Nicholas with St Mary, Chetwode:

> My own feeling is that I would far rather see an early nineteenth-century case, Gothic or Renaissance, than the average pipe-crowned hoarding that somehow manages to find its way into our churches, even in these enlightened days. The older ones may not be models for imitation, and a few were admittedly horrid, but they were and are *cases*, and they have their place in the long and honourable tradition of organ craft. Even the worst of them should not give place to what is nothing more than a pipe-rack at best, and often enough with the rack altogether omitted.[53]

The 'true principles' of Pugin, taken up by the Oxford Movement, regarded such *Gothick* design as debased, and Freeman called to mind 'the windows and doors of most of the Gothic toll-gate houses that formerly peppered the turnpike roads' (reminding us of those *ogee* arches!).[54] Such cases broke the cardinal rule that construction can be decorated, but decoration must not be constructed. He became surprisingly polemical on the topic, here offering a perfect answer to the old conundrum – the general disappearance of cases in the nineteenth century and the acceptance of the ubiquitous pipe-rack front:

> The fact of the matter is that "true principles" is the excuse, not the reason for bare-topped fronts. The Oxford Movement declared war on west-galleried choirs, – probably not without reason, for the old-time singers could be a fairly considerable thorn in the side of a fresh parson with his new-fangled ideas of what was (and what was not) seemly in worship. So the old singing club was disbanded and the less recalcitrant members, with the addition of a dozen or more boys, put into cassocks and surplices

51 Ibid., 223; Freeman's italics.

52 Second edition 1838 and also known as *The Organ-builder's Assistant*. I am obliged to the Library of the Royal College of Organists, Birmingham City University and Frances Pond, the Library Manager, for generously making available information on Freeman's personal library.

53 BOA Freeman collection, box 81 ('Notes on Organs and Organ Builders'), Freeman, Andrew, 'A holiday in North Bucks', *Musical Opinion* (December 1927), (probably) proof copy pasted in the cuttings book and numbered: 199–203.

54 Andrew Freeman, 'More Organ Cases of a Hundred Years Ago', *The Organ* 18, no. 70 (October 1938): 89 alludes and 91.

and crowded into chancels where there were no curtains to draw when they wanted to talk or fidget. Of course, the organs had to come east as well, and this is where the real mischief began. Chancels and side chapels lacked headroom, so cornices and cresting were hacked off and the bare-top case came into being. It was not an invention: it was the fruit of vandalism. "True principles" was not a discovery, but an excuse; first for destroying old case-work, and then for making new organs in conformity with the approved models. Thus did destructiveness go hand-in-hand with parsimony. Perhaps it was not so wonderful that the iconoclasts got away with it then, for they were good men as well as zealous, but it is well to remember how the ugly organs that disfigure our fine churches came into being.[55]

Another example of Freeman's developing opinions and analysis is set out in a text on concert hall cases. He noted that 'On the Continent, where large and ornate cases have been customary for some centuries, it was the usual practice to engage a master-carver and joiner (often two independent craftsmen) at the same time that the organ was given to the organ maker'. He declared:

> But a large front is a much more difficult matter, and calls for a specialist – one who knows how to group his front pipes effectively, and how to dispose his woodwork, so that the said pipes may be displayed (not hidden) to the best advantage. The man who would design a perfect organ case must go to the trouble to examine at least a few cases of the best period (1450–1750), not casually and at a distance, but at close quarters, so that he can see for himself how perfectly the woodwork of an old-time organ front was made to fit, and set off each several group of pipes. The modern practice of having the woodwork made by one firm to fit pipes made by another, in accordance with the plans of an architect who has no sympathy with the pipes which it is his business to display, is not conducive to perfection. In almost all the best of the older cases (certainly of the larger ones, English as well as Continental) the joiner and carver worked on the spot – usually after the front pipes had been set up in an agreed position.[56]

~

But now it is time to return to our conscientious and inexhaustible investigator. Sunset approaches (a dangerous time when inhabiting M.R.James' imagination!) and the sacristan shows 'signs of hurry and impatience' and heaves 'a sigh of relief when camera and note-book were finally packed up and stowed away...'[57] Turning from story-telling and his scholarly labours, James' *Prologue* expresses enthusiasm for Freeman's Father Smith researches, but anger at the loss of so many west galleries, cathedral screens and the organ cases that formerly stood on them. He sought to rein in the 'passions which have long fermented within me'.

> Let me compose my feelings and say that this book, to the attentive reader, will be a precious boon, leading him [*sic*] to see the beauty of a whole class of very fine works, and confirming him in the resolve that his word and influence shall always be on the side of preserving, and where that is possible, reinstating them in their pride of place.[58]

Amen to that.

55 Freeman, 'Some Gothic Organ Cases', 40.

56 Freeman, 'The Organ Case in British Concert Halls'.

57 M.R.James, 'The Uncommon Prayer-book (Full Text),' *A Thin Ghost*, accessed June 24, 2015, www.thin-ghost.org/items/show/161. 1921.

58 James' Prologue in Freeman, *Father Smith*, n.p.

Overleaf: Pages from Freeman's sketch books
(BOA, Freeman Collection, Box 83)

Wraxall

3445

" T. C. Bates.

Organ and Piano-Forte manufacturer

Upton on Severn

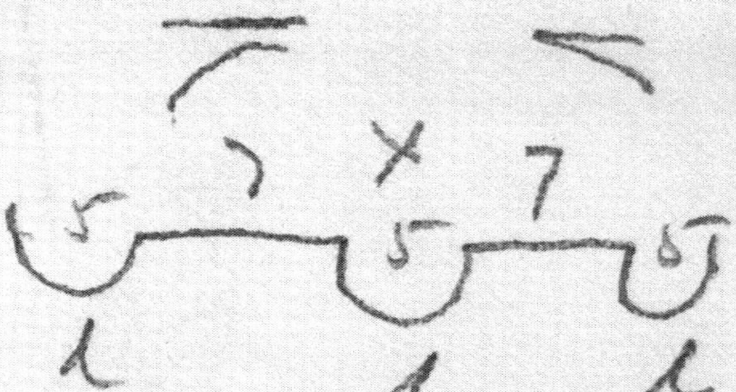

The Organ Photography of Andrew Freeman

Photographing organs is a specialised branch of architectural photography which for many years was looked down upon by historians and collectors. Only within the past three decades has it begun to be accorded the respect it deserves. Architectural photography as a whole has been easy to dismiss as an art form: the photographer traditionally has been a secondary player in a building's history. Tasked with merely recording a visual impression of the space before the camera lens, the photographer has been seen as less important than the architect, who is the designer of the space. Little thought has been given to the possibility that the image produced could, itself, be more than a visual record, and that it could tell us much about the nature of the space and the objects which inhabit it. Not only can a photograph reveal details of the historic period in which it was taken, but it can also function as the eye of the recorder, reflecting his or her familiarity and interest in the subject matter, as well as the limitations of the photographic process of the time. In the case of Andrew Freeman's photographs, all these elements combined to create images which, flawed or not, are telling documents of this most singular musical instrument.

In 1952, the eminent architectural and landscape photographer Edwin Smith wrote:

> At all hours of the day, long after I was expected elsewhere or have found a hotel for the night, I have hurried back to my car for my equipment and begun working – entranced by the sense of communion with something admired to intensity, intoxicated by the privilege of being able to pay it the homage of my craft.[1]

Smith's words expressed his excitement at the discovery of something new and the opportunity to commit it to silver. From everything we know about Andrew Freeman, these words could have been written by him. Smith was part of an emerging consciousness which saw the lack of controls over the fate of historic buildings and their frequent wholesale destruction as cultural threats, and sought to document these structures before they were reduced to rubble by the wrecker's ball. Years earlier, Freeman had also been moved by such sentiments in his work as a photographer and recorder of the English organ.

What is all the more remarkable is that Freeman worked in an age when photography as an art-form and method of pictorial record still shared so much with its antecedents: the processes involved were long and complex, equipment was relatively bulky and required a great deal of manual dexterity, and good results could not always be guaranteed. That his legacy, amounting to some 1600 glass plate negatives, is still with us is testament to his undoubted skill behind the lens and the enduring quality of his methods and visual perception. Gilbert Benham, that other doyen of the genre, wrote, 'One or two men I know have taken up this fascinating – and therefore extremely difficult – branch of photography more or less seriously.'[2]

1 E.Smith, and G.Hutton, *English Parish Churches* (London: Thames & Hudson, 1952); rev. edition with O.Cook (1976), 7.

2 Gilbert Benham, 'Organs and Their Successful Photography', *The Organ* 4, no.14 (Oct. 1924): 118.

Opposite: Westminster Abbey, London, south case (1922)
Freeman/511; plate 755

Both north and south cases are '...of excellent design and workmanship' (*The Organ* 2, no. 7 (Jan. 1923): 142.)

Christ-Church, Newgate Street
see plate 38, p.108

Staunton Harold Hall
see plate 90, p.160

Holy Trinity, Bridlington
Plate 42, p.112

There is no doubt he included Freeman among them. Who can forget the monumentality of Hill's Christ-Church, Newgate Street or the delicacy of Staunton Harold Hall seen through Freeman's eyes?

Organs are, by their nature, basically either flat or box-shaped, and this is what the eye sees. The flatness is relieved by the shape of the façade pipes and the way they are grouped in flats and towers. The eye has the advantage that it permits three-dimensional appreciation of what is before it. The success, or otherwise, of an organ photograph depends to a great extent on the photographer training his eye to shut out the stereoscopic effect and see the organ as the camera lens would. The curious lack of perspective engendered by taking a picture from a head-on position is one reason why relatively few of Freeman's pictures are taken from this standpoint. Even a relatively mundane pipe-rack such as Holy Trinity, Bridlington gains enormously in depth and perspective simply by not photographing it straight ahead, which would leave the eye clueless as to the existence of the (relatively shallow) angle of the returns at either side. In this picture Freeman demonstrated that other canon of good photography: having trained the eye to see like a camera lens, including framing the image, as it were, on the human equivalent of a rectangular glass plate, he had to reintroduce the suggestion of three dimensions on a flat surface. In this way much of the 'photography' was accomplished before the camera had even been erected on its tripod. He then transferred what he had seen to the ground-glass screen at the back, and the instrument simply had to capture it on silver halide.

Freeman faced other more fundamental challenges to capturing his images. From a technical standpoint, the lenses and sensitive materials available imposed severe limitations. The development of camera lenses, for example, belonged then to the arcanum of the optical designer: a new lens could be many months in the making and as such became a highly individual article in a way unimaginable today. Names such as Meyer's 'Aristostigmat', the Ross 'Homocentric' and the Zeiss 'Double Protar' were on the lips of every aficionado who wanted the very best in optical performance. Not for nothing did Gilbert Benham state unequivocally, 'To begin with, it must be clearly understood that for this type of photography *only* the very best of everything is good enough, and this includes skill and thought quite as much as the outfit.'[3] In addition, photographic plates were very insensitive in Freeman's day: a plate regarded as 'medium fast' would have had about the same capability as Kodachrome II (ISO25), a well-known slide film after WWII, meaning that exposures would have run into minutes, sometimes over an hour. Not for nothing did photographers joke about 'a fortnight at *f*/8'.

Even with the best equipment, stray light from a window or reflections from highly polished metalwork or a glass mirror could play havoc with the most careful composition, introducing areas of vaguely-shaped luminosity sufficient to alter or obliterate detail: stop-heads could become curiously ovoid as perspective became stretched; vertical lines could be bent weirdly out of shape

3 Ibid. Italics original.

as if the organ were reflected in a mirror out of an old-time fun-fair, and so on.

A successful photographer had to be acutely aware of all these limitations, and it is greatly to Freeman's credit that he rarely produced a picture in which these constraints were obvious. Occasionally it was unavoidable, but now, over a century later, the documentary value of the images far outweighs their faults. If some of his pictures can be criticised, it needs to be borne in mind that the photographer had to work within the rules set by the medium, much as an organist has to work with the organ if he or she is to obtain the best musical effect from it.

To us, the thought of spending as much as two hours just to obtain one photograph seems ludicrous, but a sufficient amount of time was essential, especially where light was poor or where sharpness over a considerable distance was necessary. Benham thought nothing of spending this much time to get the picture he wanted. When the photographer encountered almost complete darkness, then magnesium flash powder or ribbon might be ignited, yielding an intense white light and clouds of smoke that must have brought to mind bizarrely antique rituals redolent of sacrifice. Chemicals were expensive and dangerous, and there was always the possibility of miscalculation: too little or too much and the negative would either be unprintable or in need of complex chemical manipulation. There is no particular evidence that Andrew Freeman resorted to these or other means, but one photograph of St Mary's, Nottingham shows a large area of white cloth slung in front of the East window as if in an attempt to either diffuse the light or reflect it onto the organ. Whether this was part of Freeman's technique is difficult to say, but there is a second negative taken from a much closer viewpoint that does not show the cloth. If Freeman was the one who hung the sheet, it gives us an indication of the lengths he went to secure a usable negative (although it has to be said that this is not one of his best photographs, since large areas of the top of the organ are in deep shadow and the low viewpoint obscures some detail of the console). Nonetheless, several other points emerge, such as whether Freeman was willing, or able, to make a second longer 'bracketed' exposure

St Mary's, Nottingham
Freeman/42; plate 136
see also plate 13, p.83

(one longer than the one for which light had been measured) in an effort to secure greater shadow detail; and the probability that he did not possess a particularly wide angle lens given the distance from the organ necessary to secure the view with the sheet in it and what was lost at the top of the case in the view close up. The length of exposure must have been considerable because there are phantom shapes as if someone or something was moving at the bottom right hand corner of the cloth, and the bottom left hand corner of the cloth is very indistinct, suggesting it was being blown about or moved (had a door been left open?) (Editor's note: for more 'ghosts' indicating long exposures, see the mysterious clergyman under the organ case, p.xi; or the ghostly congregation in Plate 165, p.235) Of course, it could be there was some glazing work being undertaken to the East window and the sheet had simply been put up to stop the draughts!

We know very little about the detailed aspects of Freeman's particular method as an organ photographer, and attempts to discover what sort of camera and the materials he used have been unsuccessful. However, it would not be unreasonable to make some suppositions based on the photographs themselves, and indeed it might be instructive: in our digital mono-culture, which is so used to the hyper-instantaneity and (arguably) sterility of cheap digital image capture, highlighting the requirements for a thoroughly competent photographic technique as well as the financial outlay necessary to secure a good result may be surprising.

Very few, if any of Freeman's images show any noticeable distortion, suggesting that he was careful in his choice of equipment. Popular cameras of the time such as Newman & Guardia's 'New Ideal Sybil' and Newman Sinclair's 'Standard Una' permitted interchangeable lenses and gave a full range of movements for correcting perspective and focus.

They were, nonetheless, expensive instruments. In 1934, The 'Standard Una' outfit with a Ross 'Homocentric' lens cost £23, the price rising to £31.10s, if fitted with a Ross 'Combinable' lens permitting two focal lengths. The outfit came with three double plate holders giving six exposures. Extra plate holders cost £1.2s.6d each. A suitable wooden tripod such as a 'Sands, Hunter' weighing in at 8 lbs would cost £4.10s. The plates themselves cost in the region of 2s.0d per dozen depending on 'speed' (sensitivity) and whether they were orthochromatic (rather deficient in red sensitivity) or panchromatic (roughly equal sensitivity to all colours). Chemicals for developing and printing could either be had in proprietary form as made by Johnson's of Hendon, or the photographer could make up his own using a vast range of formulae supplied by the likes of the *Amateur Photographer* magazine, the *Ilford Manual of Photography* [4] (the photographer's bible), or the *British Journal of Photography* yearbook,[5] all aimed at producing either the finest grain, best contrast or extracting the highest speed from the plate.

Portability was obviously a consideration, since of course Freeman travelled widely to take his photographs, not only in England but also on the continent: perhaps one of the most delightful pictures in the archive is the cartoon of Freeman setting off to photograph an organ somewhere [see pp.48–49].

The 'Standard Una'

A.F. starts his Journey.

The basic outfit described above could be carried in a single leather case containing camera and probably half a dozen plate holders weighing in at around 10 pounds. The tripod would

4 C.H.Bothamley, *The Ilford Manual of Photography* (London: Brittania Works Co., 1890). In 1901, Brittania Works Co. became Ilford Ltd., and the book went into four more editions. Five subsequent editions have been published under the title *The Manual of Photography.*

5 *The British Journal of Photography* (from 1860) began as the *Liverpool Photographic Journal* in 1854. It continues to be published to this day, and is highly regarded by professionals.

obviously be a separate item but, altogether, this would amount to an outfit capable of being transported on a bicycle, if awkwardly. It is fair to surmise that this was the extent of his equipage. Freeman did not possess long telephoto lenses for capturing small details (these would have added considerably to the bulk) since almost all his photographs are views. Where there are close-ups to any degree, these would have been achieved in the enlarger, since the image quality of the best of his negatives is so good even by today's standards.

The matter of exposure, of small concern in this age of digital photography, was in Freeman's lifetime quite a complicated affair. Photographers had to rely on exposure tables provided by manufacturers of photographic plates or published monthly by *Amateur Photographer*, combined with practical considerations, such as always using the correct plate sensitivity, and familiar brands of chemicals in the developing process.[6] Careful thought and preparation would enable a reasonable degree of consistency and some certainty as to the result, even though the technology of photographic materials was not as robust as it is today. Freeman might have used an optical exposure meter, where the eye was used to judge exposure through a specially designed viewer, or a Watkins Extinction meter where the amount of time needed to darken a piece of photographic paper was used to estimate exposure. Even with this level of care, Freeman's negatives do show some variation, which suggests that his exposures were rather hit and miss and were compensated for during development in the dark room. It was here that a badly under- or over-exposed plate could be saved: one could watch the image appear by safelight in the chemical dish until a reasonable image appeared, at which point development was halted. Alternatively, images could be reduced or intensified to manipulate density after development had been completed, often using what would be considered banned substances today – mercury, uranium and chromium salts, cyanides and other chemicals of similar toxicity.

That Andrew Freeman took his equipment on foreign tours adds to the sense one has of his intense enthusiasm, interest and dedication. He needed all three because the preparation and management of the photography side of things could be quite an ordeal, as witnessed by the following advice on how to plan a foreign tour taken from the *Ilford Manual of Photography* from 1901, some six years after he began his work.

> On Tour. When away from home special difficulties arise in connection with the transport of new and exposed plates, emptying and refilling the dark slides, repacking the exposed plates, etc. The dark slides can, as a rule, be refilled, and the exposed plates repacked at night in the bedroom. A portable orange or ruby lamp will be required, and a candle is the safest illuminant to pack with other things. If there is a fan-light over the door, as frequently happens in hotels, take care that no light comes through it into the room from the corridor. Diffused light from the moon, or from street lamps, can, as a rule, be neglected, provided that the lamps are some distance below or away from the window. The blind should, of course, be pulled down, and if the window is provided with curtains or shutters they should be drawn or closed. If it seems really necessary, a sheet or coverlet from the bed may be fastened against the window by means of large drawing-pins, half a dozen of which should be carried in readiness for an emergency; but such a proceeding is rarely need, and the slides may be quite safely emptied and refilled in a room in which there seems to be a considerable amount of diffused light of the kind referred to, provided that the operation is performed quickly and the plates are not exposed to direct rays from the window. A corner of the room on the same side as the window is usually the safest place. If you are likely to need to change plates during the day it is well to carry some orange or ruby fabric, or paper, and some drawing pins, so that a small window can be effectually screened in a few minutes.
>
> Exposed plates should be packed so that they form practically a solid block of glass. To separate the plates by wedges of

6 Freeman himself recounted a story about using an unfamiliar developer on his first trip to Belgium, which caused him to lose some hard-won photographs. See *Musical Opinion* 56, no.662 (Nov. 1932): 146.

cardboard or other material at the sides, or still worse at the ends, greatly increases the risk of fracture. The best method is to use the special boxes devised by Pringle and made by Hare. They are internally of exactly the dimensions of the plates, and the latter are placed in them back to back, face to face, or face to back, strong springs attached to a false end and a false lid preventing any movement and making the plates practically a block of glass. Care must of course be taken that there is no dust or grit between the plates.......Before each plate is packed a number (corresponding to an entry in the note-book) should be written with a pencil on one corner of the film.

The packets of exposed or unexposed plates should be packed in a stout wooden box, the packages being so arranged that the plates rest on their long edges, and do not lie flat. Tightly packed in this position, so that they cannot shake about, the risk of breakages is reduced to a minimum......Development en route is not to be recommended, but it is well to develop one or two plates in order to check the exposures. The plates used for this purpose should be duplicate exposures so that they can be thrown away after being developed......

Photographers are often in doubt as to what they may or may not photograph without permission. On the Continent the permissions required vary in different countries. In all cases the neighbourhood of fortifications should be carefully avoided. In some countries permission is required in order to photograph in the streets, and is usually to be obtained from the Chief of Police. Should any difficulties arise, apply to the British Consul or Charge d'Affaires.

Considerable care is required when passing the Customs Houses, but courtesy and politeness will reduce the difficulties to a minimum. The more freely you offer your packages for inspection, the better, and if you find it difficult to prevent packages of plates from being opened, insist upon being taken to the chief officer. In some places there is a dark room in which plates can be examined. The appearance of photographic goods is now pretty well known at all the principal Customs Houses, and it is a good plan to keep the plates as far as possible in the original boxes with the original labels, and to have a spare box of plates that can be opened if necessary.[7]

If there is one picture that shows Freeman at his best, it might be St Catharine's College Chapel, Cambridge (opposite). Here, Freeman wasn't content to simply photograph the organ head-on but, instead, took account of what was the instrument's 'bright side' allowing the eye to dictate the most comfortable viewing angle while taking in the whole of the subject. For that reason, the camera was placed slightly right of centre, resulting in a pleasing asymmetry and allowing the viewer's eye to be directed to the most easily visible detail, that which is lit by the windows. At the same time, there is enough reflected light from the opposite walls to ensure that detail in the shadows remains adequate. This also assists in modelling the shape of the pipe towers giving them a roundness and depth which would be lost were they to be viewed from straight in front. If there is perhaps one criticism, it is that the viewing angle is rather low so that the foreground is slightly intrusive; but this is compensated for by the general sense of perspective. Overall, there is a balance and a range of light and shade that is eminently satisfying. It is fair to say that in this photograph, all aspects of his craft discussed in this essay have come together in a way that could not be improved.

To view Andrew Freeman's work is to enter a world which is all but lost today save in some out-of-the-way country church which has escaped the encroachments of progress. Freeman realised that the organ as he knew it was not set in stone. The removals and rebuildings of the previous century must have alerted him to the fragility of its legacy, since otherwise he wouldn't have engaged in such a precarious undertaking. What survives is testament to a man who was not only a lover of the organ but also had the resources needed, both intellectually and morally, to record what he saw for posterity.

opposite:
St Catharine's College Chapel, Cambridge (1906).
Freeman/13; plate 68

7 *The Ilford Manual of Photography* (1901), 44–46.

A.F. starts his Journey.

Arrives —
but finds himself
Locked Out.

The Key is found.

The Photograph taken.

The Organ inspected

- and A.F. returns, happy, with a few Souvenirs.

VEULES - LES - ROSES

AN ORGANIST ABROAD

Freeman's travels to the continent, 1927–46

Between the years of 1927 and 1946 Andrew Freeman joined a parade of organists and enthusiasts from England, the United States, and the continent who travelled to foreign countries to look at – and when possible, to play and hear – organs. Amongst those who came to England in the nineteenth century alone can be mentioned Felix Mendelssohn, Aristide Cavaillé-Coll, and the American organist, hymn-writer, and teacher Lowell Mason. The list of English musicians and writers who visited organs in foreign lands usually begins with Charles Burney in the eighteenth century, and moves into the nineteenth with writers and critics such as Edward Holmes, Henry Chorley, George Smart, and many others. With the explosion in writing about organs in English music journals from the mid-nineteenth century, the number of names of English travellers abroad also increased. A casual perusal in journals from the first part of the twentieth century shows articles about foreign organs by Ernest Adcock, A. Eaglefield Hull, J. Stuart Archer, Malcolm Hallowes, Gilbert Benham, Cecil Clutton, John Compton, T. F. Bumpus, J. W. Hinton, Arthur G. Colban, C. F. Abdy Williams, and a host of often chatty letters and essays whose authors are identified only by their initials or noms de plumes such as 'Magister Choralis' or 'A Naval Man'. Freeman obviously had long cherished the idea of making a pilgrimage to the continent: his photographic archive shows many drawings reproduced from books of famous organ cases in Spain, France, Germany, and other countries. In addition, he assembled and bound books made up of clippings from journals and other places about continental organs and curiosities about foreign organs and organ playing.

Clearly, money was a concern however, and his trips were hard-won and re-lived frequently after his return home. The prologue to his account of his first trip abroad in 1927 gives a clue as to his straitened circumstances:

> To visit foreign countries and to see and photograph foreign organs had been a dream of mine almost as long as I could remember. In 1927, through the generosity of a friend, the dream became a possibility. France was the obvious choice… With the gift and what Ethel had managed to put by, we had enough for a fortnight's holiday for the four of us.[1]

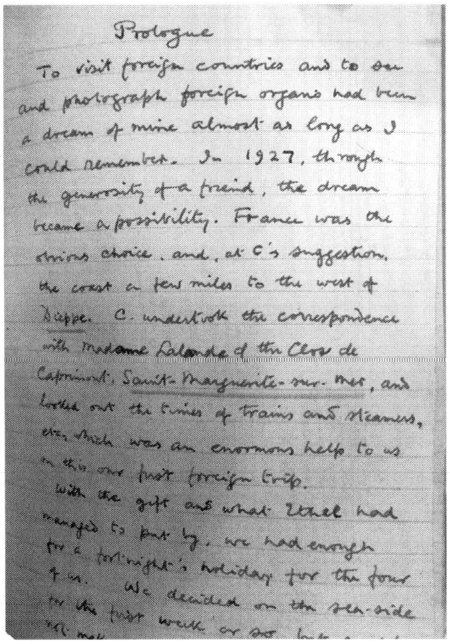

Prologue

To visit foreign countries and to see and photograph foreign organs had been a dream of mine almost as long as I could remember. In 1927, through the generosity of a friend, the dream became a possibility. France was the obvious choice. and, at C's suggestion, the coast a few miles to the west of Dieppe. C. undertook the correspondence with Madame Lalande of the Clos de Caprimont, Saint-Marguerite-sur-Mer, and looked out the times of trains and steamers, etc., which was an enormous help to us in this our first foreign trip.

With the gift and what Ethel had managed to put by, we had enough for a fortnight's holiday for the four of us. We decided on the sea-side for the first week or so

1 BOA, Freeman Collection, Box 39, 'First Impressions of French Organs'. This account, according to his hand-written notes in BOA box 40A, red book 15, was written in March 1944, 'as remembered by two of the party (G & A) [probably Greta and Andrew]… seventeen years after'.

Opposite:
Drawing of Veules-les-Roses by H. T. Lilley. Lilley's drawing was based on Freeman's photograph of the organ (see plate 102, p.172), and used as an illustration in Freeman's account of this trip in *Musical Opinion*, 1928. It also appears as a drawing in Freeman's diary; see p.57.

Freeman by no means squandered these opportunities, and his travels were unique and particularly valuable today because of the detail and thoroughness with which he documented his visits – and of course, because of his photographs.

In all, Freeman took six trips to the Continent, each lasting a minimum of two weeks, and a few as many as four or even more: 1927, 1929, 1932, 1935, 1939, and 1946. His practice was to keep a careful diary during the trips, complete with drawings and diagrams, called a 'rough book'; then upon his return (perhaps the following winter, as his trips abroad took place in the summers) he would write the journal up more neatly, including his photographs. The number of photographs in the archive shows that he took anywhere from 33 to 83 pictures of organs on each trip.

Sichem Church, Belgium (1929): *(Freeman/768; plate 1049)*

Freeman's sketch of this organ is on p.59.

These accounts appeared as short articles in *Musical Opinion* and *The Organ* magazine over the course of several subsequent years. Later still he would use the galley proofs from these articles as the basis for further home-made accounts of his trips, which often included more photographs and details, and which he carefully bound himself. (For example, his account of the 1932 trip to Austria, called 'Some Austrian Organs: Being Notes of a Tour in June 1932' bears the following note at the bottom of the title page: 'Made at Standish vicarage, GLOS, March 1938.' From the several different versions of each trip which exist in the Freeman archive, it is unclear what Freeman's intended audience was for these accounts: certainly the enthusiasts who read the journals were the most obvious beneficiaries, but it is also evident that he relished going over and over the details of his trips himself, perhaps re-living each day from the distant remove of his study in Standish. More than once he remarked on the fact that while there were many travel books about visiting churches and historic towns, monuments, and works of art on the continent, there was precious little mention of organs or organ cases. He complained that travel books might describe the interior fittings of a church, but even though the pulpit, altar, or windows might be exhaustively described, the organ was scarcely remarked upon. In the early 1930s Freeman carefully annotated in astonishing detail a published book by G.E.R Gedye titled *A Wayfarer in Austria*.[2] Onto every spare page and empty space Freeman neatly pasted in typewritten paragraphs about the organs in the places discussed by the author. Margins are filled with his tiny, neat handwriting, with photographs and drawings filling spaces inside covers and between chapters. His note at the beginning of the book reveals his mission: 'Austrian Organ Cases are amongst the finest of the fittings in their churches: they are amongst the finest in the world. Mr Gedye's fascinating book contains no mention of their existence. It is to repair this

2 4th ed., revised (London: Methuen and Co. Ltd., 1931).

omission that the copy in my possession has been extra-illustrated but the subject requires more pictures (and of larger size) than could be crowded into the available nooks and corners.'

His journals and articles from all his tours (except perhaps the last one in 1946) betray his delight at being abroad and 'organ-hunting': they are filled with good-natured anecdotes about the places he visits and the people he meets, as well as free-hand drawings and diagrams in the margins, all which combine to make them colourful, engaging, and very readable. A sample from his journal from the 1935 car trip to Austria sings out with his good mood, as well as reveals his inability to resist looking at organs on the way to the ferry before even leaving England:

July 8 1935 (Monday). A really hot day. Ethel and I left Standish for Witham at 12. Matilda had just been decarbonised and fitted with new piston rings, etc., so we had to drive rather slowly – not over 30 miles, we were told, though I fear we exceeded it a bit without noticing. We had lunch in the Cotswolds, some 5 or 6 miles beyond Seven Springs. The route we took was Gloucester, Air Balloon, Seven Springs, Northleach, Witney, the new Eynsham-Oxford Bypass (we avoided both places), Aylesbury, St Albans, Epping, Writtle *(no case to organ)* and Chelmsford. We arrived at 6.30 to find the Avenue in possession of the Road Makers, but managed to get Matilda into the garden where she stayed the night. [italics mine]

Loading 'Matilda' onto the boat at Dover

Below: Annotated pages from Gedye's *A Wayfarer in Austria.*

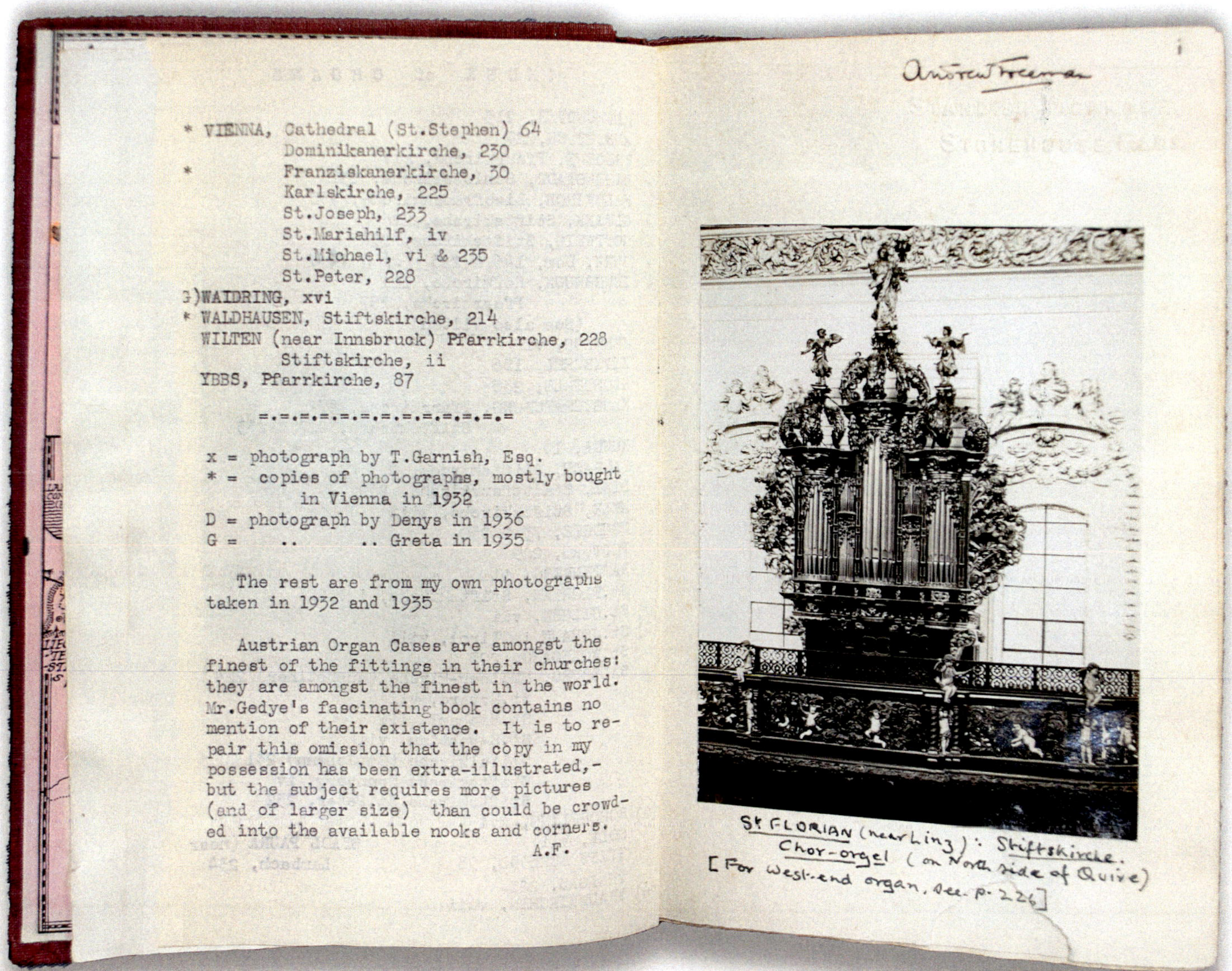

* VIENNA, Cathedral (St.Stephen) 64
Dominikanerkirche, 230
* Franziskanerkirche, 30
Karlskirche, 225
St.Joseph, 233
St.Mariahilf, iv
St.Michael, vi & 235
St.Peter, 228
G)WAIDRING, xvi
* WALDHAUSEN, Stiftskirche, 214
WILTEN (near Innsbruck) Pfarrkirche, 228
Stiftskirche, ii
YBBS, Pfarrkirche, 87

=.=.=.=.=.=.=.=.=.=.=.=.=

x = photograph by T.Garnish, Esq.
* = copies of photographs, mostly bought in Vienna in 1932
D = photograph by Denys in 1936
G = ... Greta in 1935

The rest are from my own photographs taken in 1932 and 1935

Austrian Organ Cases are amongst the finest of the fittings in their churches: they are amongst the finest in the world. Mr.Gedye's fascinating book contains no mention of their existence. It is to repair this omission that the copy in my possession has been extra-illustrated,- but the subject requires more pictures (and of larger size) than could be crowded into the available nooks and corners.
A.F.

Andrew Freeman

St FLORIAN (near Linz): Stiftskirche.
Chor-orgel (on North side of Quire)
[For West-end organ, see p. 226]

opposite: Frutigen Church, Switzerland (1946): *(Freeman/1397; plate 1669)*

Freeman's sketch of this organ is on p.66.

below: Offranville Church *(Freeman/674; plate 933)*

Freeman's sketch of this organ is on p.57.

Whatever his purpose, Freeman's handwritten accounts are impressively neat and easy to read, and his narrative almost always genial, positive, interesting, and full of gentle good humour. Mostly he writes about the organs, but occasionally about the health of one or other of his travelling companions (when he wasn't travelling alone, his companions were often his wife Ethel, his daughter Greta, and his son Denys). Even though his travels took place in the tense inter-war years in the war-torn places of Europe, he rarely makes a comment about the political goings-on, unless it has to do with areas he is unable to visit. His trip to Switzerland in 1939, for example, came about only after a planned 'saunter down the Moselle; thence to Bavaria' was scuppered owing to 'the alarms of early spring'. In the opening sentence of his published article on the trip he says only, 'If I know about ten times as much about Swiss organs as I knew last year, I have to thank the one and only Fuehrer for the fact.' [3] Freeman was not a commentator on international policy or war-time society: he perhaps deliberately turned a blinkered eye from the distress, dismay, and destruction of daily life, to the wonderful organs and organ cases in foreign churches. His accounts must have been a much-welcomed view of an entirely different slice of Europe than that which was so prominent in the news otherwise: a separate and slower world, anchored in the distant past, and carrying on without regard to the exigencies of current affairs.

Extraordinarily, Freeman's earliest trip, in 1927 to France, was taken on a bicycle, with his wife and two children. When one considers the weight and fragility of his camera(s) and glass slides, one wonders how this could have been possible (though see Andrew Hayden's reasoned explanation in Chapter 4). In his self-bound book on a later trip to Belgium, he said that he usually tried to expose two plates of each organ, in case 'an accident to one may not leave me utterly bereaved'[4] – thus, if he followed his own best practice he would have to carry twice the number of plates as one might expect. Added to the logistical difficulty must be counted the presumed patience of his family: we have 33 photographic plates from the 1927 French trip (there may have been more photographs taken) of which almost every shot is from a different angle, and if each view was a half-hour in the setting up and exposure alone, (leaving aside the time necessary to find the priest or other responsible person, the explaining and requesting permission, sometimes by gesticulations only, the exchange of pleasantries, and so on) that is a considerable amount of time carved out for this pastime in what was ostensibly a family holiday. Freeman himself says about his visit to Antwerp in 1929 that 'Of two-and-a-half-days exploring

---

3 Freeman's clipping is from his article "Some Swiss Organs", in *The Organ* 19, no.75 (Jan. 1940): 138.

4 BOA, Freeman Collection, Box 39, "An Organ Tour in Belgium, Vol. I", p.122.

the city and its numerous churches, eight photographs swallowed up six whole hours for exposure alone.'[5]

Most of Freeman's other trips were taken by train, which freed him up to carry heavy weights, but also restricted him to the towns that were on the train line. About his 1932 train trip to Austria, Freeman wrote, 'I had reduced my luggage to the utmost minimum, – a stand camera and one large portmanteau, whose ballast was ten dozen 5 by 4 plates. (It was heavy!)'[6] His trip to Austria in 1935, by car, allowed him more freedom to travel where and when he liked, and presumably to carry more equipment.

We have seen that Freeman himself was an accomplished organist, and in fact he not only photographed organs but he also played them as often as he could. Indeed, there is at least one account in his reports that he played the closing voluntary to a Mass (in Bruges, 1929).

Freeman's travels to the continent were extraordinary in several ways: first, the pictures document not only some important and magnificent lost organs, but also, through the warmth and personality which Freeman was able to capture in them, bear witness to the tragic destruction of war which reaches even into the hidden by-ways of pipe organ cases. Second, they are a testament to the energy, persistence, and love Freeman held for the artistry of pipe organs, both visually and aurally; and third, they bring to the attention of a wider public the beauty of an under-appreciated craft. By gently but passionately drawing attention to these works of art, Freeman played a role in their preservation, even if only in image and memory, as well as in the preservation of similar works of art in the future. In his photographs he certainly has shown us not only beautiful organs of the past, but also the promise and pleasure of this special art.

5 *The Organ* 11, no.44 (April 1932): 200.
6 *The Organ* 12, no. 48 (April 1933): 236.

1927 – France

26 July to 12 August
France Seine Inférieure (since 1955 called Seine-Maritime) and Eure

Freeman's first trip abroad was a family holiday, with his wife Ethel and two children, Greta and Denys. By his own account, he cycled about 250 miles in fifteen days; looked inside 50–60 churches; saw 42 organs; examined 29 of them; played 'a round dozen'; and photographed a score (there are 33 photographs from this tour). In the archive is a small (purchased) lined notebook into which Freeman wrote his account of the trip, and drew pictures of the organs he had seen. Articles from this account were first published in *Musical Opinion* between January 1928 and September 1930. Later, the galley proofs of the articles were annotated and carefully pasted into a hand-sewn book, which is dated at the back in Freeman's tiny but perfectly legible handwriting: 'Made & Bound at Standish, Glos., Jan. 1931'.

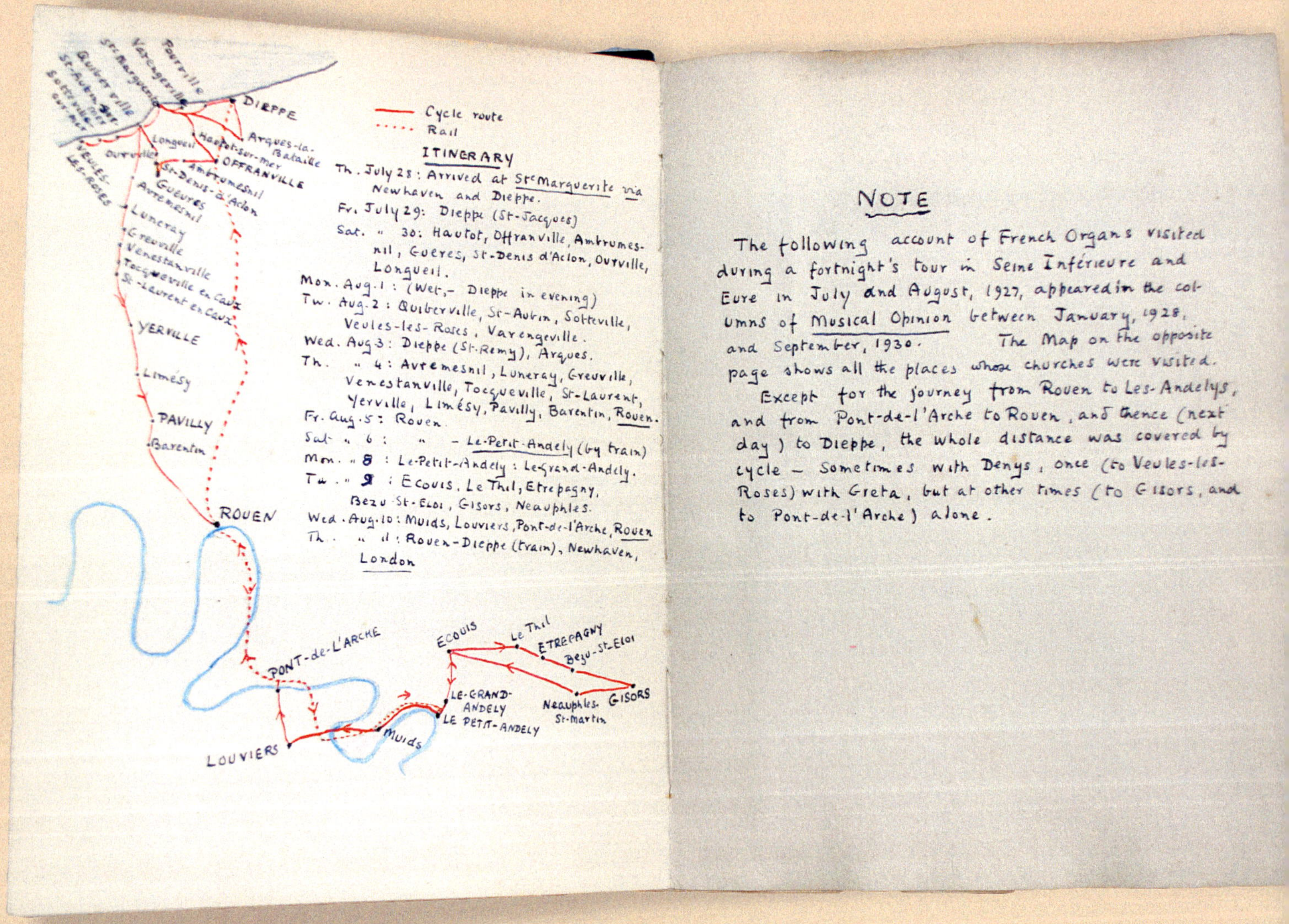

3231

(... pipes). The case is only about 3 ft 6 inches thick.

3227

8 ft (Gr. O.) was a very poor Open diap. The Trompette was very loud and raucous and the Clairon no better. The Tremolo was not much better than a similar stop on a harmonium.

The Touch of both claviers was springy & heavy, especially that of the Gr. O.

3242

Saint-Laurent-en-Caux.

At the west end is an organ case with no pipes in it. Style – "French Norman Gothic!" c. 1850.

The wood work is apparently oak.

The pipe racks to the front are still there (not drawn) from which the number of the front pipes has been deduced.

[4.8.27]

3255

[5.8.27]

Rouen – St. ~~Germain~~ Romain.

At the east end, behind the Altar, is a beautifully encased organ, with its wood work much gilded. Front pipes of tin.

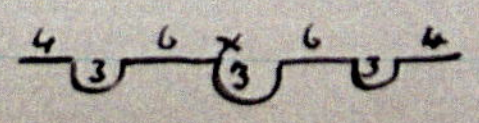

1929 – Belgium

6–28 June
Bruges plus 25 other towns and villages

On this second trip abroad, Freeman travelled alone by train, returning with 65 images on glass plates. By his own account he played 25 out of the nearly 100 instruments he had seen. In the first of several articles he wrote about the trip for *The Organ* magazine, he said that he had photographed 'five fine cases belonging to the sixteenth century, nine belonging to the seventeenth, and another dozen and a half belonging to the eighteenth, besides others of more recent date. In all I took upwards of 60 photographs of cases and consoles in the space of three weeks.'[1]

In the introduction to his diary of the journey, Freeman related stories about people he encountered, as well as his impressions of the town, the opening hours of the post office, what letters he received, and other commonplace details. Among other stories, he told of a conversation with a priest in one of the churches he visited, who looked at his clerical collar in a perplexed manner, and said that he had thought that the English clergy 'had no valid orders'. Freeman reportedly 'smiled, and said we hoped we had, and anyhow I was hoping for Reunion'.

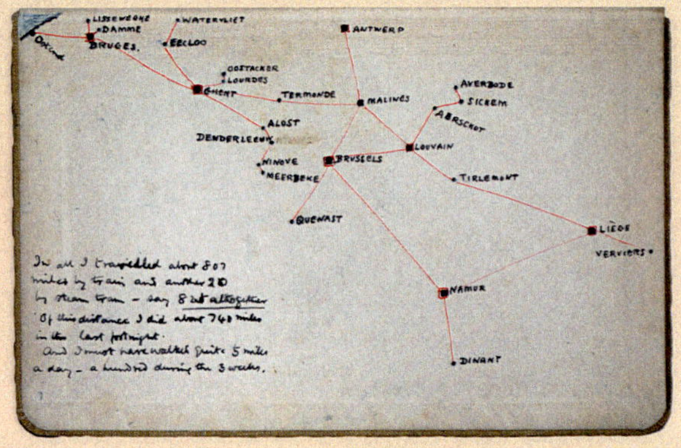

1 *The Organ* 9, no. 34 (Oct. 1929): 79–83; Other articles can be found in *The Organ* 9, no. 36 (April 1930): 226–30; and Vol. 10, no. 39 (July 1930): 162–5. There was also a series of articles about the trip in *Musical Opinion*, from November 1930 to March 1933.

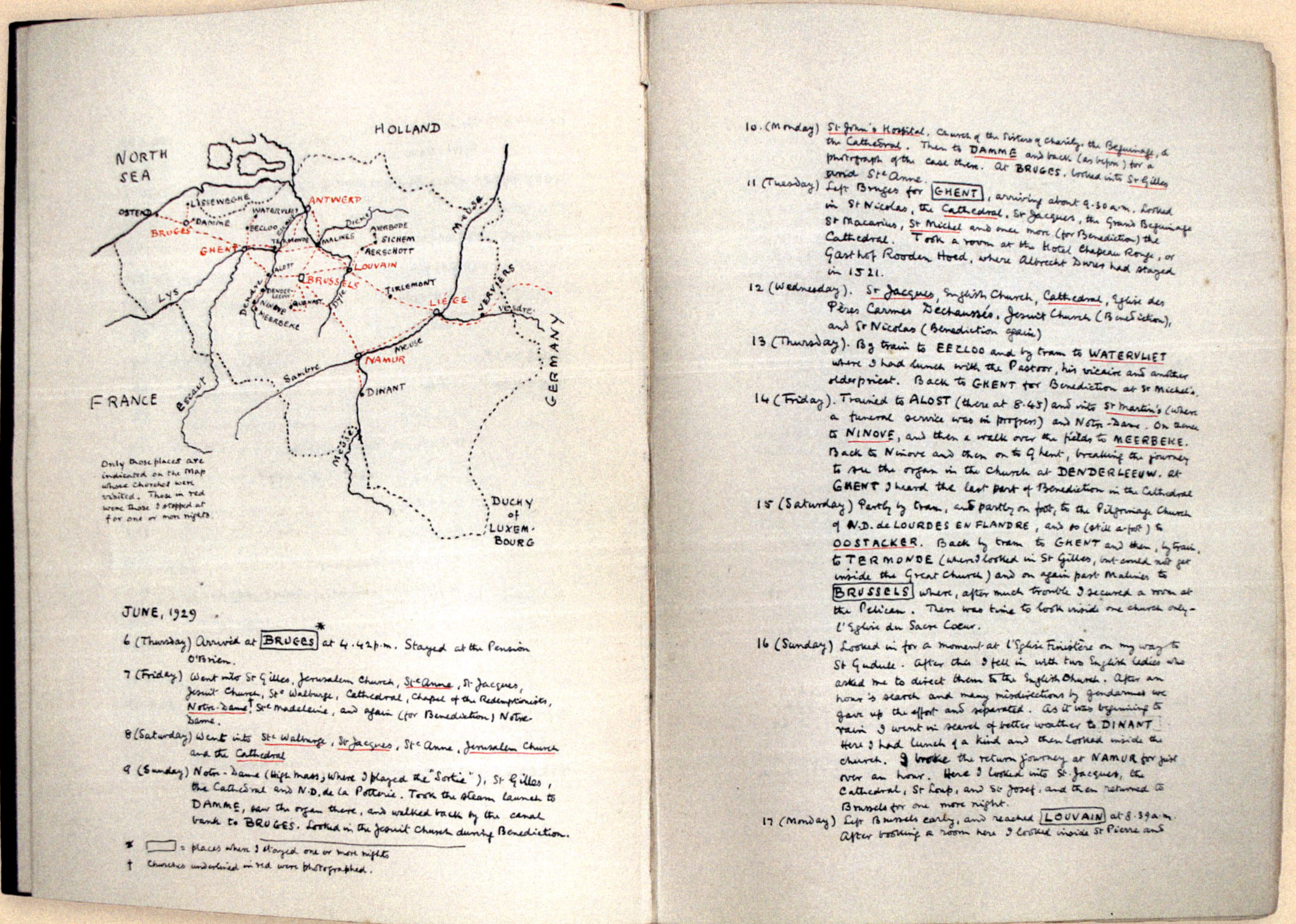

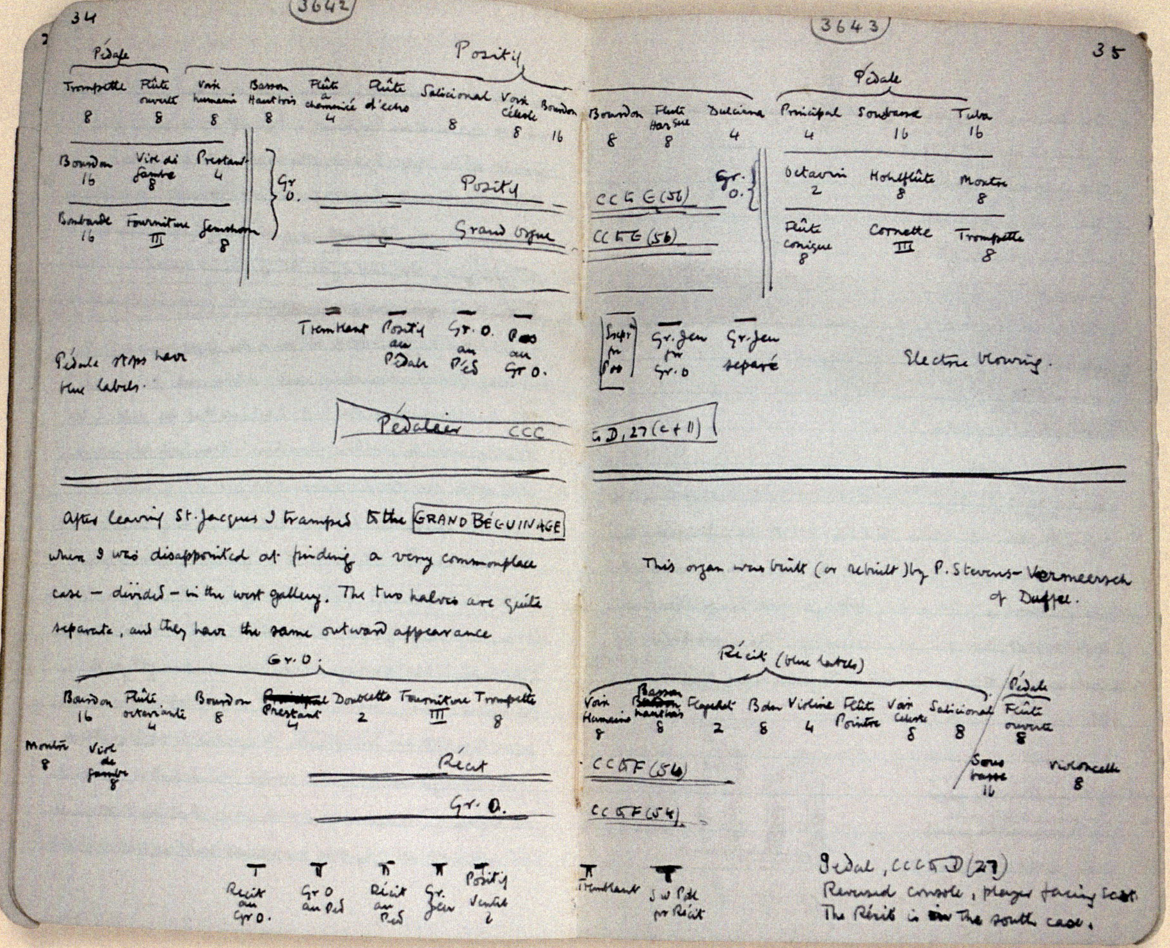
34 (3642)

Pédale: Trompette 8, Flûte ouverte 8

Positif: Voix humaine 8, Basson Hautbois 8, Flûte à cheminée 4, Flûte d'écho, Salicional 8, Voix Céleste 8, Bourdon 16, Bourdon 8, Flûte Harm. 8, Dulciana 4

Bourdon 16, Viol di Gambe 8, Prestant 4
Bombarde 16, Fourniture III, Gemshorn 8
} Gr. O.

Positif CCGG (56)
Grand Orgue CCGG (56)

Trembleur, Positif au Pédale, Gr. O. au P.d., Pos au Gr O., Suppr. pr Pos, Gr. Jeu pr Gr. O, Gr. Jeu separé

Pédale stops have blue labels.

Pédalier CCC–G D, 27 (c+11)

Electric blowing.

(3643) 35

Pédale: Principal 4, Soubasse 16, Tuba 16, Octavin 2, Hohlflûte 8, Montre 8, Flûte conique 8, Cornette III, Trompette 8

After leaving St. Jacques I tramped to the GRAND BÉGUINAGE when I was disappointed at finding a very commonplace case – divided – in the west gallery. The two halves are quite separate, and they have the same outward appearance.

This organ was built (or rebuilt) by P. Stevens-Vermeersch of Duffel.

Gr. O.: Bourdon 16, Flûte octaviante 4, Bourdon 8, ~~Principal~~ Prestant 4, Doublette 2, Fourniture III, Trompette 8, Montre 8, Viol de Gambe 8

Récit (blue labels): Voix Humaine 8, Basson ~~Bourdon~~ Hautbois 8, Flageolet 2, Bdn 8, Violine 4, Flûte Pointue, Voix Celeste 8, Salicional 8

Pédale: Flûte ouverte 8, Sous basse 16, Violoncelle 8

Récit CCGF (56)
Gr. O. CCGF (54)

Récit au Gr O., Gr O au Ped, Récit au Ped, Gr. Jeu, Positif Vent 2, Tremblant, Sw Pdl pr Récit

Pedal, CCC–D (27)
Reversed console, player facing east.
The Récit is in the south case.

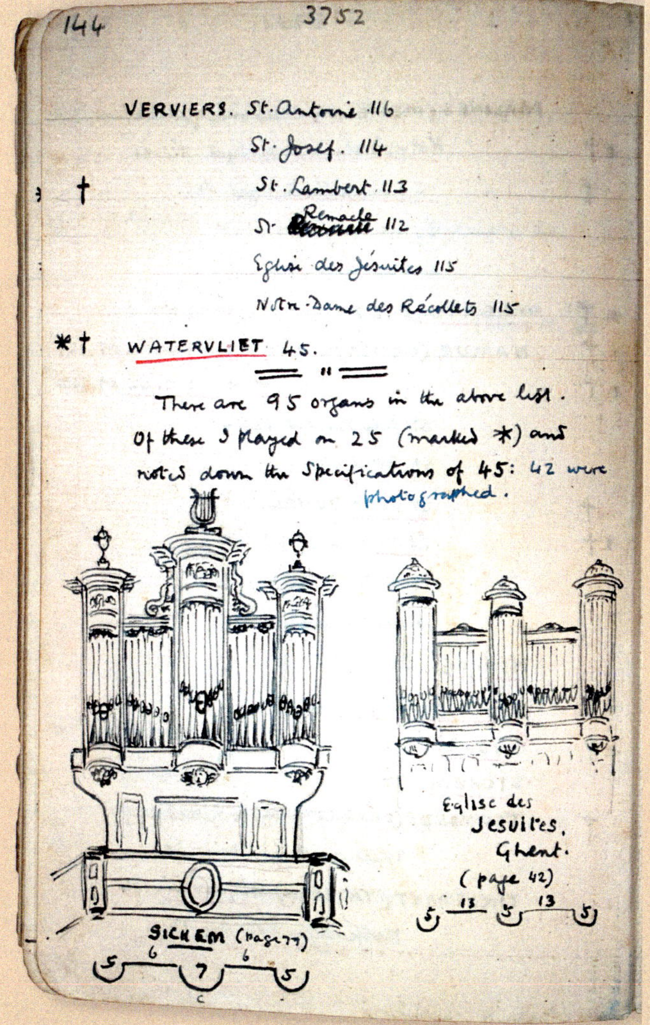
144 3752

VERVIERS. St. Antoine 116
St. Josef 114
† St. Lambert 113
St. Remacle 112
Eglise des Jésuites 115
Notre-Dame des Récollets 115

*† WATERVLIET 45.

There are 95 organs in the above list. Of these I played on 25 (marked *) and noted down the Specifications of 45: 42 were photographed.

Eglise des Jesuites, Ghent. (page 42)

SICHEM (page 77)

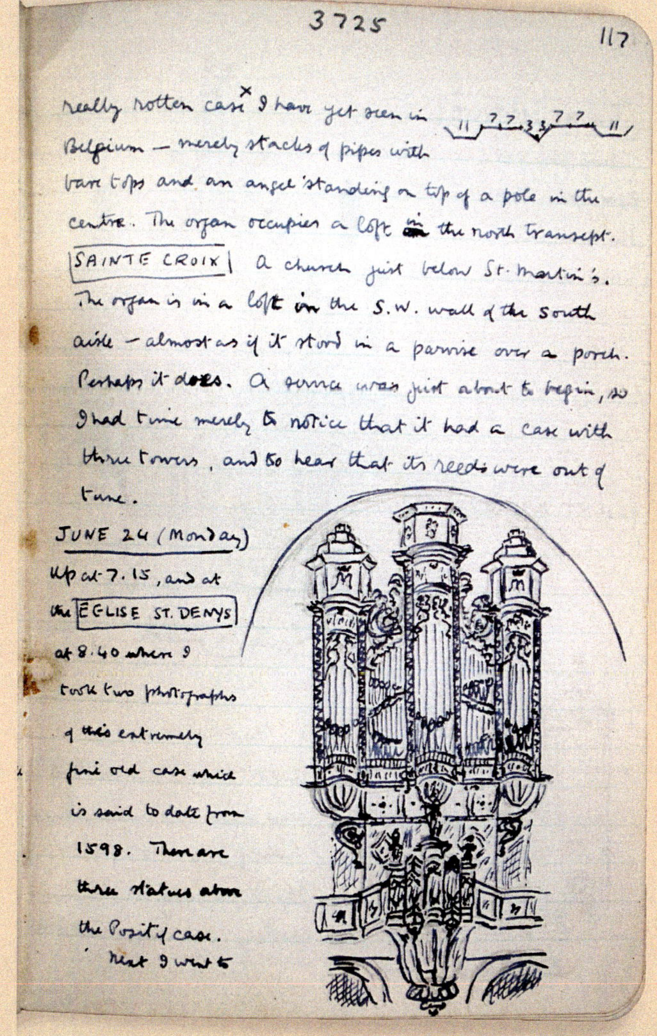
3725 117

really rotten case× I have yet seen in Belgium – merely stacks of pipes with bare tops and an angel standing on top of a pole in the centre. The organ occupies a loft in the north transept.

SAINTE CROIX A church just below St. Martin's. The organ is in a loft in the S.W. wall of the south aisle – almost as if it stood in a parvise over a porch. Perhaps it does. A service was just about to begin, so I had time merely to notice that it had a case with three towers, and to hear that its reeds were out of tune.

JUNE 24 (Monday)

Up at 7.15, and at the EGLISE ST. DENYS at 8.40 when I took two photographs of this extremely fine old case which is said to date from 1598. There are three statues atop the Positif case. Next I went to

1932 – Belgium, Germany, and Austria

24 May to 18 June

Bruges - Brussels – Cologne – Passau – Munich – Salzburg – Vienna

As in 1929, Freeman travelled alone by rail. Articles stemming from his account of this trip appeared in *The Organ* from April 1933 to April 1937. Freeman later formed two separate books, the first combining accounts from his 1929 and 1932 trips through Belgium, and the second about his trip to Austria. There are 82 glass plate negatives in the archive from this journey, taken in fifty-four different churches.

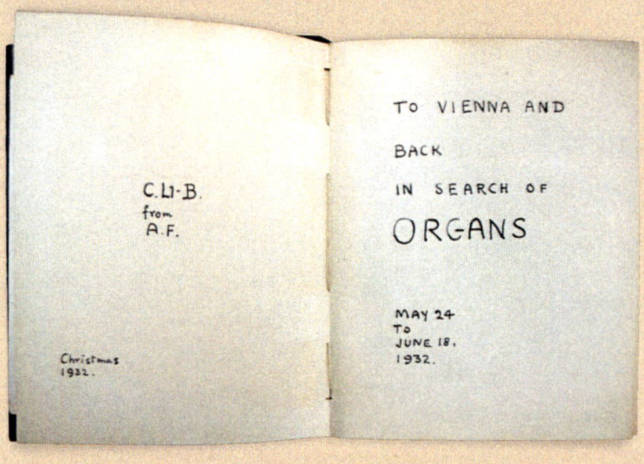

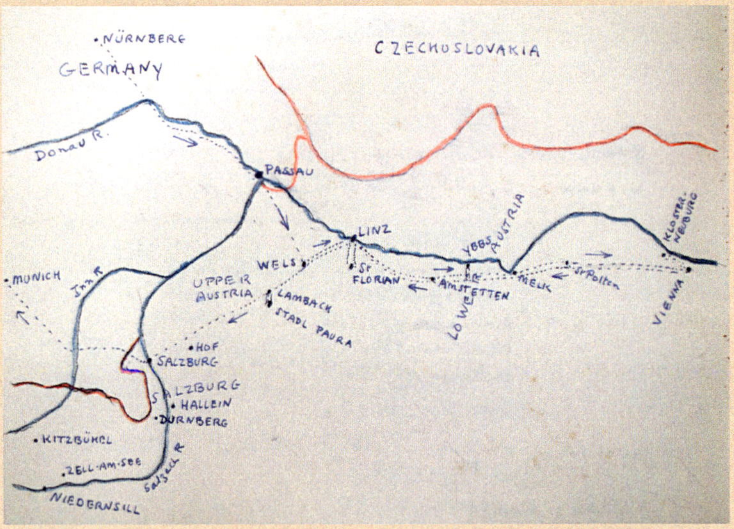

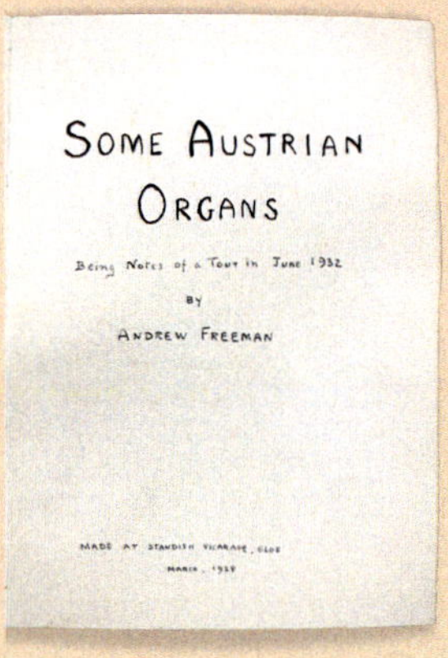

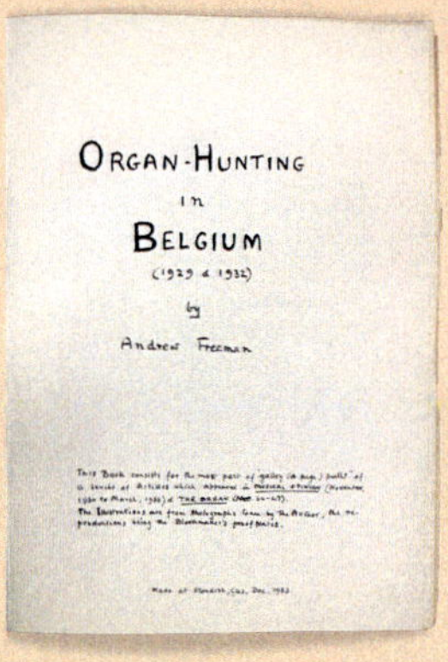

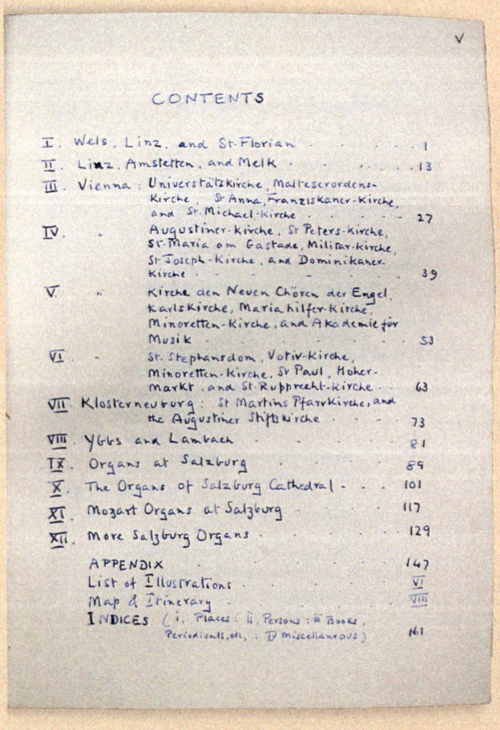
v

CONTENTS

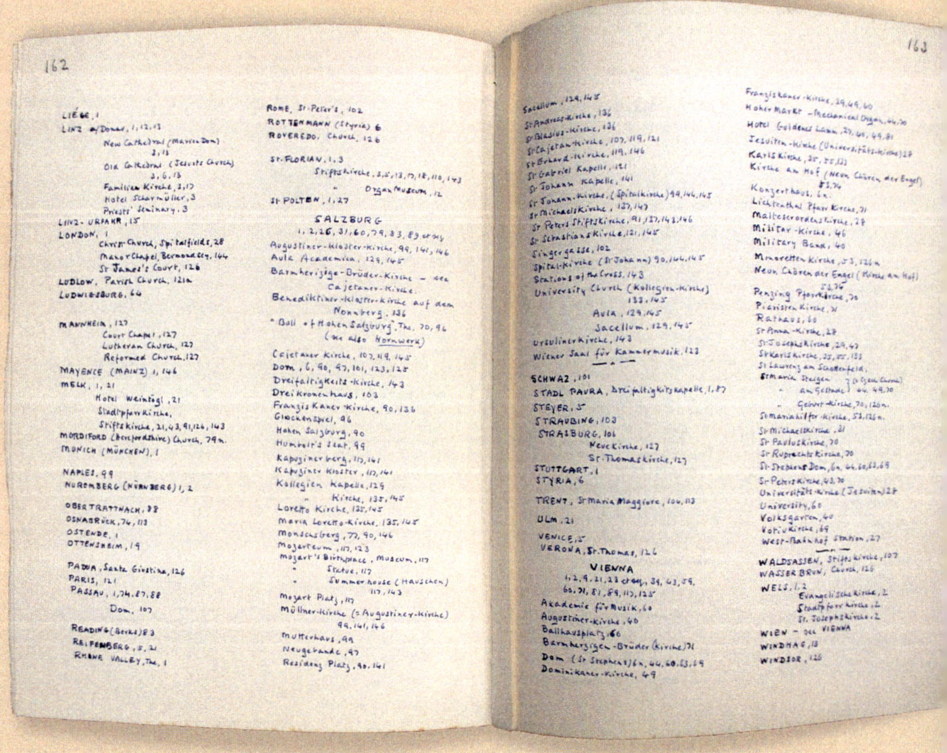
162

163

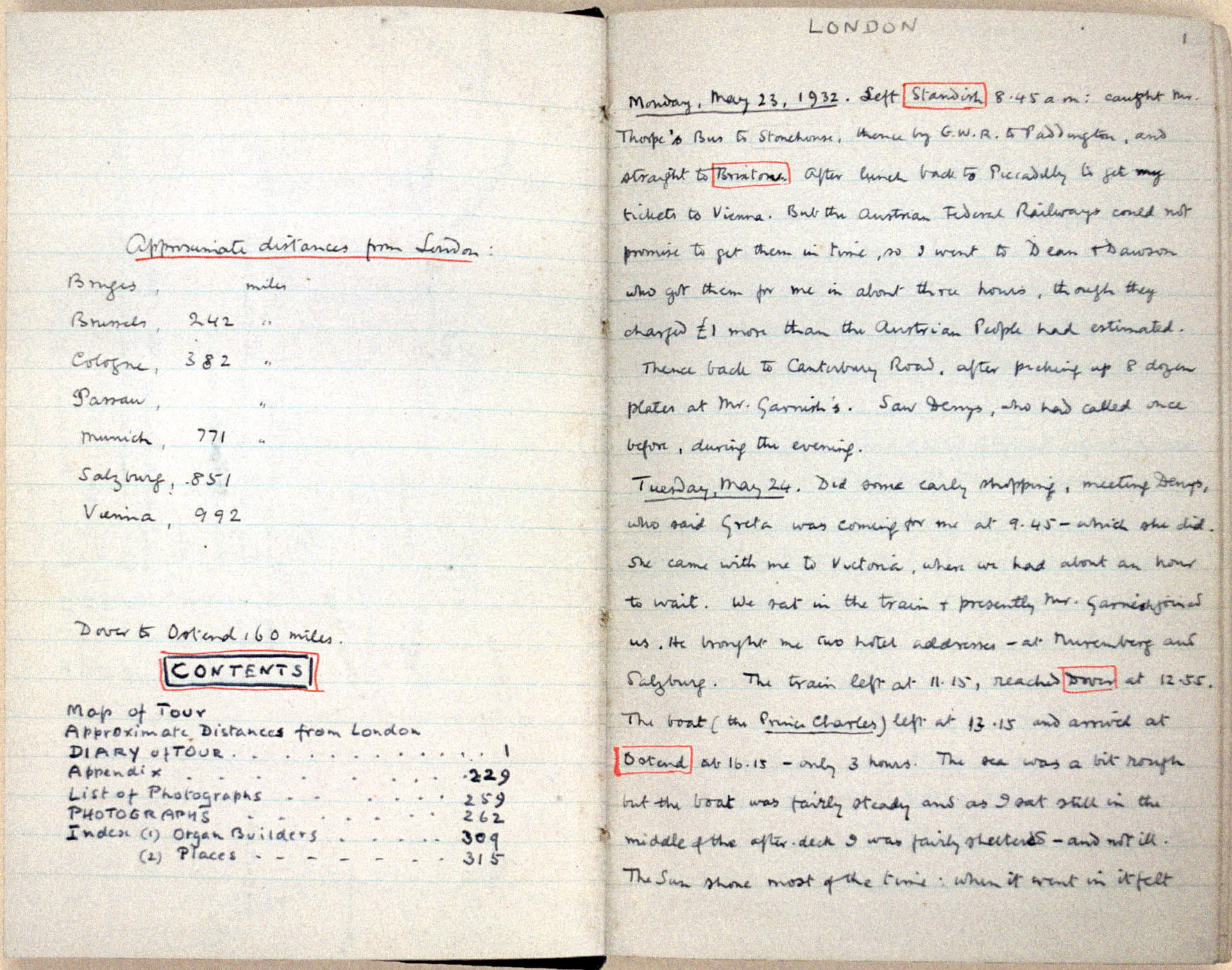

Approximate distances from London:

Bruges, miles
Brussels, 242 "
Cologne, 382 "
Passau, "
Munich, 771 "
Salzburg, 851
Vienna, 992

Dover to Ostend: 60 miles.

CONTENTS

LONDON 1

Monday, May 23, 1932. Left Standish 8.45 a.m.: caught Mr. Thorpe's Bus to Stonehouse, thence by G.W.R. to Paddington, and straight to Brixton. After lunch back to Piccadilly to get ~~my~~ tickets to Vienna. But the Austrian Federal Railways could not promise to get them in time, so I went to Dean + Dawson who got them for me in about three hours, though they charged £1 more than the Austrian People had estimated.

Thence back to Canterbury Road, after picking up 8 dozen plates at Mr. Garnish's. Saw Denys, who had called once before, during the evening.

Tuesday, May 24. Did some early shopping, meeting Denys, who said Greta was coming for me at 9.45 – which she did. She came with me to Victoria, where we had about an hour to wait. We sat in the train + presently Mr. Garnish joined us. He brought me two hotel addresses – at Nuremberg and Salzburg. The train left at 11.15, reached Dover at 12.55. The boat (the Prince Charles) left at 13.15 and arrived at Ostend at 16.15 – only 3 hours. The sea was a bit rough but the boat was fairly steady and as I sat still in the middle of the after-deck I was fairly sheltered – and not ill. The Sun shone most of the time: when it went in it felt

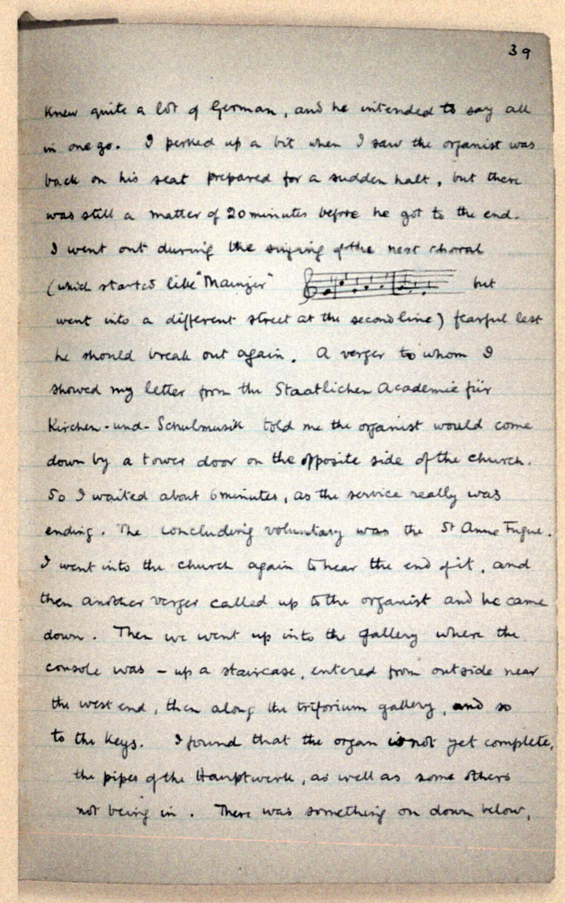

39

knew quite a lot of German, and he intended to say all in one go. I perked up a bit when I saw the organist was back on his seat prepared for a sudden halt, but there was still a matter of 20 minutes before he got to the end. I went out during the singing of the next choral (which starts like "Mainzer" [music] but went into a different street at the second line) fearful lest he should break out again. A verger to whom I showed my letter from the Staatlichen Academie für Kirchen-und-Schulmusik told me the organist would come down by a tower door on the opposite side of the church. So I waited about 6 minutes, as the service really was ending. The concluding voluntary was the St Anne Fugue. I went into the church again to hear the end of it, and then another verger called up to the organist and he came down. Then we went up into the gallery where the console was – up a staircase, entered from outside near the west end, then along the triforium gallery, ~~and~~ so to the keys. I found that the organ ~~is~~ not yet complete, the pipes of the Hauptwerk, as well as some others not being in. There was something on down below,

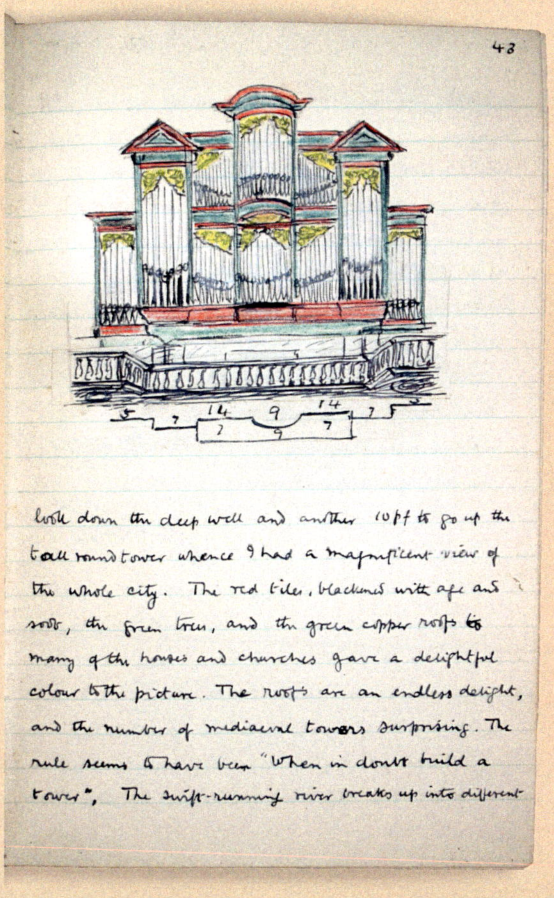

43

look down the deep well and another 10 pf to go up the tall round tower whence I had a magnificent view of the whole city. The red tiles, blackened with age and soot, the green trees, and the green copper roofs ~~to~~ many of the houses and churches gave a delightful colour to the picture. The roofs are an endless delight, and the number of mediaeval towers surprising. The rule seems to have been "When in doubt build a tower". The swift-running river breaks up into different

1935 – France, Belgium, Germany, Austria, Switzerland

8 July to 8 August

Calais – Ypres – Dinant – Luxembourg – Trier – Coblenz – Mainz – Frankfurt – Rothenburg – Augsburg – München – Salzburg – Mondsee – Bad Ischl – Bischofshofen – Innsbruck – Bregenz – Brunnen – Schaffhausen – Freudenstadt – Karlsruhe – Saarbrücken – Rheims – Boulogne

Freeman undertook this journey by car with Ethel, Greta, and a friend. Rather charmingly, Freeman wrote in his diary, 'Matilda had just been de-carbonized and fitted with new piston rings, etc., so we had to drive rather slowly – not over 30 miles, we were told, though I fear we exceeded it a bit without noticing.' The account was published in *The Organ* in installments between 1936 and 1939. There are 58 images of organs from this trip.

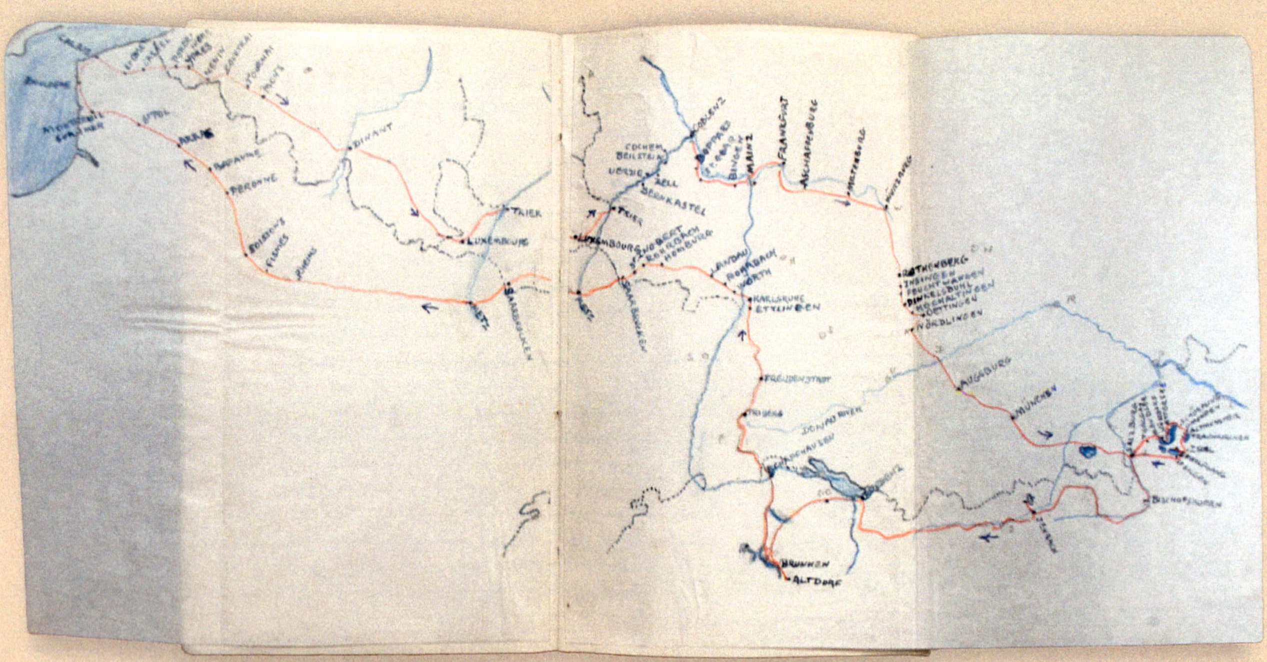

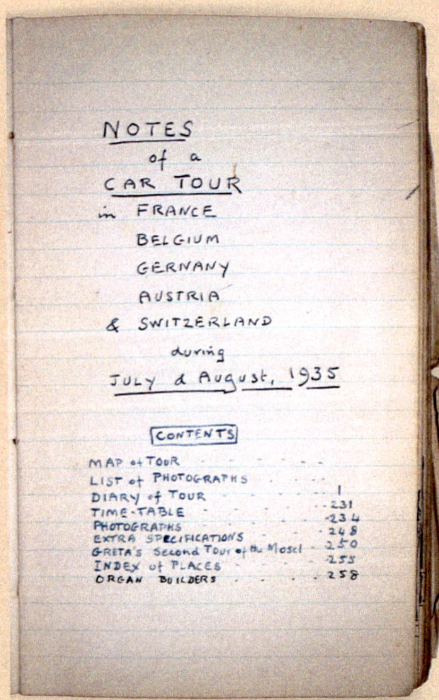

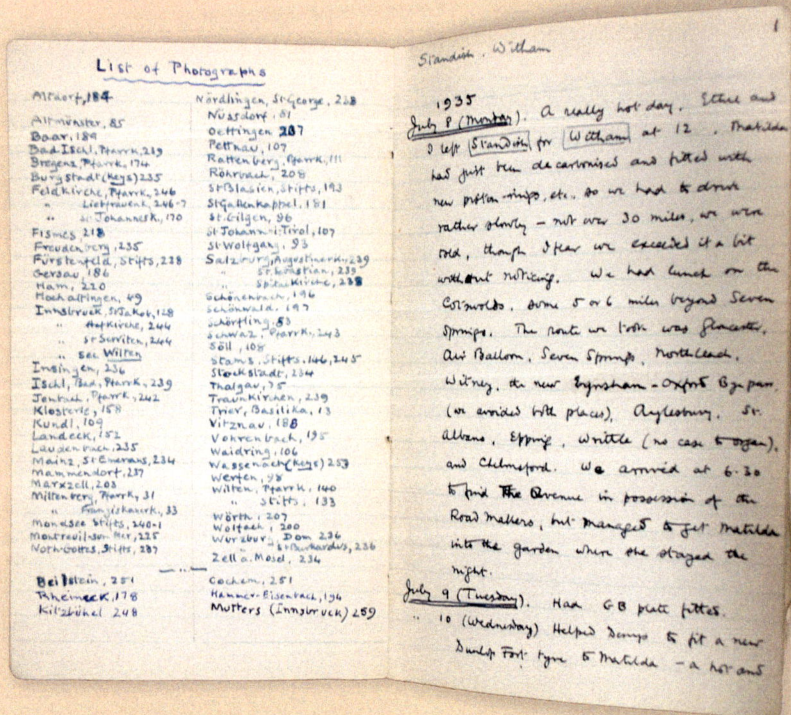
List of Photographs

Standish . Witham

1

1935

July 8 (Monday). A really hot day. Ethel and I left Standish for Witham at 12. Matilda has just been de-carbonised and fitted with new piston-rings, etc. so we had to drive rather slowly – not over 30 miles, we were told, though I fear we exceeded it a bit without noticing. We had lunch on the Cotswolds, some 5 or 6 miles beyond Seven Springs. The route we took was Gloucester, Air Balloon, Seven Springs, Northleach, Witney, the new Eynsham – Oxford By-pass (we avoided both places), Aylesbury, St. Albans, Epping, Writtle (no case to organ), and Chelmsford. We arrived at 6.30 to find The Avenue in possession of the Road Makers, but managed to get Matilda into the garden where she stayed the night.

July 9 (Tuesday). Had GB plate fitted.

" 10 (Wednesday) Helped [illegible] to fit a new Dunlop Fort tyre to Matilda – a hot and

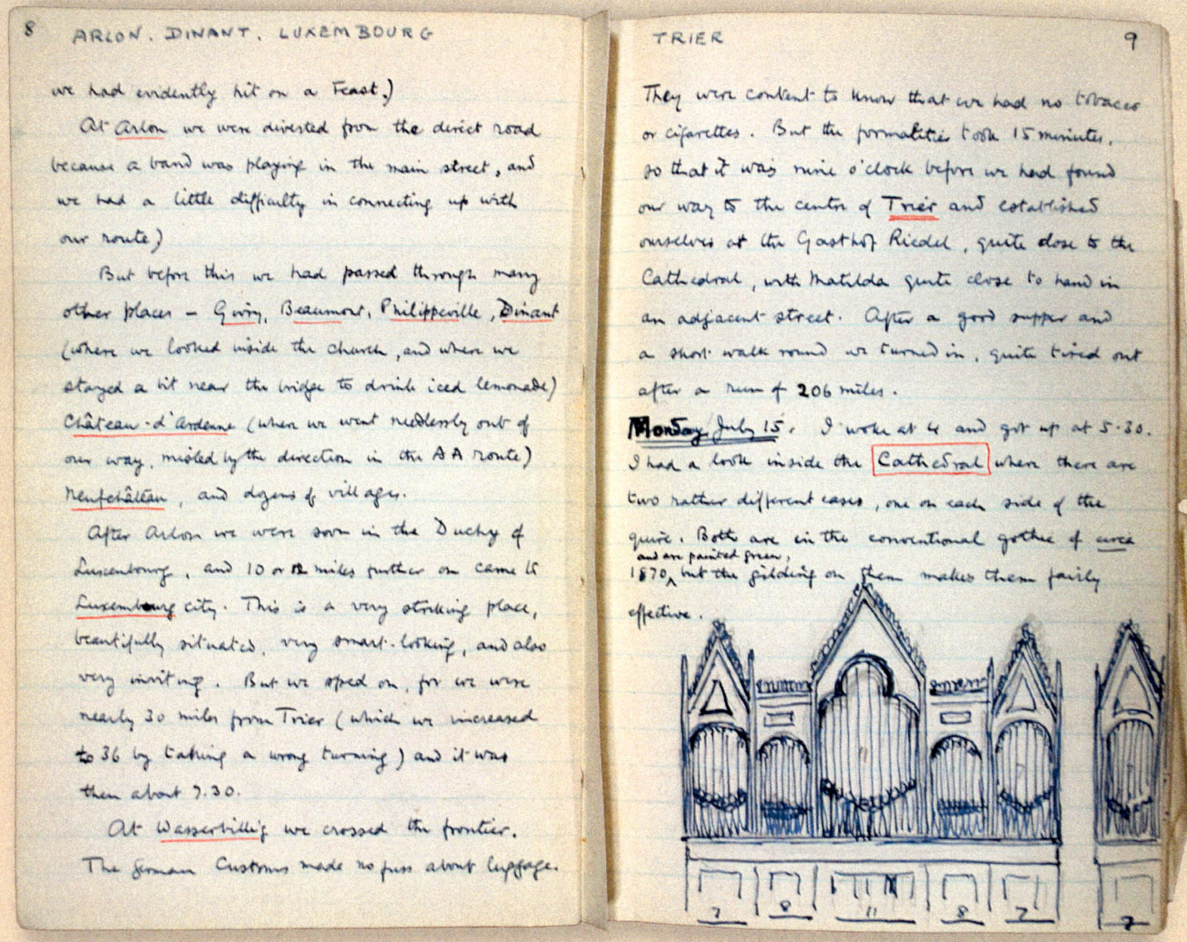

8 ARLON. DINANT. LUXEMBOURG

we had evidently hit on a Feast.)

At Arlon we were diverted from the direct road because a band was playing in the main street, and we had a little difficulty in connecting up with our route)

But before this we had passed through many other places – Givry, Beaumont, Philippeville, Dinant (where we looked inside the church, and where we stayed a bit near the bridge to drink iced lemonade) Château-d'Ardenne (when we went needlessly out of our way, misled by the direction in the AA route) Neufchâteau, and dozens of villages.

After Arlon we were soon in the Duchy of Luxembourg, and 10 or 12 miles further on came to Luxembourg city. This is a very striking place, beautifully situated, very smart-looking, and also very inviting. But we sped on, for we were nearly 30 miles from Trier (which we increased to 36 by taking a wrong turning) and it was then about 7.30.

At Wasserbillig we crossed the frontier. The German Customs made no fuss about luggage.

TRIER 9

They were content to know that we had no tobacco or cigarettes. But the formalities took 15 minutes, so that it was nine o'clock before we had found our way to the centre of Trier and established ourselves at the Gasthof Riedel, quite close to the Cathedral, with Matilda quite close to hand in an adjacent street. After a good supper and a short walk round we turned in, quite tired out after a run of 206 miles.

Monday July 15. I woke at 4 and got up at 5.30. I had a look inside the Cathedral where there are two rather different cases, one on each side of the quire. Both are in the conventional gothic of circa 1870, and are painted green, but the gilding on them makes them fairly effective.

7 8 11 8 7 7

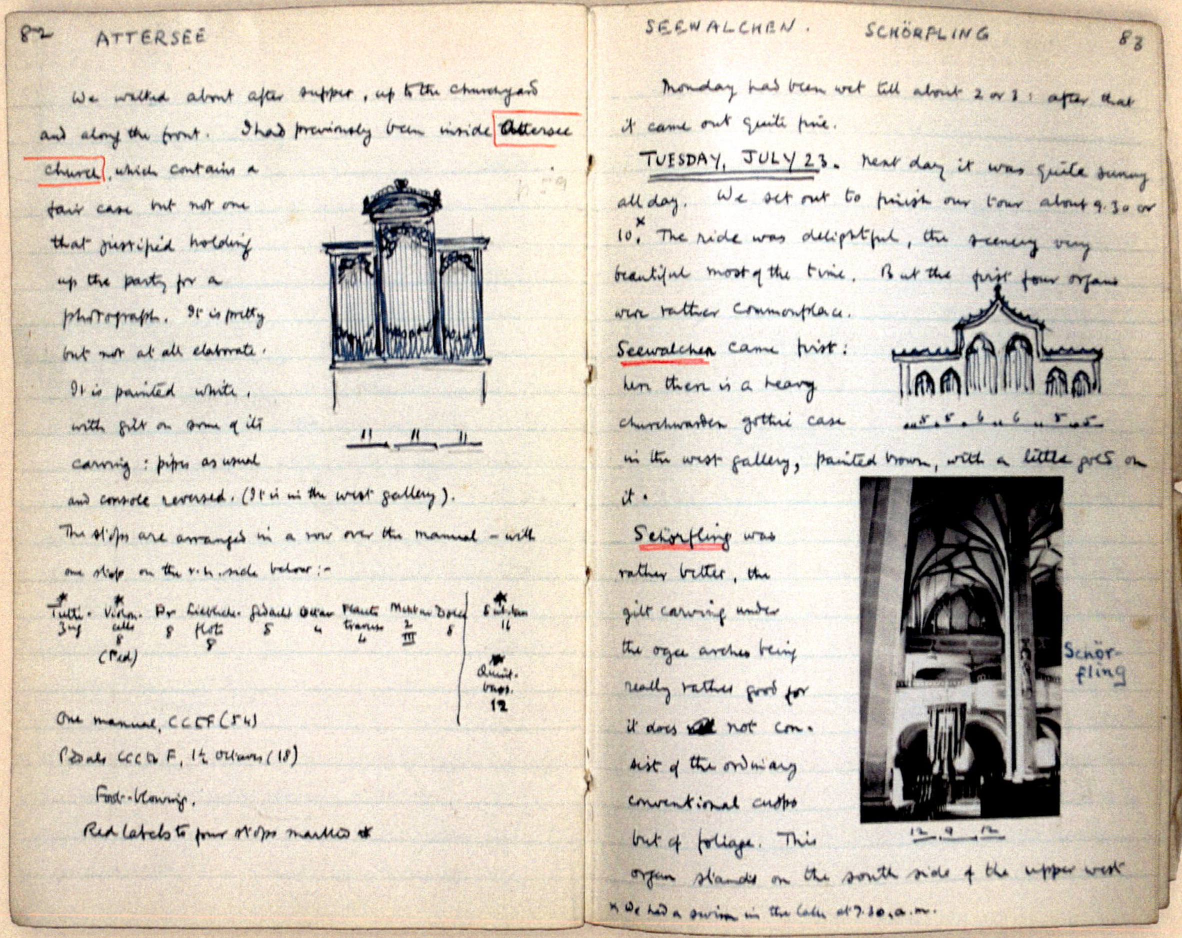

82 ATTERSEE

We walked about after supper, up to the churchyard and along the front. I had previously been inside Attersee church, which contains a fair case but not one that justified holding up the party for a photograph. It is pretty but not at all elaborate. It is painted white, with gilt on some of its carving: pipes as usual and console reversed. (It is in the west gallery).

11 11 11

The stops are arranged in a row over the manual – with one stop on the r.h. side below:–

*Tutti-Zug · *Violon-cello 8 (Ped) · Pr 8 · Lieblich-Flöte 8 · Gedackt 8 · Octav 4 · Flauto traverso 4 · Mixtur 2 III · Dolce 8 | *Subbass 16 · *Quint-bass 12

One manual, CC–F (54)

Pedals CCC to F, 1½ octaves (18)

Foot-blowing.

Red labels to four stops marked *

SEEWALCHEN. SCHÖRFLING 83

Monday had been wet till about 2 or 3: after that it came out quite fine.

TUESDAY, JULY 23. Next day it was quite sunny all day. We set out to finish our tour about 9.30 or 10.* The ride was delightful, the scenery very beautiful most of the time. But the first four organs were rather commonplace.

Seewalchen came first: here there is a heavy churchwarden gothic case in the west gallery, painted brown, with a little gilt on it.

5 5 6 6 5 5

Schörfling was rather better, the gilt carving under the ogee arches being really rather good for it does not consist of the ordinary conventional cusps but of foliage. This organ stands on the south side of the upper west

Schörfling

12 9 12

* We had a swim in the lake at 7.30 a.m.

1939 – Switzerland

4–27 May

Bern – Lake Thun – Interlaken – Lucerne – Lugano – Locarno – Einsiedeln – Fribourg

Once again, Freeman travelled by train, and his companions were Ethel and Greta. His rough notebook – the handwritten journal with sketches – was lost, so there are a number of blank pages in the neatened account. As was his usual practice, Freeman later used galley pulls from his published articles in *The Organ* and *Musical Opinion* to form a larger book with pictures. In the archive are fifty-eight glass-plate negatives, covering about thirty-six locations from the trip.

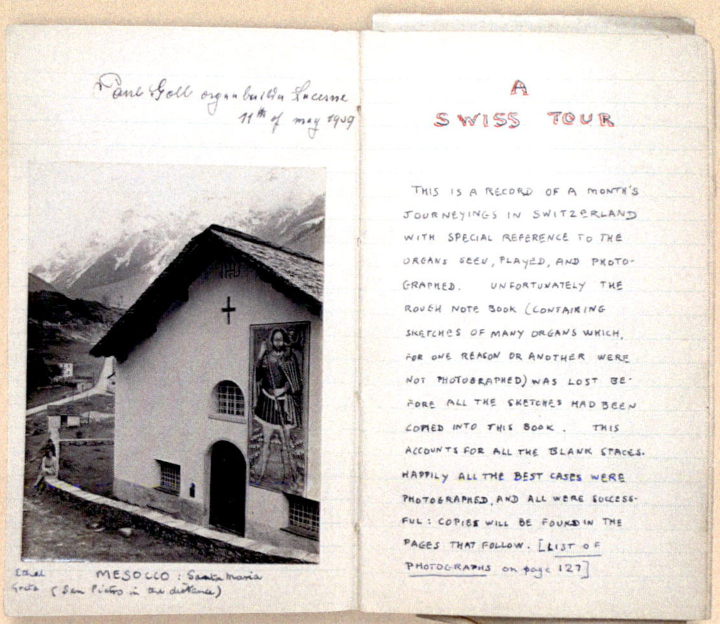

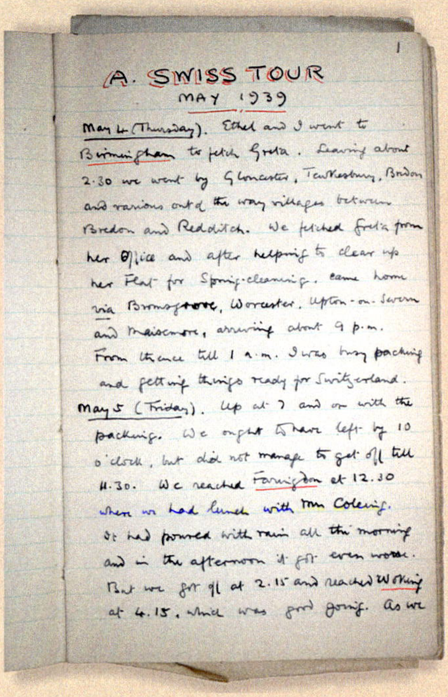

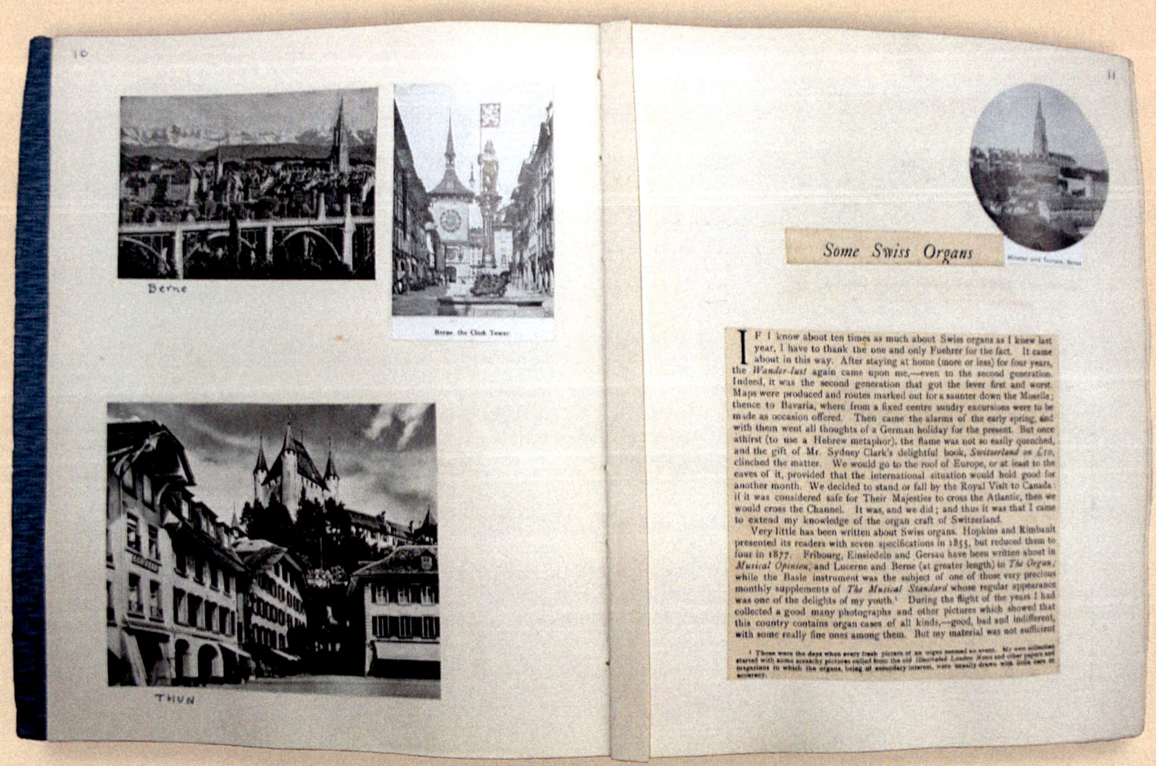

If I know about ten times as much about Swiss organs as I knew last year, I have to thank the one and only Fuehrer for the fact. It came about in this way. After staying at home (more or less) for four years, the *Wander-lust* again came upon me,—even to the second generation. Indeed, it was the second generation that got the fever first and worst. Maps were produced and routes marked out for a saunter down the Moselle; thence to Bavaria, where from a fixed centre sundry excursions were to be made as occasion offered. Then came the alarms of the early spring, and with them went all thoughts of a German holiday for the present. But once athirst (to use a Hebrew metaphor), the flame was not so easily quenched, and the gift of Mr. Sydney Clark's delightful book, *Switzerland on £10*, clinched the matter. We would go to the roof of Europe, or at least to the eaves of it, provided that the international situation would hold good for another month. We decided to stand or fall by the Royal Visit to Canada: if it was considered safe for Their Majesties to cross the Atlantic, then we would cross the Channel. It was, and we did; and thus it was that I came to extend my knowledge of the organ craft of Switzerland.

Very little has been written about Swiss organs. Hopkins and Rimbault presented its readers with seven specifications in 1855, but reduced them to four in 1877. Fribourg, Einsiedeln and Gersau have been written about in *Musical Opinion*; and Lucerne and Berne (at greater length) in *The Organ*; while the Basle instrument was the subject of one of those very precious monthly supplements of *The Musical Standard* whose regular appearance was one of the delights of my youth.[1] During the flight of the years I had collected a good many photographs and other pictures which showed that this country contains organ cases of all kinds,—good, bad and indifferent, with some really fine ones among them. But my material was not sufficient

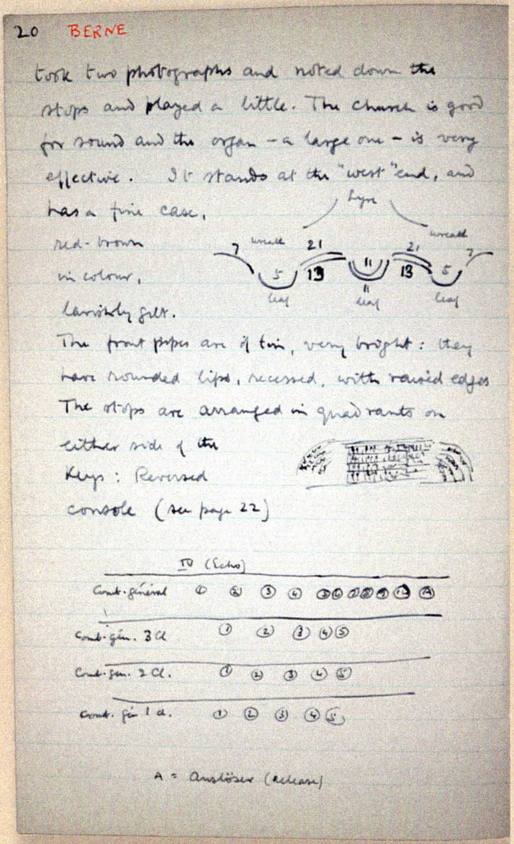
20 BERNE
took two photographs and noted down the stops and played a little. The church is good for sound and the organ – a large one – is very effective. It stands at the "west" end, and has a fine case,
red-brown in colour, lavishly gilt.
lyre
wreath
7 wreath 21 11 21 7
5 13 13 5
leaf leaf leaf
The front pipes are of tin, very bright: they have rounded lips, recessed, with raised edges
The stops are arranged in quadrants on either side of the
Keys: Reversed console (see page 22)
IV (Echo)
Cont. général
Cont. gén. 3 Cl.
Cont. gén. 2 Cl.
Cont. gén. 1 cl.
A = Auslöser (action)

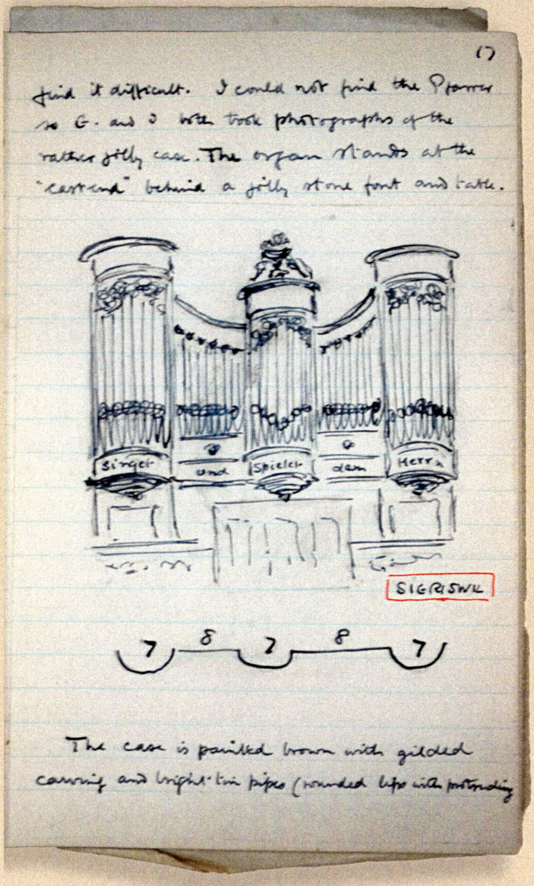
17
find it difficult. I could not find the Pfarrer so G. and I both took photographs of the rather jolly case. The organ stands at the "east end" behind a jolly stone font and table.
Singet und Spielet dem Herrn
SIGRISWIL
7 8 7 8 7
The case is painted brown with gilded carving and bright tin pipes (rounded lips with protruding

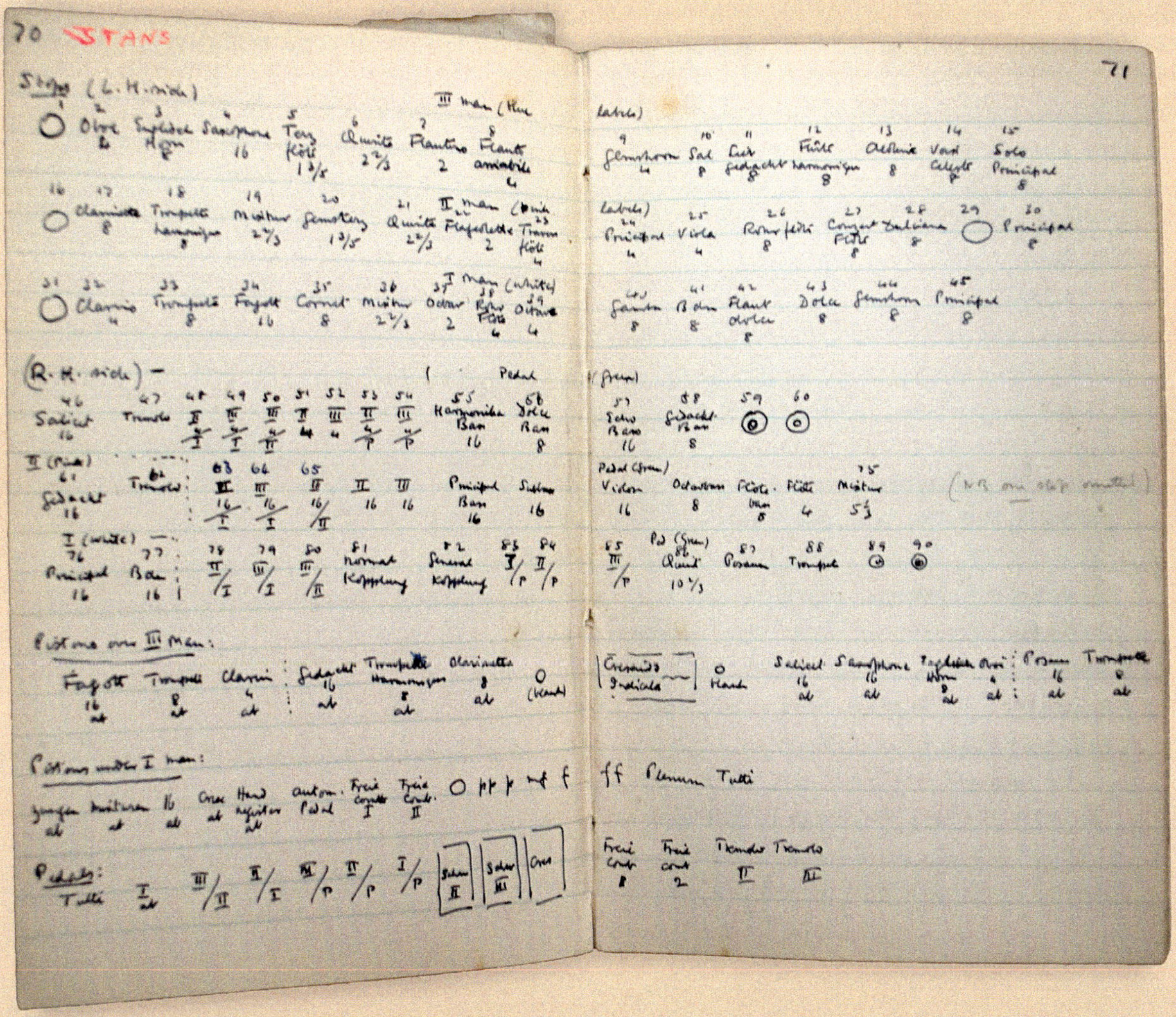
70 STANS
Stops (L.H. side)
III man (blue labels)
1 ○ 2 Oboe 8 3 Englisch Horn 8 4 Saxophone 16 5 Terz Flöte 1 3/5 6 Quinte 2 2/3 7 Flautino 2 8 Flaute amabile 4
9 Gemshorn 4 10 Sal 8 11 Lieb gedackt 8 12 Flûte harmonique 8 13 Aeoline 8 14 Voix Celeste 8 15 Solo Principal 8
16 ○ 17 Clarinette 8 18 Trompette harmonique 8 19 Mixtur 2 2/3 20 Gemsterz 1 3/5 21 Quinte 2 2/3
II man (pink labels)
22 Flageolette 2 23 Traversflöte 4
24 Principal 4 25 Viola 4 26 Rohrflöte 8 27 Concert Flöte 8 28 Dulciana 8 29 ○ 30 Principal 8
31 ○ 32 Clarino 4 33 Trompette 8 34 Fagott 16 35 Cornet 8 36 Mixtur 2 2/3 37 Octav 2
I man (white labels)
38 Rohr Flöte 4 39 Octave 4
40 Gamba 8 41 Bordun 8 42 Flaute dolce 8 43 Dolce 8 44 Gemshorn 8 45 Principal 8
(R.H. side) –
46 Salicet 16 47 Tremolo
Pedal (green)
55 Harmonika Bass 16 56 Dolce Bass 8
57 Echo Bass 16 58 Gedackt Bass 8 59 60
II (pink) 61 Gedackt 16 62 Tremolo 63 64 65
Principal Bass 16 Subbass 16
Pedal (green)
Violon 16 Octavbass 8 Flöte 8 Flöte 4 75 Mixtur 5 1/3
(NB one stop omitted)
I (white) 76 Principal 16 77 Bass 16 78 79 80 81 Normal Koppelung 82 General Koppelung 83 84
85 Ped (green) 86 Quint 10 2/3 87 Posaune 88 Trompete 89 90
Pistons over III man:
Pistons under I man:
Pedals:
Tutti
ff Plenum Tutti
71

1946 – Switzerland

17 June to 25 July

On his final trip abroad, Freeman again travelled by train, accompanied by his daughter Greta. He reported trouble sourcing as many photographic plates as he would have liked. In one of his last articles for *The Organ*, Freeman wrote, 'In June and July, 1946, it was my good fortune to make a third trip to Switzerland, lasting rather over a month. This, in normal times, would have been long enough to collect a full bag of organ photographs, but despite persistent efforts to obtain plates, all I could muster was a beggarly three dozen, and these included some that I had taken to the same country in 1939, and had not been able to use; the rest were of a brand quite strange to me... Foreign travel is easier now than it was last year, when rules and regulations were altering almost daily, and final obstacles were surmounted but a few hours before we found ourselves at Victoria en route for Dover and Calais. One could forgive the slow journey through France when one caught sight of the havoc all along the line, but the incompetence of the French officials at Basle, where we arrived at eight o'clock in the morning and were kept waiting in a seething crowd for an hour, was unforgettable.'[1]

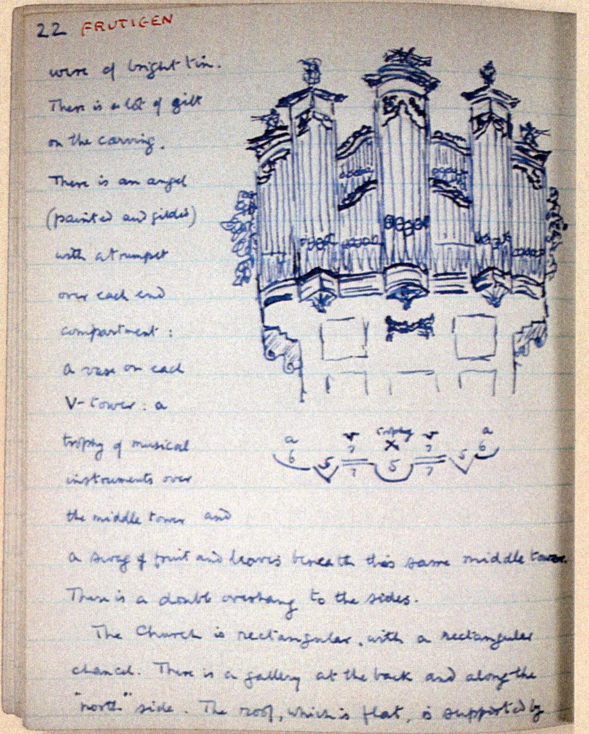
22 FRUTIGEN

were of bright tin.
There is a lot of gilt
on the carving.
There is an angel
(painted and gilded)
with a trumpet
over each end
compartment:
a vase on each
V-tower: a
trophy of musical
instruments over
the middle tower and
a swag of fruit and leaves beneath this same middle tower.
There is a double overhang to the sides.
The Church is rectangular, with a rectangular
chancel. There is a gallery at the back and along the
"north" side. The roof, which is flat, is supported by

Overall, Freeman's tone was slightly peevish during this trip, and betrayed a weariness that had not been evident before. In an excerpt from his journal, Freeman wrote, '7. (Sunday) It rained heavily in the night and has rained all day. I went to the English Church in the morning (10.30, Matins & H.C.). The lady organist was tame. She went from one manual to another, but they all sounded alike. – the same mf quality – and she scarcely touched a stop. One of the tunes was a bete noir of mine – Elliot's tune to 'O Jesus I have promised'. The 1st lesson was about Hannah and Samuel. I wonder how long we shall go on reading O.T. Lessons of that sort. What is there in a lesson of that type? The service was perfunctory. Ugly organ in a recess... No proper case. The centre compartment (two stories, the lower with bearded pipes), is unpleasant looking.'

In another place, Freeman complains about the trains in Basel: 'The muddle at Basle station was as bad as ever – incompetence which is due, one would think, to spite as much as to ignorance...Any village station-master in England would have done the job which these wretched duffers watched and left alone. No wonder they muddled their part of the War.'

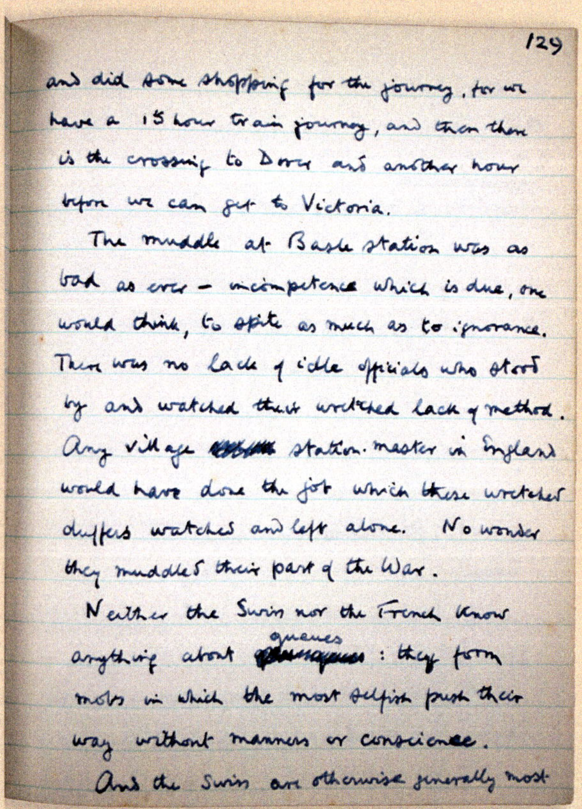
129

and did some shopping for the journey, for we have a 15 hour train journey, and then there is the crossing to Dover and another hour before we can get to Victoria.
The muddle at Basle station was as bad as ever – incompetence which is due, one would think, to spite as much as to ignorance. There was no lack of idle officials who stood by and watched their wretched lack of method. Any village station-master in England would have done the job which these wretched duffers watched and left alone. No wonder they muddled their part of the War.
Neither the Swiss nor the French know anything about queues: they form mobs in which the most selfish push their way without manners or conscience.
And the Swiss are otherwise generally most

1 *The Organ* 26, no. 104 (April 1947): 145.

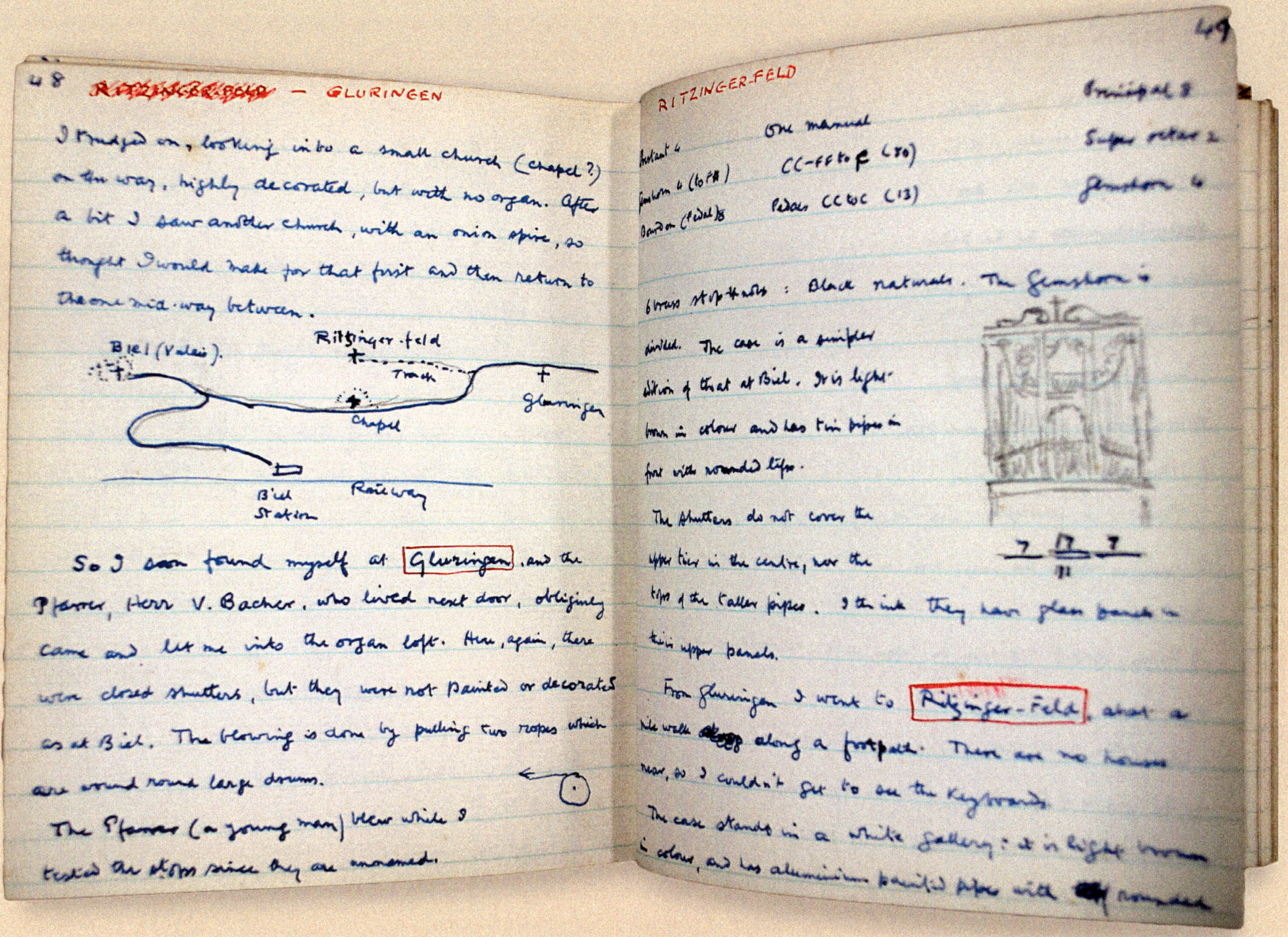

48 ~~RITZINGER-FELD~~ – GLURINGEN

I trudged on, looking into a small church (chapel?) on the way, highly decorated, but with no organ. After a bit I saw another church, with an onion spire, so thought I would make for that first and then return to the one mid-way between.

So I soon found myself at Gluringen, and the Pfarrer, Herr V. Bacher, who lived next door, obligingly came and let me into the organ loft. Here, again, there were closed shutters, but they were not painted or decorated as at Biel. The blowing is done by pulling two ropes which are wound round large drums.

The Pfarrer (a young man) blew while I tested the stops since they are unnamed.

49

RITZINGER-FELD

Principal 4 / Gemshorn 4 (to F#) / Bourdon (Pedal) 8 — One manual CC–FF to F (30) / Pedals CC to C (13) — Principal 8 / Super octave 2 / Gemshorn 4

6 brass stop-knobs : Black naturals. The Gemshorn is divided. The case is a simpler edition of that at Biel. It is light brown in colour and has tin pipes in front with rounded lips.

The shutters do not cover the upper tier in the centre, nor the tops of the taller pipes. I think they have glass panels in their upper panels.

7 · 17 · 7 / 11

From Gluringen I went to Ritzinger-Feld, about a mile walk ~~along~~ along a footpath. There are no houses near, so I couldn't get to see the keyboards. The case stands in a white gallery: it is light brown in colour, and has aluminium painted pipes with ~~[illegible]~~ rounded

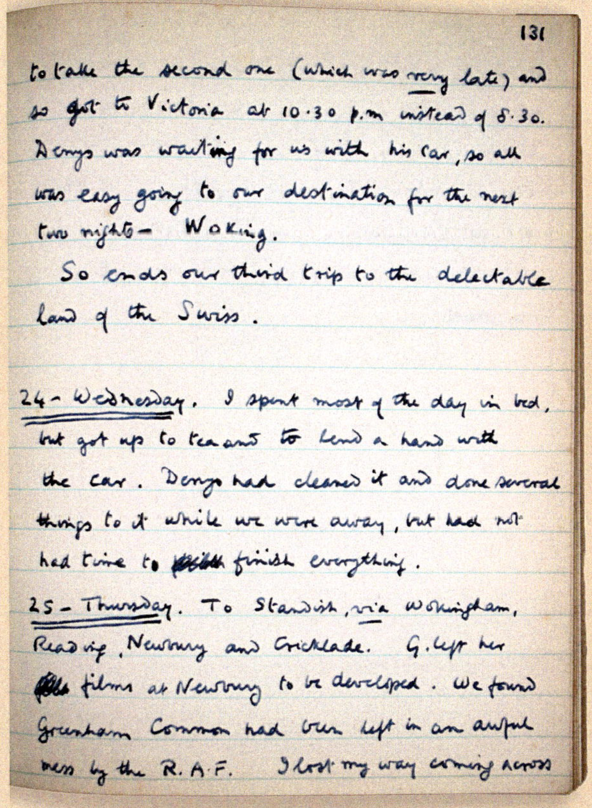

131

to take the second one (which was very late) and so got to Victoria at 10.30 p.m. instead of 8.30. Denys was waiting for us with his car, so all was easy going to our destination for the next two nights – Woking.

So ends our third trip to the delectable land of the Swiss.

24 – Wednesday. I spent most of the day in bed, but got up to tea and to lend a hand with the car. Denys had cleaned it and done several things to it while we were away, but had not had time to ~~[illegible]~~ finish everything.

25 – Thursday. To Standish, via Wokingham, Reading, Newbury and Cricklade. G. left her ~~[illegible]~~ films at Newbury to be developed. We found Greenham Common had been left in an awful mess by the R.A.F. I lost my way coming across

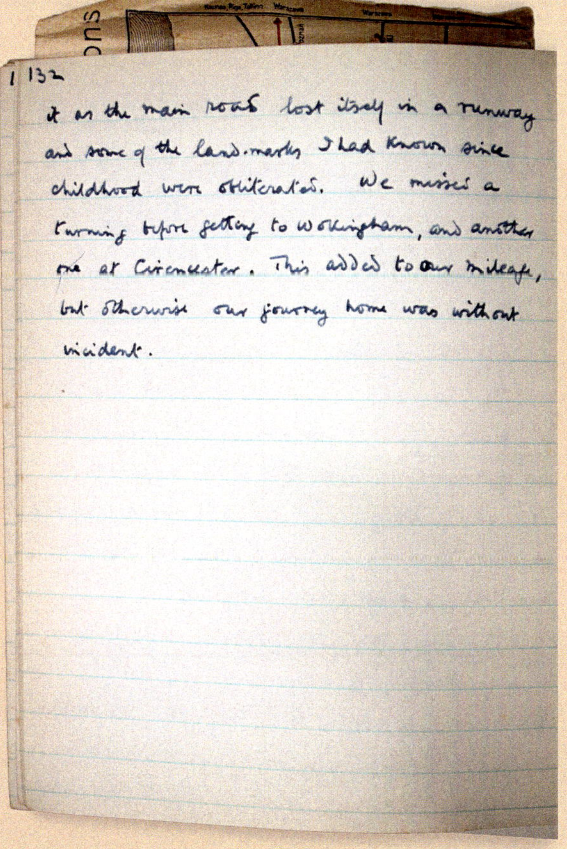

132

it as the main road lost itself in a runway and some of the land-marks I had known since childhood were obliterated. We missed a turning before getting to Wokingham, and another one at Cirencester. This added to our mileage, but otherwise our journey home was without incident.

Sketch of St Mary's, Rotherhithe. *Freeman's photograph can be found in the CRL online catalogue at Freeman/439; plate 671.*

The Plates

These plates can also be viewed on the website of the Cadbury Library (Birmingham University (UK) libraries Special Collections): www.birmingham.ac.uk/facilities/cadbury. Each plate is assigned a Freeman number and a plate number. The date following the place and name identification is the year the photograph was taken; thus the list of photographs is in roughly chronological order. (Because the original plates were not themselves dated, some years may have been estimated). While most quotations in the captions are from Freeman's articles in *Musical Opinion* and *The Organ*, some are taken from other sources, including his handwritten notes in the British Organ Archive, and his book, *English Organ Cases* (London: Geo. Aug. Mate & Son, 1921).

Plate 1 — Wesleyan Church, Newbury, Berkshire (1895)

Freeman/1; plate 3

Freeman's church as a boy. 'A very usual type of case for an organ of moderate dimensions during the latter half of the period – from 1820 to 1860...It consists of three ogee arches bounded by pinnacled buttresses, arches and pinnacles being alike crocketed and crowned with finials. When the designer managed to hit on the right proportions and proper curves the result, as in this instance, was both pleasing and picturesque, and infinitely preferable to the bald boxes of whistles which found their way into our Churches during the same period through the parsimony and ignorance of the authorities concerned.'

Freeman, *English organ cases*, 63

Plate 2 — Hobson Street Wesleyan, Cambridge (1895)

Freeman/4; plate 7

'It is not easy to achieve a satisfactory result by filling up one or more rectangular openings with pipes of the same length but of varying diameters, but the case of the old organ at Hobson Street Wesleyan Chapel, Cambridge, serves to show what can be done under this limitation. It had gilt pipes and green-painted wood-work. Both chapel and organ-case have been destroyed.'

Freeman, *English organ cases*, 76

Plate 3 — Holy Trinity Church, Cambridge (1896)

Freeman/7; plate 16

'The design, though conventional, is not without charm. The three gables are well proportioned, and the pinnacle buttresses play their part (a purely ornamental one) unobtrusively. The cusping below the arches and the crockets and finials above the gables are on the right scale, and the general effect is extremely good. I could wish that panelling had been inserted at the sides instead of the three pipes; failing the panels, a carved and gilded pipe-shade would take away the unpleasant effect of the straight edge along the top of these pipes. I think, too, that if space allowed the base of the organ to be brought out so that it joined up with the lower edge of the overhang, there would be a feeling of complete homogeneity, which at present is lacking. With these alterations, I think the case would be a perfect example of its type.'

The Organ 18, no. 70 (Oct. 1938): 90

Plate 4 — Cambridge Guildhall (1906)

Freeman/12; plate 67

'[Case by A. G. Hill]. The projecting tubas are a somewhat unnecessary feature, and there is but little in the way of ornamentation, but there are many points about this excellently proportioned 16ft. case, which might well serve as a model where the space allowed is wide in proportion to its height and where an expensive case is out of the question.'

Freeman, *English organ cases*, 73

Plate 5 — St John's College Chapel, Cambridge (1906)

Freeman/16; plate 74

'1889, a twin-fronted case… by Mr. J. Oldrid Scott [son of Sir Gilbert]'

Freeman, *English organ cases*, 68

Plate 6 — Trinity College Chapel, Cambridge (1906)

Freeman/21; plate 92

'Smith 1708 finished by Shrider. Till 1870 the Main Case consisted of four towers and three flats. Of these the two inner towers were semicircular and contained three pipes each while the two flanking towers (of five pipes) were flat. There are now six towers. The Choir Case has a flat tower at either end joined to a centrally placed semicircular tower by means of a flat. Each tower displays five pipes.'

Freeman, *English organ cases*, 46

Plate 7 — Jesus College Chapel, Cambridge, Chancel Organ (1906)

Freeman/25; plate 100

'...captivating...A beautiful little work, as satisfying today as it was in 1849, the year it was made and set up. The design is very simple, for it will be seen that the front pipes, nineteen in number rake from the largest pipe in the centre to the smaller ones at the two sides. The V-tower allows more pipes to stand in the given width, and it certainly adds to the interest of the design. The winged doors, overhanging sides and carving – all of them skilfully and appropriately decorated – are admirably conceived. The design is closely in accord with the Decorated Gothic in vogue in England during the period 1307–77—the Middle Pointed, so greatly beloved of the Camden Society... Seeing how few examples of organ cases of this early date were available for his guidance, even in pictorial form, it is really rather wonderful that Pugin should have succeeded in devising a thing that seems true and beautiful to us...'

The Organ 18, no. 71 (Jan 1939): 142

Plate 8 — Jesus College Chapel, Cambridge, West End Organ (1906)

Freeman/26; plate 101

case designed by G. F. Bodley, painted to match the chancel organ

Freeman, *English organ cases*, 28

Plate 9 — St Andrew the Less (Abbey Church), Cambridge (1906)

Freeman/31; plate 109

'...a charming little organ case that is perfectly in keeping with its place and office. If one were to write its epitaph in a line the words that suggest themselves would be "mediaeval without affectation." And so it is, with its rich yet unobtrusive colouring its overhanging front, and its folding shutters. If one thing is certain about the instrument it is that the Suttons (and possibly Pugin) had a great deal to do with its installation...In default of definite information one would hazard the guess that it was between 1850 and 1870. As in other instances where the Rev. F. H. Sutton was the ruling genius, the organ is placed in a shallow chamber, which has two openings into the church, one above the other, the upper one for the case, and the lower for the keyboards.'

Musical Opinion 50, no. 591 (Dec. 1926): 277

Plate 10 — St Laurence Church, Reading, Berkshire (1907)

Freeman/33; plate 111

Byfield organ, 1741

Freeman, *English organ cases*, 59

Plate 11 — Congregational, Newbury, Berkshire (1907)

Freeman/36; plate 116

Plate 12 — Wesleyan, Newbury, Berkshire (1907)

Freeman/39; plate 119

This case is an enlargement of the one seen in Plate 1, p.71.

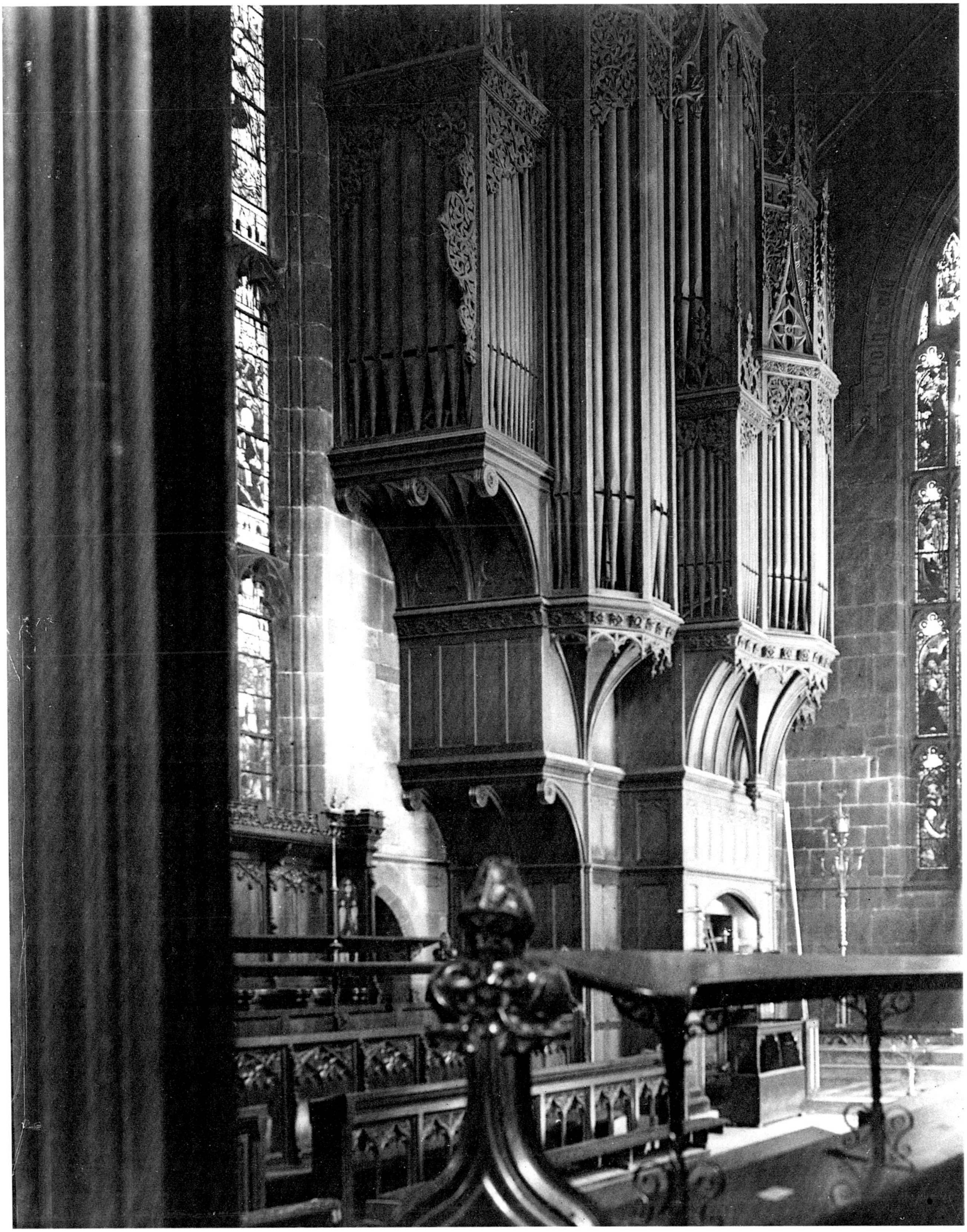

Plate 13 — St Mary the Virgin, Nottingham (1907)

Freeman/43; plate 137

'Sir Gilbert Scott's case at Nottingham would have been enormously improved if the pipe-feet had varied inversely with the length of their bodies. By this means a certain gauntness which is especially noticeable about the pipes of the end towers and (to a lesser extent) bracketed sides would have been avoided, and the one defect of the composition remedied.'

Freeman, *English organ cases*, 27

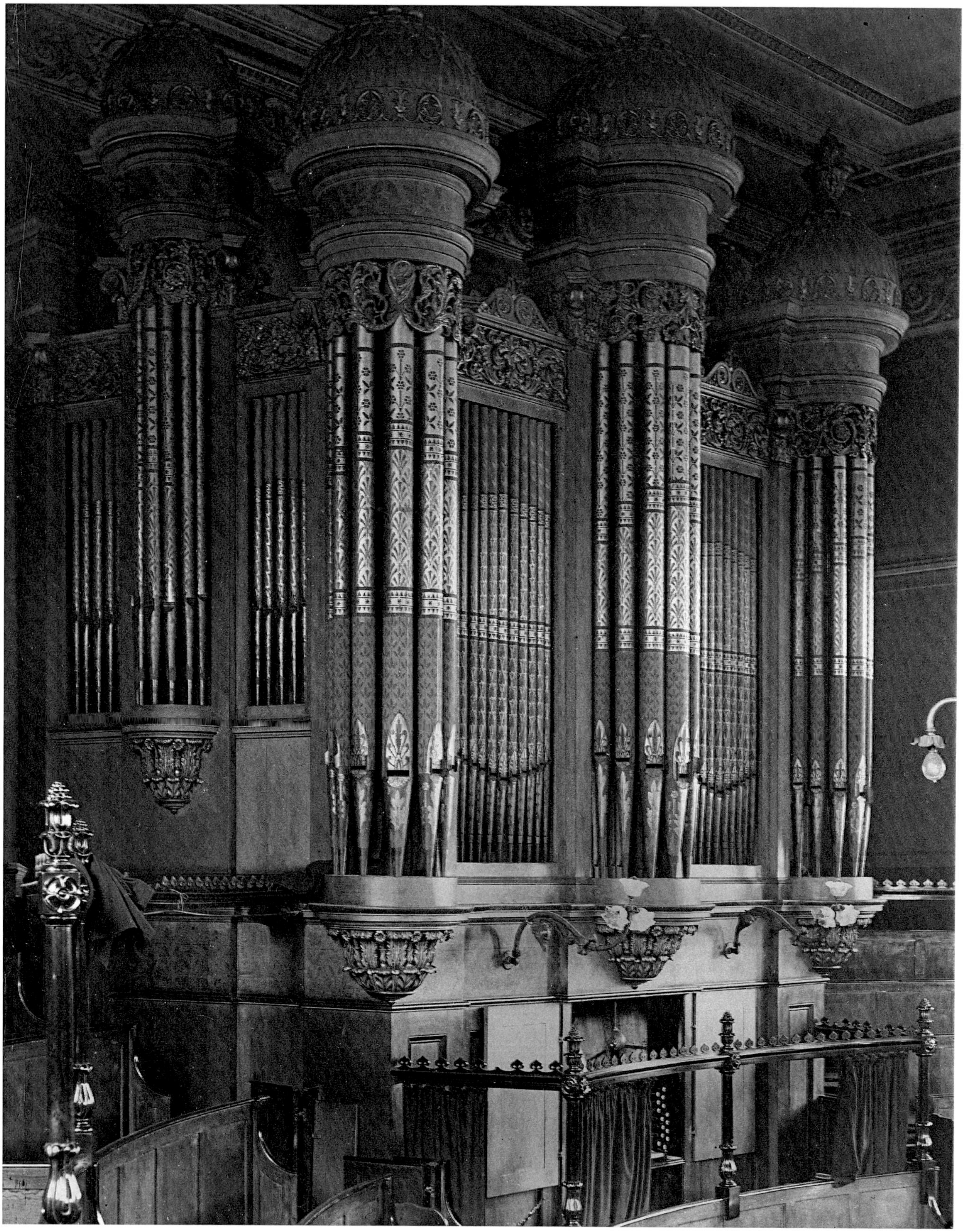

Plate 14 — Halifax Place Wesleyan Church, Nottingham (1907)

Freeman/47; plate 141

'[This organ] is quite effective. It belongs to that type which is generally improved by being somewhat lavishly decorated – a procedure which has been followed out in this instance as regards both wood-work and pipes.'

Freeman, *English organ cases*, 75–6

Plate 15 — St Mary the Virgin, Finedon, Northants (1907)

Freeman/48; plate 143

'"It would not be easier to plan a finer architectural effect than the grand old organ at Finedon Church produces." Such is the testimony of the late Frederick Heathcote Sutton, Vicar of Theddingworth, author of *Church Organs: their position and construction*, and an enthusiast in the matter of preserving old organs and designing beautiful cases. Though it is nineteen years since my one and only visit to Finedon, I still have a vivid recollection of the delight I felt when, on turning round halfway up the church, I first set eyes on the organ…It was certainly a goodly and pleasurable sight…Its plan – a central rounded tower flanked by a flat and flat tower – is extremely rare. Its overhanging sides will not pass unnoticed, though these were by no means unusual at the beginning of the eighteenth century. The carving over the two "flats" is more uncommon, though some of Father Smith's were so provided. But the really distinctive note in the design is struck by the broken circular pediments, – very bold, very excellent and yet rarely introduced into the components of an English organ case. There remains but one thing to add: that the workmanship is carefully and skilfully wrought and in every way worthy of the design, of the instrument, and of the place it occupies in the church and in the church's services.'

The Organ 6, no. 21 (July 1926): 33–5

Plate 16 – Holborn Town Hall, London (1907)

Freeman/51; plate 146

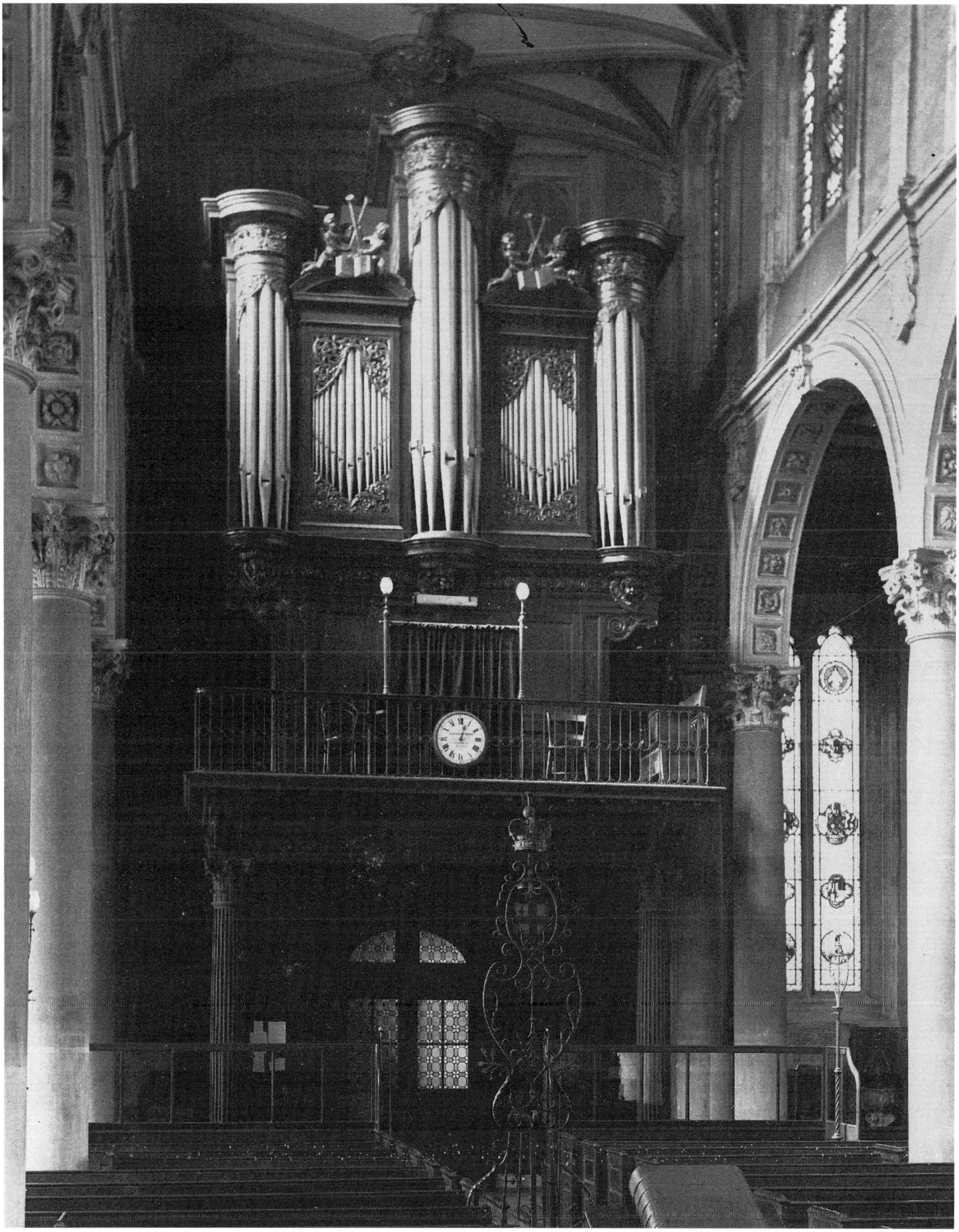

Plate 17 — St Katherine Cree, London (1907)

Freeman/52; plate 149

'Smith, 1683. [An example in which] the cornice was a horizontal straight line, parallel with the impost…[and also] in which the cornice took the form of, or was surmounted by, a pediment.'

Freeman, *English organ cases*, 52–3

Plate 18 – St John the Baptist, Cirencester, Gloucestershire (1908)

Freeman/55; plate 159

Plate 19 — All Hallows, Barking, London (1908)

Freeman/58; plate 180

'This is a fine and dignified example of late seventeenth or early eighteenth century design and workmanship. It is usually considered to be the case of the original Renatus Harris organ of 1675....I think it much more likely that it was supplied by Gerard Smith in 1720... There is no organ case quite like it that is known to me, the nearest in form being the one built by (George?) Dallam for St Martin-in-the-Fields, now – much altered and considerably spoilt – at St Peter-in-the-East, St Albans, Herts...Both designs are good, but that at All Hallows strikes one as the finer, particularly in the arrangement of the lower flats. The engrailing of the pipe shades of the three towers is a pleasing and noteworthy feature. The gilt pipes and the oak framing look extremely well; and the west gallery is so obviously the place for it, both musically and architecturally, that one wonders what can have possessed architects, clergy and vestrymen that they should have wrought such senseless destruction in churches where the effect was comparable with that still to be experienced here...'

The Organ 8, no. 30 (Oct. 1928): 91–2

Plate 20 — St Olave, Hart Street, London (1908)

Freeman/60; plate 182

In 1944 Freeman wrote, 'This organ had one of the best of [Samuel] Green's cases, a very delightful little thing, and a perfect example of the best work of its period.'

The Organ 23, no.92 (April 1944), 162

The organ and church were destroyed in the Blitz of 1941.

Plate 21 — St Edmund King and Martyr, Lombard Street, London (1908)

Freeman/63; plate 185

'The original case, which still exists, has a most unusual design. Its front pipes are divided into three compartments – a central flat and two towers – all contained under a single curved pediment. The base-line of the pediment is limited to a short length at either end, – just sufficient to form caps for the two semi-circular towers. In this way the two towers are made to serve as columns supporting the entablatures, and the segmental pediment connecting them. Though the design is not one that would commend itself to a purist, it is not without its merits. Carving and a profusion of gilding give it a rich appearance. In 1880, when the organ was removed from the west gallery to its present position on the north side of the church, a replica of the original case was made, so that the organ has now twin-fronts, standing side by side.'

Musical Opinion 48, no. 566 (Nov. 1924): 172

Plate 22 — All Hallows, Lombard Street, London (1908)

Freeman/64; plate 186

'Case by Harris, c.1695. This organ has two large semicircular towers with five pipes in each. The space between them is divided into two stories, the lower of which is occupied by a rectangular frame of caring with a large circular opening in which are displayed twenty-seven small pipes. The upper story consists of a small semicircular tower with five pipes, flanked by two flats with fourteen pipes each. The carving is rich and excellent, though the designer was not inspired when he decided upon the circular flat, nor in his treatment of the cornice above the three upper compartments. But it is a fine case despite these faults.'

Freeman, *English organ cases*, 45

The church was demolished in 1937.

Plate 23 – High Wycombe Town Hall, Buckinghamshire (1908)

Freeman/66; plate 203

Plate 24 — St Peter's Moravian Church, Bedford (1908)

Freeman/73; plate 212

Plate 25 — St Michael and All Angels, Brownsover, Rugby, Warwickshire (1908)

Freeman/77; plate 216

Plate 26 — St John the Baptist, Thaxted, Essex (1908)

Freeman/82; plate 221

Lincoln organ, c.1820, moved to this church in 1858.

Plate 27 — St Paul's Church, Cambridge (1908)

Freeman/86; plate 225

'[The case], for its period, is extremely good... It has faults, of course, notably in the too-numerous raking lines which destroy all feeling of repose without giving it a sense of life. But it also has a certain dignity, and when it stood in the west gallery, as it did till 1905, it looked really effective. On the ground floor at the east end of the north aisle (where it now is) it looks somewhat ungainly. This is partly due to an excessive overhanging of the front (there is *really* not room for it here), but even more to the hideous pedal pipes that form a hoarding to its side.'

Musical Opinion 50, no. 589 (Oct. 1926): 56

Plate 28 — King's College, Cambridge (from antechapel) (1908)

Freeman/97; plate 238

'...one of the loveliest organ cases in England, graceful in design and superbly carved...It is difficult to speak of the case of the King's organ save in superlatives...Each of its three component parts differ entirely from the other two [Freeman describes three 'fronts': one facing west (pictured) and two facing east] in design, yet combine with them to form a perfect whole. A more graceful outline could hardly be imagined, nor one more in keeping with its position and surroundings. The west front has the more uncommon design; indeed I know of no existing case at all like it...The carving is superb, being well conceived and cunningly wrought; while the little figures that are to be found at various points of the case, particularly those in the panels under the pipes of the west case, are real works of art.'

The Organ 8, no. 31 (Jan. 1929): 129, 138

Plate 29 — All Saints, St Ives, Huntingdonshire (1908)

Freeman/100; plate 240

Case by G. F. Bodley. 'The organ is very curiously and exceptionally placed above the screen where it entirely blocks out the view of the upper part of the Chancel. The ingenious way in which the organ-front is made to embody the Holy Rood with the attendant images of the Virgin and S. John is worthy of notice. The wood-work of organ and screen is elaborately decorated in gold, white, and red on a green ground, and the general effect is rich, though with a tendency to gaudiness.'

Freeman, *English organ cases*, 28–9

Plate 30 — St Helen's Parish Church, Abingdon, Oxfordshire (formerly Berkshire) (1908)

Freeman/103; plate 243

'...built by Abraham Jordan in 1725...The gilded representation of King David and his harp once adorned the west gallery (where the organ stood until its removal to its present position in the south Chancel Aisle), It scarcely merits its prominent place on this fine old organ-case.'

Freeman, *English organ cases*, 59

Plate 31 — Reading Town Hall, Berkshire (1908)

Freeman/115; plate 257

'A fine and imposing oak case, with a 16ft. speaking-front of plain metal pipes. It is so planned that a considerable number of the larger pipes are displayed on its three sides without any of its compartments being broken up into stories. It was designed by Mr. Lainson.'

Freeman, *English organ cases*, 74

Plate 32 — St Andrew's Parish Church, Enfield, Middlesex (1909)

Freeman/119; plate 263

case by Richard Bridge (1753). 'The ogee curve was a favourite one in work of this period, and used with discretion, as at Enfield, was a means of beauty. (Its use in the *plan* as well as in the elevation of the curtains between the towers should be noticed.)'

Freeman, *English organ cases*, 59

Plate 33 — Brasenose College Chapel, Oxford (1910)

Freeman/155; plate 316

case by T. G. Jackson. '...constructed in 1892. It is placed on a screen dividing the chapel from the ante-chapel, to each of which it presents a differently planned front of gilded pipes. The east, or chapel front, has three rounded towers. Above the central one, which is the smallest, is seated an angel, playing on a viol. Two peacocks are to be seen in the pipe-shades of each of the three towers.... The case is of light oak, embellished with gold, and the overhanging sides add to its graceful and refined appearance.'

Freeman, *English organ cases*, 72–3

Plate 34 — Parish Church, Quendon, Essex (1910)

Freeman/168; plate 335

Compare with Plate 210, p.280: the organ, enlarged, re-using some elements of this case.

Plate 35 — Holy Trinity Church, Clapham, London, Chancel Organ (1910)

Freeman/170; plate 337

'...an excellent modern organ in a solidly-wrought oak case, made by the builders [A. Hunter & Son, 1909] in accordance with the designs of Mr. Beresford Pite. Personally, I do not like to see the tops of the pipes showing above the wood-work of the case, and I cannot say that I admire either the fret-carving which is so much in evidence, or the curve given to the cornices which connect the towers with the wings, but these blemishes – and blemishes they are – are not sufficient to nullify the air of great strength conveyed by what is really a very original case. I have nothing but admiration to express for the fine quality of workmanship both of case and instrument.'

Freeman, *English organ cases*, 74–5

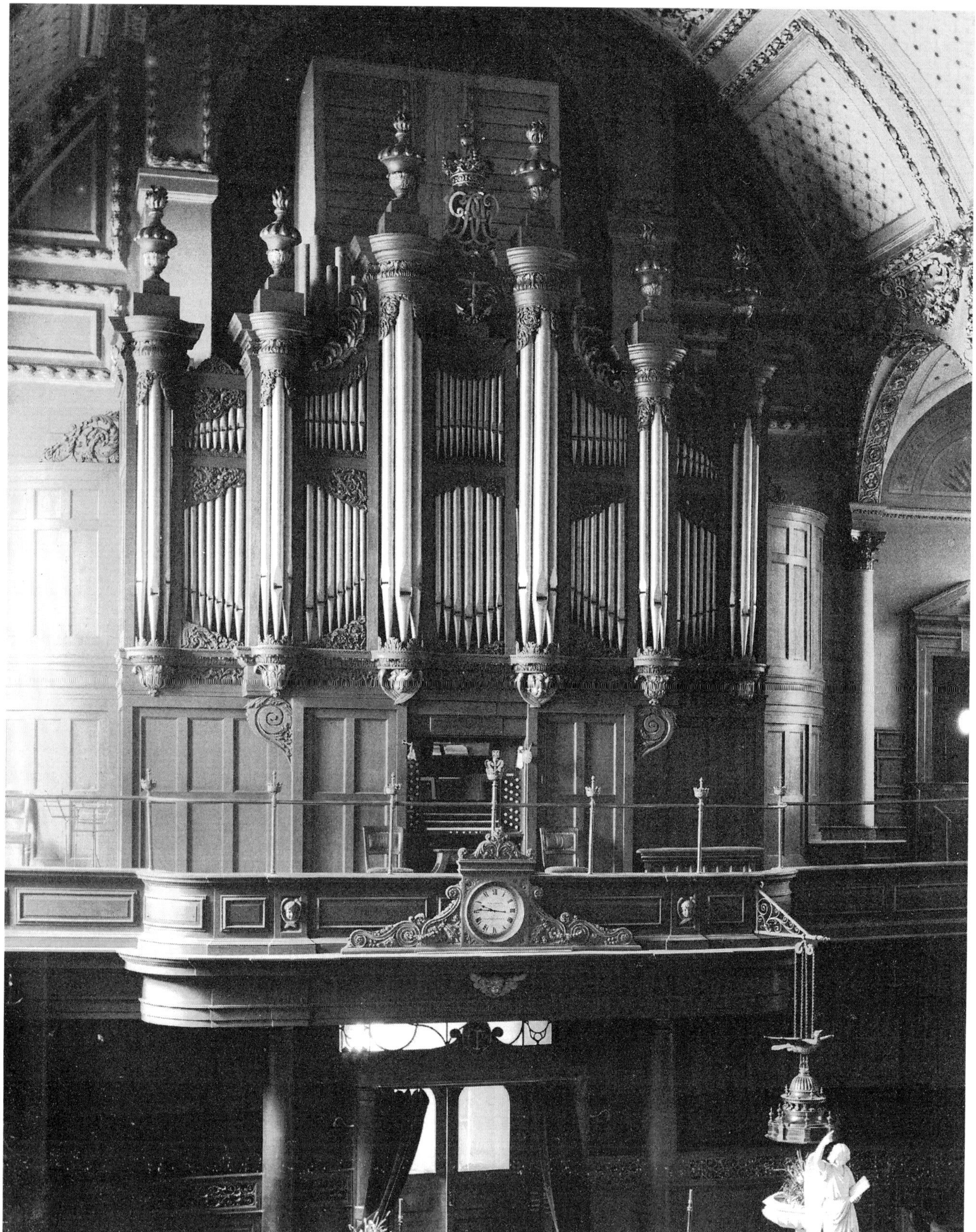

Plate 36 — St Clement Danes, Strand, London (1911)

Freeman/191; plate 360

The organ, along with the interior of the church, was destroyed during the 1941 London Blitz.

Plate 37 — St James, Piccadilly, London, from gallery (1911)

Freeman/200; plate 371

The church was heavily damaged during the Blitz of 1940; however, the organ case, apparently carved by Grinling Gibbons, had been protected prior to the raid and survived.

Plate 38 — Christ Church, Newgate Street, London (1911)

Freeman/213; plate 384

Destroyed by bombing in 1940.

Plate 39 — St Vedast, Foster Lane, London (1911)

Freeman/216; plate 387

The church was gutted during the Blitz, and reordered after the war to a design by Stephen Dykes Bower.

Plate 40 — St Mary Parish Church, Lambeth, London (1911)

Freeman/232; plate 406

'...It was my pleasure to play...the organ at Lambeth Parish Church for some five or six years....The lower part of the case is excellent late seventeenth century work, but all above the impost, except for a few fragments of carving, belongs to the middle of the last century (1851–2). The new work is well carried out but its design is crude and faulty to a degree...'

Musical Opinion 49 (May 1926): 839–40

Plate 41 — Clare College, Cambridge (1911)

Freeman/235; plate 409

'[Case designed by] J. W. Simpson, a very successful recasting and enlargement of an old-fashioned case, the towers being increased from four to six.'

Freeman, *English organ cases*, 76

Plate 42 — Holy Trinity Church, Bridlington, Yorkshire (1911)

Freeman/248; plate 440

Plate 43 — Quay Wesleyan Church, Bridlington, Yorkshire (1911)

Freeman/254; plate 446

Plate 44 — St Mary's, Plaistow, Bromley, Kent, transept (1911)

Freeman/263; plate 455

Plate 45 — St John's Parish Church, Hackney North, London (1912)

Freeman/304; plate 505

'The case, massive in appearance, is in keeping with the architecture of the church.... The fluted supports to the four towers attract attention: their form is probably unique.'

The Organ 21, no. 82 (Oct. 1941): 46

Plate 46 — Christ Church Cathedral, Oxford (1912)

Freeman/308; plate 509

'[Father Smith's] case [(1680)] has survived, though not without alteration. Thus wings have been added to the east front, which originally consisted of four towers and the three inner flats only. The choir case is also an addition, – pleasing, although not quite so successful as one could wish. (For one thing, the towers require deeper pipe shades, while the horizontal line of the pipe mouths in its towers is not at all happy ...)'

The Organ 11, no. 41 (July 1931): 38

Plate 47 — St Alkmund, Whitchurch, Shropshire (1912)

Freeman/318; plate 519

Plate 48 — Tewkesbury Abbey, Gloucestershire (1912)

Freeman/320; plate 523

'This case is a magnificent example of pre-Restoration design and workmanship, strongly Elizabethan in character...There are thirty-seven pipes in front, all of the gilt and ten of them beautifully embossed...They present a wonderfully rich appearance.'

The Organ 3, no. 11 (Jan. 1924): 154

Plate 49 — St Laurence, Ludlow, Shropshire (1912)

Freeman/326; plate 529

'The organ, enclosed in its original case, is placed in the North Transept, beyond the aisle. The console is detached, and situated under the tower arch, near the NW pier. The case, which is a fine one (one of Snetzler's best) has overhanging aisles and front, stands high up, and looks very dignified, with its gilt front pipes, but the 26 Tuba pipes, placed fan-wise on either side of the central tower, are not in keeping with the rest, and their removal would not be a matter for regret... These are really good bold cornices and with carved pipe-shades to the 3 towers and to the two lower flats, but the upper flats are spoilt by having their pipes (20, in all) of exactly the same length – a great mistake, as they are "short and stubby". Moreover the cornice above the upper tier of pipes has been destroyed to make way for the Tubas – unless, indeed, the upper tiers are themselves an addition, taking the place of some former shield of carved work. Either way these upper tiers are the most unsatisfactory feature in an otherwise fine case.'

From Freeman's hand-written notes in the British Organ Archive: Box 83, 'Notebooks (organ visited)', vol. 4: 629–32

Plate 50 — St Martin in the Fields, London (1912)

Freeman/332; plate 535

Plate 51 — The Queen's College, Oxford (1912)

Freeman/314; plate 515

Plate 52 — St George's, Camberwell, London (1913)

Freeman/343; plate 551

Plate 53 — St Margaret Pattens, London (1913)

Freeman/345; plate 563

Plate 54 — St Ethelburga's, Bishopgate Street, London (also spelt Bishopsgate) (1913)

Freeman/362; plate 578

Plate 55— St Paul's Parish Church, Deptford, London (1913)

Freeman/364; plate 580

Plate 56 — St Mary the Virgin, Islington, London (1913)

Freeman/365; plate 582

Plate 57 — St Mildred's, Bread Street, London (1913)

Freeman/367; plate 584

The church was destroyed by bombs in 1941.

Plate 58 — St John's, Waterloo Rd, Lambeth, London (1913)

Freeman/370, plate 594

'[In 1889] Messrs Hele & Co. added a solo organ [to the original J. C. Bishop organ of 1824]...which was placed in a separate swell box in a case of its own, behind the organist's back. It will be noticed that the newer case is less ornate than the older ones above it. It also contains plain metal pipes with rounded lips whereas those in the main case are decorated and have leaf lips. A little more gilt on the woodwork would undoubtedly improve the appearance of the organ, whose case is in keeping with the architecture of the church and better than most of the other fittings. If a "square" case of this kind seems somewhat dull and commonplace in comparison with those of the latter half of the seventeenth century, it is immeasurably superior to those of the pipe-rack period, from which only a few church organs have as yet been rescued.'

Musical Opinion 50, no. 599 (Aug 1927): 1091–3

Plate 59 — St John, Wapping, London (1913)

Freeman/376; plate 601

Plate 60 — Dulwich College Chapel, London (1913)

Freeman/384, plate 609

'The case [by George England, 1760] stands in a class by itself, for it is an example, not of the Gothic revival, but of the "Gothic survival". In some parts of England the Gothic tradition never quite died out... There is an antique feeling about the lower tiers of the flats that is very pleasing, and the curve of the cornice above the upper ones is very graceful, even though quite ordinary. The decorative carving is well designed and executed, though the arched mouldings above the pipes in the towers strike one as not being perfectly happy, due chiefly to the fact that the pipes of the towers are slightly in advance of their buttresses, and so the pipe shades have to be brought forward to enfold them... Noteworthy features...are three spirettes above the three towers. These are not mere gables, but proper four-sided spires of pierced work, quite in the tradition of such early cases as those at Zaragoza and Palma (Majorca), which date from the fifteenth century. The pinnacles, too, which stand on top of the six buttresses, have the same affinity with the past. No revivalist would have tolerated them, nor could anyone before the time of Pugin bettered them.'

The Organ 20, no. 80 (April 1941): 139–141

Plate 61 — Summer Drawing Room, Hatfield House, Hertfordshire (1913)

Freeman/388; plate 618

'...probably built by T. Dallam...The case is square but really very beautiful. It is divided rather less than half-way up by the impost on which rest the two pillars which support the overhanging cornice. Between these two pillars the upper portion is divided into five flats of gilt pipes, of which those in the three central compartments stand higher than the two end ones. There are carved and gilt pipe-shades beneath as well as above the pipes. The sides and lower portion of the front are panelled with much inlaid work, while the whole case is richly decorated in black, white, colours, and gold.'

Freeman, *English organ cases*, 36

Plate 62 — St Mary the Virgin, West Tofts, Norfolk, looking west (1913)

Freeman/394; plate 624

'...a really lovely Pugin case...one of the most successful of all his works.'

The Organ 18, no. 71 (Jan 1939): 142

'...an altogether delightful little case, suspended, with its tribune, from the north wall of the Chancel... Every detail seems to have been carefully thought out. Even the front edges of the naturals belonging to the manuals are carved – those of the swell displaying a series of ogee arches, and of the great a similar series of arches with cusps...This charming composition is another of those cases which can be directly traced to the Sutton influence. It was erected, presumably, c.1857...'

Freeman, *English organ cases*, 24–5

Plate 63 — St Phillip's Cathedral, Birmingham, Warwickshire (1913)

Freeman/404; plate 636

Plate 64 — Parish Clerks Hall, Silver St., London (1921)

Freeman/457; plate 694

Plate 65 — St Mary's, Petworth, Sussex (1921)

Freeman/486; plate 728

'It was at Petworth that my persistence in carrying a camera on several fruitless trips was at last rewarded to the full. For the case of the instrument in this church, though not perfect in every respect, is exceedingly fine, and of a striking and original design, being bold in outline, yet refined in its intricate detail. As the casework is of dark oak, with the front pipes silvered, and the carving lavishly gilt, the whole composition has a brilliant appearance which is quite in keeping with the rest of the internal decorations...The case looks at its best when viewed at an angle, for the side pipes of the end tower are then in evidence, and the fine effect of the two square towers can be properly appreciated. From the front, the one weakness of the design – the four flats almost exactly alike – is so obvious that one wonders how the architect came to let it stand in his drawing. But most astonishing of all, is to find the effect of this beautiful case seriously marred by the unsightly and quite unnecessary protrusion of four or five large metal pipes above the top of it.

Musical Opinion 52, no. 619 (April 1929): 651

Plate 66 — Holy Trinity, Bramley, Surrey (1921)

Freeman/490; plate 732

'...What was more to my liking was its very pleasing case, painted green and red and enriched with much gilding. Designed by Mr. W. Tapper, this case would as certainly be an addition to the furnishing of almost any village church, as it is an eloquent memorial to those who took thought for the appearance of this particular instrument. It is indeed strange how much time diocesan chancellors and advisory boards will spend fussing over the style of lettering ...of a memorial brass that nobody looks at six months after it has been put up, and how readily they will pass any old thing labelled "design for a new organ". They do not know, and because they do not know they think it does not matter. Hence the rare delight of a really beautiful organ case.'

Musical Opinion 52, no. 617 (Feb. 1929): 416

Plate 67 — Marylebone Presbyterian, London (1921)

Freeman/492; plate 735

Plate 68 — Organ in Bevington's Factory, Manette Street, Westminster, London (1921)

Freeman/494; plate 738

'...organs with toe pedals are very rare indeed. I happened to have dropped in at Messrs Bevington & Sons, [organ builders] in Soho, and chanced to speak about the extreme rarity of organs with toe pedals. Mr Lewis Bevington agreed, but added. "We've one of them in our workshops at the present time." Mr Bevington allowed me to examine and play this little instrument –a chamber organ made by his grandfather c. 1830—and on another occasion to photograph it. It stood originally in a private house in Suffolk, but was afterwards removed to Kent. It was quite well made and had been carefully used. The case is of debased Gothic, with three flats of dummy pipes, gilt, in front.'

Musical Opinion 49, No. 582 (March 1926): 614

Plate 69 — St Anselm & St Cecilia, Kingsway, London (1921)

Freeman/495; plate 739

Plate 70 — Bristol Cathedral (1922)

Freeman/505; plate 749

'Though the two fronts bear a strong resemblance to each other in their general arrangement, there is a marked difference in the treatment of the woodwork between the two towers. The western case (the old west front) is distinctly more architectural in feeling, – note the Corinthian columns on either side of the flats, with the broken entablature and segmental pediment above, and the swags of foliage over the pipes. Though the eastern case is less formal than the other it has a profusion of carving, the latter being so arranged as to emphasize the arch-like appearance of the openings through which the pipes in the flats are displayed. The binding together of the two flats under the bold segmental moulding – a feature that is almost exclusively confined to cases by Thomas and Renatus Harris, and for that reason typical of their work – certainly makes for unity; but in this particular example there are two rather large expanses of uncarved wood which detract somewhat from the otherwise good effect, not so much because they are destitute of embellishment as because they are of an awkward shape.'

The Organ 2, no.6 (Oct. 1922): 72

Plate 71 — Christ Church, Bristol (1922)

Freeman/508; plate 752

'The case undoubtedly belongs to the original organ, circa 1700–09, so that it is older than the church, which was built in 1784. ...I think the two vases standing on either side of the organ originally stood above the side towers.'

Musical Opinion 53, no. 628 (Jan. 1930): 343

Plate 72 — St Peter, Bristol (1922)

Freeman/510; plate 754

'The case...falls short both in general design and intricacy of details. Not that its workmanship is at fault, but rather because its author tried to make the towers into Corinthian pillars and pilasters. The thing cannot be done, and the best that can be said for this effort is that it is a worthy failure.'

Musical Opinion 53, no. 628 (Jan. 1930): 344

The church was destroyed in the bombing of Bristol in 1940.

Plate 73 — St Mary Magdalene, Willen, Buckinghamshire (1922)

Freeman/519; plate 763

'I feel convinced that organ and case were not made for each other... The organ is clearly not modern. Some of its pipes are decidedly old, possibly as old as the church. It may be that the wood-work was not originally designed to form a case (the half round openings on each side are exceedingly poorly contrived) which means that its constituent parts may have been assembled to encase a caseless organ. If, on the other hand, the case is original, its original front pipes have given place to others that are too long to be slightly. These front pipes are composed of soft plain metal, with lips pressed out from solid. One or two which have soldered lips are evidently replacements. Some of the pipes at the sides are dummies.'

Musical Opinion 49, no. 586 (July 1926): 1022

Plate 74 — St Mary & St Lawrence, Great Waltham, Essex (1922)

Freeman/525; plate 770

Plate 75 — St Mary Magdalene, Upton, Torquay, Devon (1922)

Freeman/526; plate 772

Plate 76 — St Matthias, Richmond, Surrey (1923)

Freeman/532; plate 778

Plate 77 — St Mary Magdalene, Richmond, Surrey (1923)

Freeman/533; plate 779

'This is a very simple, but not ungraceful, front, with three flat towers and sufficient carving to make it interesting and worthy of its position. The instrument was rebuilt by J. W. Walker in 1907.'

The Organ 7, no. 26 (Oct. 1927): 124

Plate 78 — Gloucester Cathedral, Gloucester, east front (1924)

Freeman/568; plate 815

'...The quire front is one of the most beautiful examples of the Renaissance period now extant. [It] is much more closely related to the pre-Restoration type of organ case than to anything subsequently made by Father Smith or Renatus Harris. This is even more true of the little chaire organ case, which seems to have a more antique feeling, both in design and treatment, than the great case above it. Though the two cases harmonise perfectly, the one differs so completely from the other in the matter of its carving and general detail that it is difficult to believe that they were designed by the same hand...The cresting of the chaire organ case and the ingenious way in which the central pipe is singled out from its neighbours, and yet supported by them, should be noticed. But indeed, the more this delightful little case is examined, the more it pleases.'

The Organ 4, no. 13 (July 1924): 9

Plate 79 — Gloucester Cathedral, Gloucestershire, west front (1924)

Freeman/569; plate 816

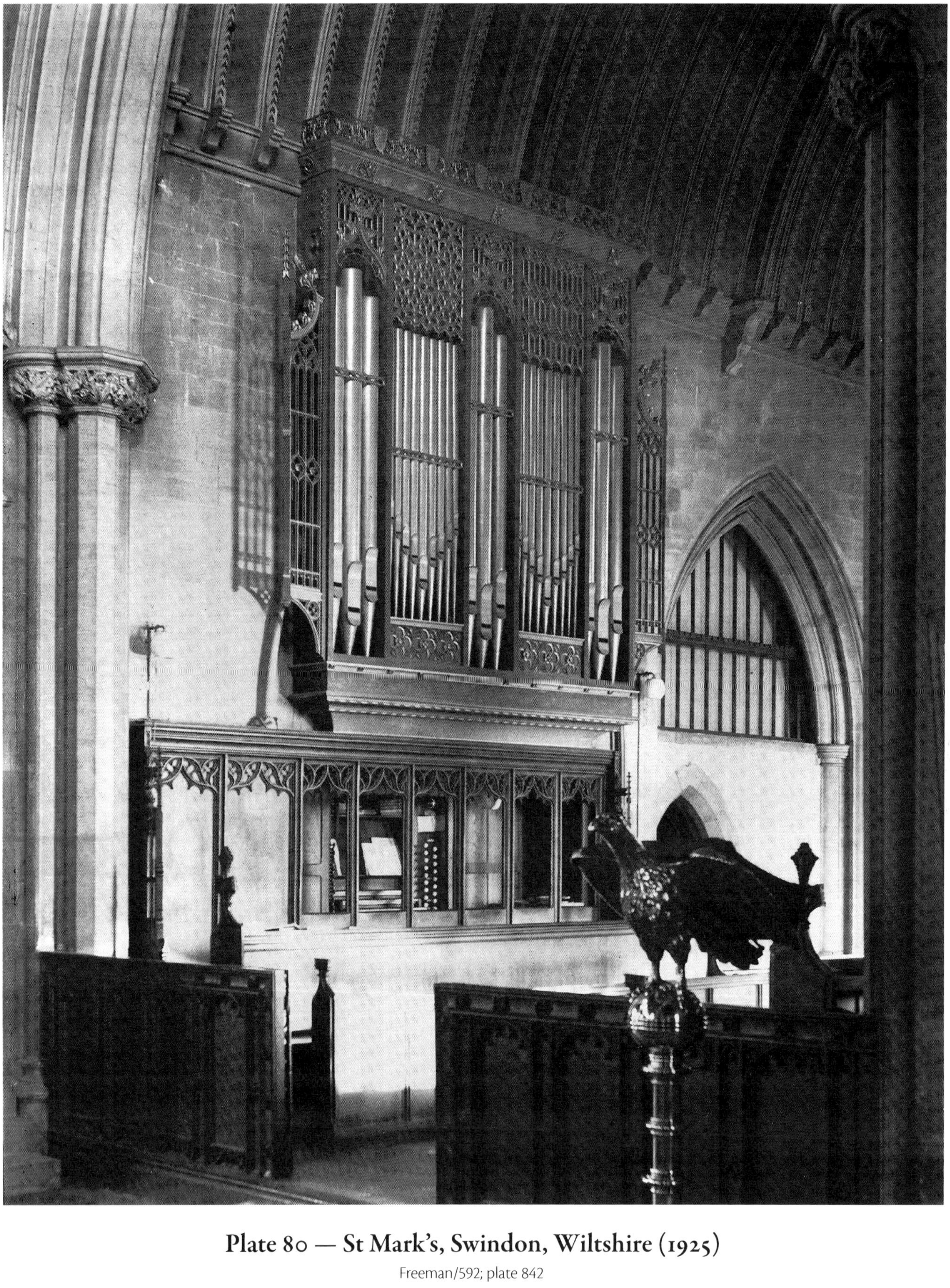

Plate 80 — St Mark's, Swindon, Wiltshire (1925)

Freeman/592; plate 842

Plate 81 — St Peter & St Paul, Blandford, Dorset (c.1925)

Freeman/599; plate 850

'The case is of oak, with some of the carvings slightly gilt. The carved scrolls on either side are rather unusual, they are also very well done. Mr. Lilley [H. T. Lilley was an artist, friend, and frequent collaborator with Freeman in organ case designs] has directed my attention to the kinship of the case with some of Heppelwhite's furniture. (Notice especially the treatment of the ovals and cornices). The crown over the centre tower is, of course, frequently met with; but the Prince of Wales' feathers over the side towers are extremely rare.'

Musical Opinion 50, no. 596 (May 1927): 801

Plate 82 — St Mark's, Kingsholm, Gloucester, Gloucestershire (1925)

Freeman/603; plate 856

Plate 83 — St Mary, Mistley, Essex (1925)

Freeman/611; plate 864

Plate 84 — St Mary Magdalene, Paddington, London (1925)

Freeman/613; plate 866

The case is by Ninian Comper

Plate 85 — St George, Southall, Middlesex (1925)

Freeman/616; plate 869

'...an instrument that is historically of interest and very handsomely encased in oak that is delicately carved, dark with age, yet excellently preserved.'

Musical Opinion 50, no. 595 (April 1927): 706

Plate 86— Worcester Cathedral, north case, Worcestershire (1925)

Freeman/619; plate 872

'...designed by Sir Gilbert Scott'

The Organ 5, no. 18 (Oct. 1925): 72

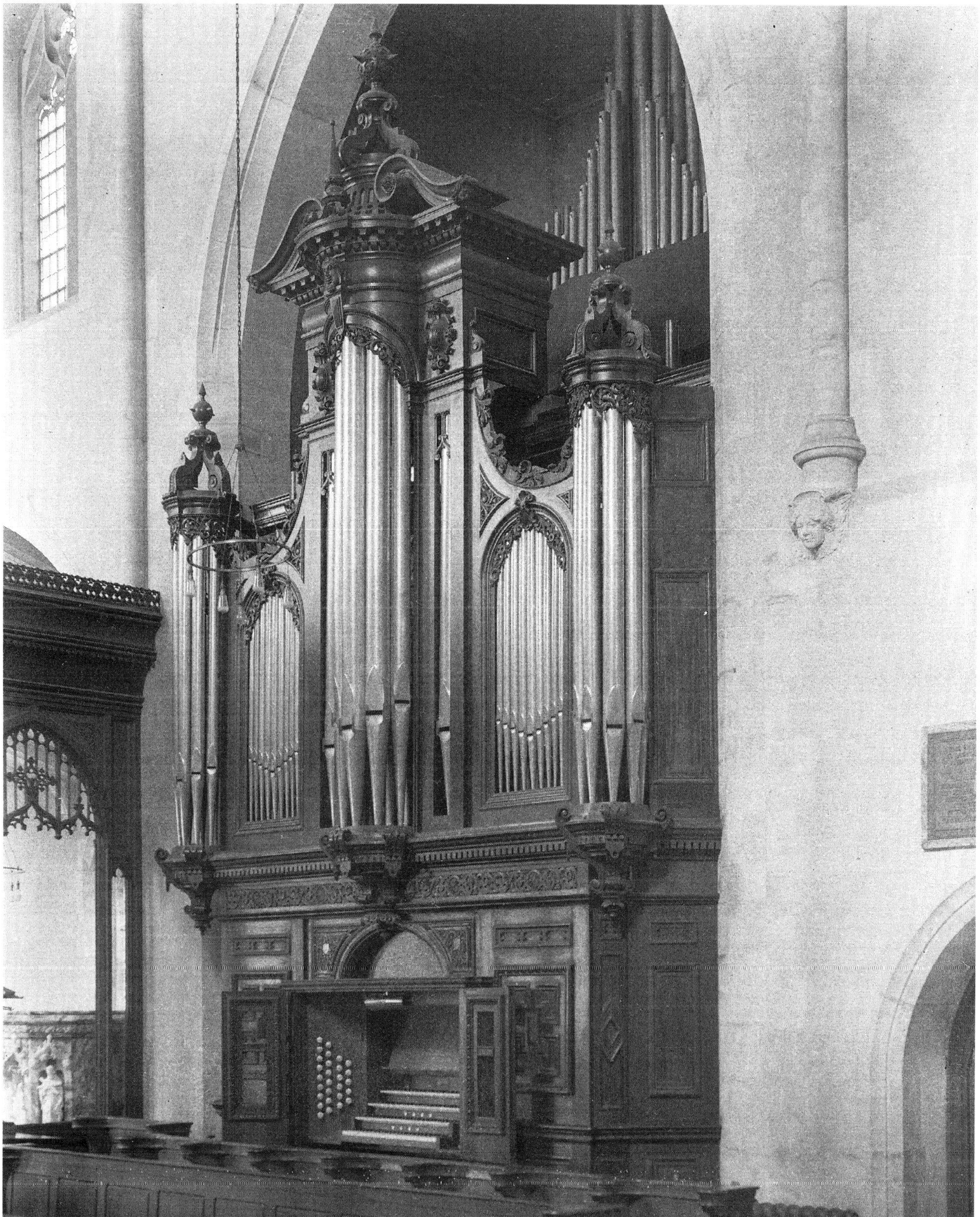

Plate 87 — St Paul, Weston Super Mare, Somerset (1925)

Freeman/623; plate 876

The church was destroyed by enemy bombing in 1941.

Plate 88 — Holy Rood Church, Southampton, Hampshire (1926)

Freeman/632; plate 885

This church was destroyed by enemy bombing in 1940.

Plate 89 — Bishop Street Wesleyan Church, Leicester, Leicestershire (1926)

Freeman/635; plate 888

Plate 90 — Staunton Harold private chapel, Leicestershire (1926)

Freeman/640; plate 893

Plate 91 — St Modwen, Burton on Trent, Staffordshire (1926)

Freeman/644; plate 897

Plate 92 — St Rose's Convent, Stroud, Gloucestershire (1926)

Freeman/646, plate 899

See the nearly identical case in St George, King Stanley: Plate 234, p.304.

Plate 93 — St Mary's Parish Church, Chepstow, Monmouthshire (1926)

Freeman/649, plate 902

'[The case dates] somewhere about the period 1790–1820. It is an elaborate specimen of its class, but not quite so sophisticated as the examples pictured in Faulkner's "Organ-Builder's Assistant," published in 1823. Though I cannot say that I admire this Chepstow effort, I infinitely prefer it to no case at all. [It is} an interesting example of a period which, for all its dullness, was not without its effect in leading to an appreciation of better things.'

Musical Opinion 52, no. 613 (Oct. 1928): 52–3

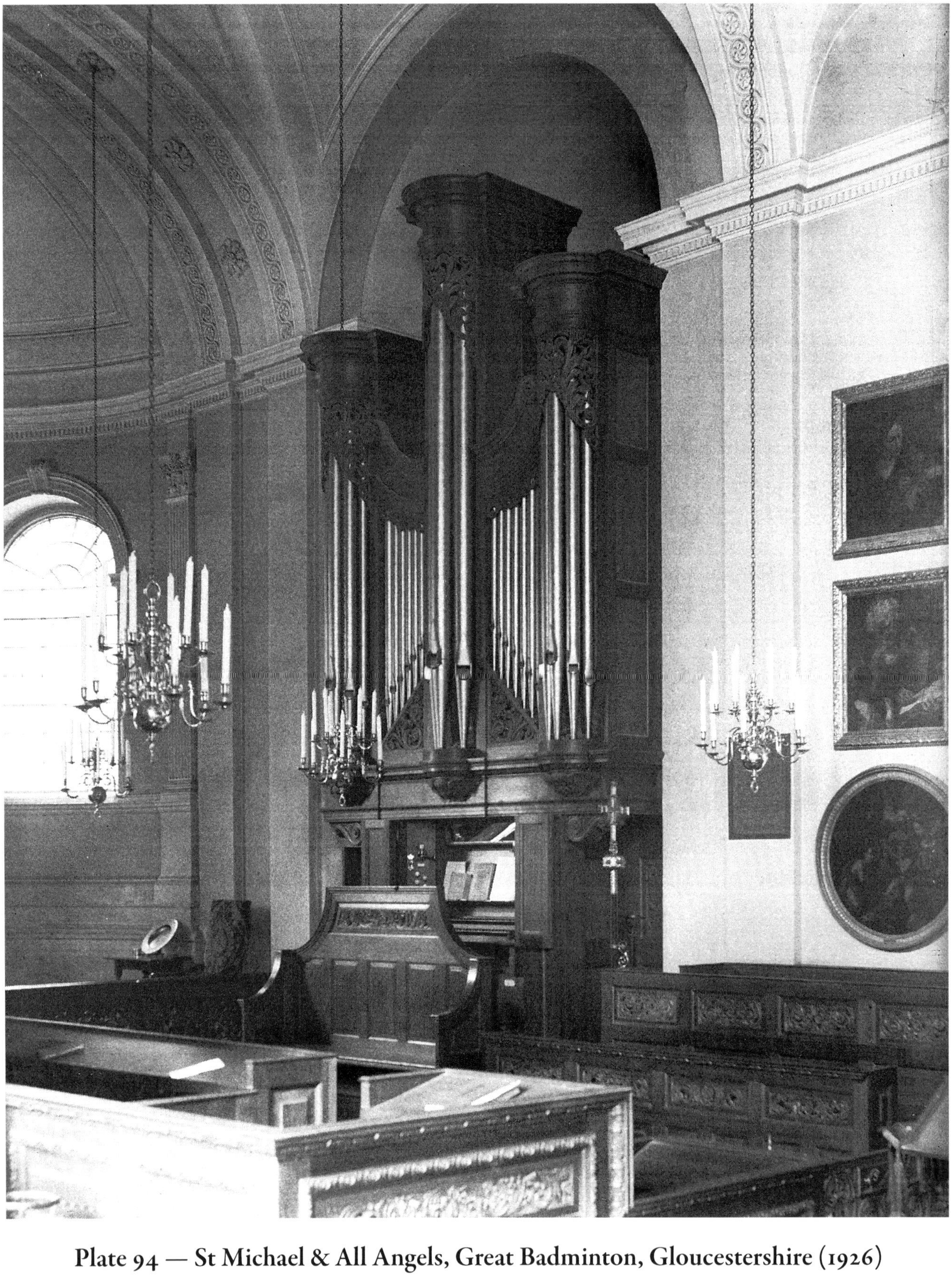

Plate 94 — St Michael & All Angels, Great Badminton, Gloucestershire (1926)

Freeman/651, plate 904

Plate 95 — St Peter's Cathedral, Exeter, Devon, from quire (1926)

Freeman/652, plate 905

'This is one of the finest to be seen in any of our great churches, though how it escaped destruction at the instance of those who, through ignorance or bad taste think that the whole of a cathedral should be seen at a glance from one end of it is somewhat of a miracle. There are many points of interest about it, such as the little turrets high up on the eastern front and the projecting central pipe in the highest tower on the same face. The small circular frames of pipes, quite different on one side from the other, are very happily conceived, while the lower flats in both fronts are stately and graceful, – an effect that is due partly to the shape of the shades (whose engrailed edges should be noticed), and partly to the proportions between the bodies of the pipes and their feet. (The flats of the choir case are similarly treated as regards their shades, but have a different curve at the level of the pipe mouths, affording a pleasing contrast of method.) The effectiveness of their overhanging sides can scarcely be overlooked; but the subtle influence of the pipe mouths, both as regards the curves made by them and the shape of their lips, is a thing that may be felt long before it is noticed. The engrailing of nearly all the pipe shades – that is, cutting them in notches to fit each individual pipe – is rather remarkable; But perhaps the most peculiar and characteristic feature of this case is that it is entirely lacking in figure carving: its ornamentation is composed almost exclusively of flowers and foliage. If there is one defect in this very noble composition it is that the caps of the side towers are somewhat heavy: they would have been more satisfactory if, instead of being completely circular in shape, they had run back into the case in accordance with the more usual custom.'

The Organ 6, no. 22 (Oct. 1926): 110–11

Plate 96 — George St Unitarian Chapel, Exeter, Devon (1926)

Freeman/653, plate 907

[G. P. England organ, c. 1790]. The pipe shades to the towers are rather poor (though I have seen many worse) and the lower part of the case is severely plain, but the design of the central portion is really attractive. The case would have been good even if the upper stories had been omitted (provided the central cap had been dropped to fit on the lower group of pipes). But the designer evidently felt that this was too commonplace an effort, so he exerted himself to achieve something more worthy, and in this he certainly succeeded. It is one of the best small cases of its type and date.'

Musical Opinion 50, no. 594 (Mar. 1927): 600

Plate 97 — St Mary Arches, Exeter, Devon (1926)

Freeman/654, plate 908

'The design is straightforward and the effect pleasing. It may be argued that the carving of the pipe shades lacks delicacy, but they are in admirable keeping with the massive cornices of the upper structure, whilst the lines formed by the pipe mouths – particularly the graceful curves of those in the flats – effectually prevent any feeling of monotony or stiffness which would have been apparent if the feet had been of equal length. It is a pity that the pipe maker is not called upon to cooperate in this way more often.'

Musical Opinion 50, no. 594 (Mar. 1927): 599

Plate 98 — St Nicholas Church, Gloucester, Gloucestershire

Freeman/661, plate 916

'The painted pipes (red, blue, and gold decorations on a grey ground) do not go very well with the casework, which is of mahogany. On the other hand, the painting and gilding of the crown and vases above the towers is quite effective.'

Musical Opinion 56, no. 672 (Sept. 1933), 1043–4

Plate 99 — Christ Church, Chalford, Gloucestershire (1926)

Freeman/665, plate 920

'...a very effective design, marred only by one or two idiosyncracies. Chief of these was the stopping short of the pipes in the side flats some inches below the shades whilst letting those in the central compartment run up behind the carved work. This destroys the unity of the design. A bar of wood across the front of the pipes is also an unnecessary and mistaken feature.'

BOA Freeman collection, box 83, vol. 9: 1, 471-3

Plate 100 — Eton College Provost's Lodge, Eton, Buckinghamshire (1927)

Freeman/667, plate 922

Snetzler organ, c.1760; 'Built for King George III, who gave it to Queen Charlotte, who subsequently gave it to the Princess Amelia as a birthday present. Early in the nineteenth century, it was purchased by the Earl of Egremont, then living at Bromley, Kent, and was subsequently lent to the Church of St Decuman, Watchet, Somerset, where it remained until 1923. In November of that year, its owner, Mr W. Wyndham, presented it to Eton College, where it now stands in the dining room of the Provost's Lodge.'

The Organ 14, no.54, (Oct. 1934): 92

M. R. James was the Provost of Eton College at the time of the acquisition of the Snetzler organ: see Chapter 3, p.23

Plate 101 — St Jacques, Dieppe, France (1927)

Freeman/672, plate 931

'The case [is] beautifully designed and magnificently carved…Attention may be directed to the extreme richness of the body of the case, the overhanging sides, and the trumpeting angels who recline against the larger end towers.'

Musical Opinion 51, no.605 (Feb. 1928): 506–7

Plate 102 — Veules-les-Roses Church, France (1927)

Freeman/678, plate 937

Compare to Lilley's drawing on p.50, and Freeman's drawing in his diary of the trip p.57.

'The moment I caught sight of the organ I realised that here was a rich reward for so small an effort as an eight-mile ride…Here was something of distinction and real beauty. Not large, for the pipes are only of eight feet speaking length; nor yet complex in design, for there are only five compartments of pipes; but finely proportioned and well thought out in all its details, – overhanging sides, tower brackets, scroll work above the flats, and panelling.'

Musical Opinion 51, no. 606 (March 1928): 606

Plate 103 — St Eloi, Rouen (1927)

Freeman/685, plate 944

'The organ case…presents an admirable appearance. The carving on it is good rather than elaborate, most of the labour and skill in this respect having found an outlet in the large figures and other work above the tops of the towers. The most peculiar feature of the design is the treatment of the two brackets under the end towers of the main case: each bracket is composed of something that is probably intended to represent a palm tree standing on the floor of the loft and reaching upward to a height of some ten or twelve feet, the foliage getting larger and thicker near the top. The idea struck me as being original rather than happy.'

Musical Opinion 51, no. 609 (June 1928): 910

Plate 104 — St Vincent, Rouen (1927)

Freeman/688, plate 947

'The organ case is laid out on much the same lines as that at St Eloi (plate 103). But no two renaissance cases could be much farther apart in spirit. For whereas the older case [St Eloi] gives one the impression of a noble and dignified reserve, the Saint-Vincent front, though quite a "fine" one in its way, is a little lacking in restraint. No one with an eye for organ cases can look on this one without being struck with its brilliance, and a moment's reflection serves to show that this is not so much due to the gilding of certain parts of the carving as it is to the entire absence of uprights between the various compartments. Too large a mass of metal pipes, as here, is always a mistake: it would be much better if broken up by framing of some kind.'

Musical Opinion 51, no. 609 (June 1928): 910

Plate 105 — Notre Dame, Le Grand Andely (1927)

Freeman/695; plate 954

'In the west end, in an elaborately carved organ loft, stands one of the oldest and grandest of French organ cases. In spite of its great age – it was made in 1573—the pipework is in an excellent state, and the case almost if not quite intact. Each [of the four towers] is surmounted by a campanile of a light and pleasing design, to which the more heavily carved pipe shades act as an excellent foil. The body of the case below the impost is divided into five compartments, corresponding exactly in width with the five inner compartments of pipes in the upper part. Each of these panels contains a three-quarter length figure. Only three of these are named – Daniel on the extreme left, David in the centre, and Solomon on the extreme right. Along the gallery front is a range of full-length allegorical figures, all of whom are provided with musical instruments, even Geometry being represented *playing a triangle!*'

Musical Opinion 52, no. 621 (June 1929): 541

Plate 106 — Ecouis Church, France (1927)

Freeman/698; plate 957

'A fine organ case (1622–7). The bright light from the great west window did not help my photograph...Characteristic features of the case [are] three campaniles above the large towers, [and] three pendants beneath the small ones. The tin pipes stand up well against the dark-coloured wood in which they are framed...'

Musical Opinion 52, no. 624 (Sept. 1929): 1114

Plate 107 — St Patrick's, Soho Square, London (1928)

Freeman/707; plate 966

Plate 108 — St Saviour Cathedral, Southwark, London, figures from Jordan organ (1928)

Freeman/711; plate 970

'[The old Jordan organ] stood in a gallery that divided the nave into two parts...The oak case was extremely lofty, for it had a 16ft. front of gilded pipes. Above the central tower was a figure of King David with his harp; and above the side towers were large angels (or "fames," as they were called) holding trumpets. These three figures are now all that remain of the magnificent case.'

The Organ 7, no. 28 (*April 1928*): 196

Plate 109 — St Mary le Savoy, Marylebone, London (1928)

Freeman/714; plate 973

Plate 110 — St Mary's Parish Church, Cheshunt, Hertfordshire, barrel organ (1928)

Freeman/725; plate 985

A.F. on barrel organs:
'There was a church near Tenbury where the barrel organ ground out the correct number of verses while the people *said* the hymns silently to themselves! There is a moral to be drawn from this, but wild horses will not make me draw it.'

Musical Opinion 49, no. 581 (Feb 1926): 503

Plate 111 — St Swithun, Worcester, Worcestershire (1928)

Freeman/734; plate 995

Plate 112 — St Mary Magdalene, Rodborough, Gloucestershire (1928)

Freeman/735; plate 996

Plate 113 — St Mary's Parish Church, Newent, Gloucestershire (1928)

Freeman/739; plate 1000

'A case of some distinction, pleasing and well made.'

Musical Opinion 52, no. 622 (July 1929): 932

Plate 114 — George Street Chapel, Plymouth, Devon (1929)

Freeman/746; plate 1012

Destroyed during the bombing of Plymouth in 1941.

Plate 115 — Notre Dame, Bruges (1929)

Freeman/754; plate 1019

'As can be seen in the photograph, the case consists of five towers and four connecting incurving curtains, so set that only the large central tower faces directly west, the remaining compartments being bent back till the end towers stand almost at right angles with the one in the middle. This device enables a large number of pipes (fifty-three) to be effectively displayed in a relatively small case; it also gives the design an attractive individuality and an excellent appearance from every angle of view.'

The Organ 9, no. 34 (Oct 1929): 82

Plate 116 — St Jacques, Bruges (1929)

Freeman/761, plate 1025

The case 'bears a strong formal likeness to the west front of the organ at St Sauveur, though in detail, and indeed in character, the difference between the two is very marked....There can be little doubt that one of the two served as a model for the other...The cathedral (St Sauveur) undoubtedly possesses the richer and more striking case, but the parochial church has one that is extremely fine in every respect, a case of quality and dignified restraint.'

The Organ 9, no. 36 (April 1930): 227

Plate 117 — St Sauveur, Bruges (1929)

Freeman/763, plate 1027

'...excellently proportioned and sumptuously carved.'

The Organ 9, no. 34 (Oct 1929): 80

Plate 118 — Damme Church (near Bruges)(1929)

Freeman/768, plate 1032

'one of the most delightful organ cases imaginable, and quite three centuries old...The whole of the front, from the top of the music desk upwards, is a mass of carving in which figures of angels, cherubic heads, fruit, and conventional foliage, are riotously but charmingly mixed.'

The Organ 12, no. 47 (Jan. 1933), 162–3

Plate 119 — St Jacques, Antwerp (1929)

Freeman/795, plate 1058

'...the east front is made continuous by means of a full-sized positif with four towers and four flats. The positif is placed at a lower level than the rest of this front, so that the complete cornice line of this front makes a series of sweeps downwards from the lofty end towers at either end to the medallion carving of Saint Cecilia in its centre.'

The Organ 11, no.44 (April 1932), 202

Plate 120 — St Germain, Tirlemont, Belgium (1929)

Freeman/801, plate 1063

'The organ stands in a loft high up at the west end of the church. The case dates from the early years of the sixteenth century – say, circa 1520. This was a period when, as the late Dr Hill remarked in his short description of this case in the second volume of his great work on organ cases,[1] the Gothic style "had well nigh given place to Renaissance forms. Though no details other than the Gothic are here manifest, yet evidence of the coming change is seen in the circular plan of the choir organ, and in the somewhat peculiar treatment of the mouldings. The pipe shades appear to have been replaced by others of a debased kind, designed in feeble imitation of the originals. There are considerable traces of gilding and colouring, and the whole case was, no doubt, at one time decorated in this manner, though at present the prevailing tone is a yellow brown." Although the design of the case as a whole is by no means perfect, it has many admirable points of extreme interest. Taking the main case first it will be noticed that the tall central tower is supported on either side by two double-tiered flats, and that all the pipes that stand along the impost have been so arranged that they diminish in length and diameter from the largest pipe in the middle to the smallest at the sides. But whereas the under edges of the pipe shades of the two (lower) flats sweep downwards and outwards in an almost continuous curve, the pipe mouths have been so contrived that they form *two* opposing upspringing curves instead of one. That this is not a mere whim of the designer can be easily discerned by noticing how he has deliberately broken the horizontal line that separates the two lower flats from the two upper ones. A few seconds study will serve to show that he has by these means secured a unity of purpose in each pair of flats without sacrificing their rightful individuality. The means are a simple and as successful as the touch is certain and masterly. The unity of the whole composition is effected by the elaborate, bracket-shaped gable whose sides are supported by uprights of archaic design, though of somewhat slender proportions for so mighty a burden. Beneath this cornice are the four upper flats. Taken by themselves these are very undistinguished members of the body corporate, and it almost looks as if the designer's skill failed him when he came to deal with them. But his right instinct came to the rescue: by filling in the gaps with small pipes he made these upper flats unobtrusive and subservient to the rest of the scheme.'

Musical Opinion 56, no. 664 (Jan. 1933): 335–6

1 Hill, Arthur George, *The Organ-Cases and Organs of the Middle Ages and Renaissance: a Comprehensive Essay on the Art Archæology of the Organ...* Second series (London: Printed for the author by Charles Whittingham, 1891).

Plate 121 — St Jacques, Liège (1929)

Freeman/803; plate 1064

'The organ occupies a sumptuously carved western gallery, where it presents a superb appearance. The case bears two dates, – 1600, the year of its erection, and 1669, the year when the instrument it held was reconstructed...A French traveller, Philippe de Hurges, who wrote about the close of the seventeenth century, speaks of this case as one of the most beautiful imaginable, so richly was the woodwork gilded and coloured. Some of this decoration yet remains; but the large doors, adorned with pictures attributed to Lambert Lombard (1505–56) were unfortunately taken away in 1854, when the organ was undergoing repairs. The case must have looked much finer when these were attached to its sides. Their absence accentuates a certain squareness about the upper half of the main case that would not have been noticed when they were in position. I think, too, that the central tower contains larger pipes than it would have had if the designer had not counted upon them to stand up against its large wings. Thus the removal of the wings, besides being an act of gross vandalism, was also an artistic blunder, quite altering the balance of the composition and doing an injustice to the genius of its architect.'

The Organ 11, no. 42 (Oct. 1931): 106

Plate 122 — St-Denys, Liège (1929)

Freeman/806; plate 1067

'The organ, sumptuously encased, stands in the west gallery...I do not think the word *sumptuous* is a bit too strong. Almost every part of the framework is carved, some more, and some less elaborately, but all alike with skill and an unerring instinct for the right thing. Some would doubtless have the three turrets removed from above the towers, but I find them pleasing. They give height to the case, and they give a distinctive character to it which I should be sorry to see taken away.'

The Organ 11, no. 42 (Oct. 1931): 108–9

Freeman's sketch of this organ is on p.59.

Plate 123 — Quenast Church (Console and Detail of Case) (1929)

Freeman/816; plate 1076

'It is the richness and character of the carvings that give this case its distinctiveness, and especially the remarkable series of heads in high relief.'

The Organ 12, no.46 (Oct. 1932): 106

Plate 124 — Wickwar Church, Gloucestershire (1929)

Freeman/821, plate 1081

Freeman was involved in the design of this case. He wrote that it was designed 'on lines suggested by A.F. & H. T. Lilley, and made by Wake & Dean of Yatton. Cost £200. Light oak, well carved: zinc pipes in front, with bright tin lips, rounded.'

BOA Freeman collection, box 83, volume 9: 1,613–17, entry number 1,312. See Chapter III, p.34–5

Plate 125 — St Eustace, Tavistock, Devon (1930)

Freeman/829; plate 1089

'What shall we say of this curious contraption at Tavistock? It would be quite easy to call it opprobrious names; but ...I think it would be quite mistaken. For though the idea is all wrong, it has been carried out with great care and skill. It dates, of course, from the time when architects tried their best to make organs look like anything else on earth except organs. If we say that this one at Tavistock looks like nothing on earth, I for one would add that its originality and its uniqueness together give it the right to be considered a success. It is probably the best of its kind: up to a point it may be admired: but it must be taken as a warning, and not as an example to be copied.'

Musical Opinion 58, no. 693 (June 1935): 786

Plate 126 — St Saviour, Townstal, Dartmouth, Devon (1930)

Freeman/834; plate 1095

'[The organ] is worthy of a better position. Stuffed, as it is, into a chamber on the north side of the chancel, less than half of the front can be viewed, even from the top of the screen, where the photograph was taken. The design is well thought out and the composition nicely balanced. The only thing to which exception might be taken is the little oval frame of pipes above the middle tower...I should not be surprised to learn that the case had been designed (and perhaps made) by the younger Chippendale, for it is clearly a clever cabinet-maker's idea of an organ case, and not an organ builder's.'

Musical Opinion 58, no. 693 (June 1935): 785

Plate 127 — St Paul, Parkend, Gloucestershire (1930)

Freeman/838; plate 1099

'I had heard that there was an old organ here..., but was quite unprepared for the discovery of a genuine Harris organ of the earliest period... Both case and front pipes suggest this as their origin. The case is unmistakeably of the old English type: that is, it show no trace of either Dutch or French influences which made themselves felt when Smith and Renatus Harris had been established long enough to impress their own preferences upon their clients...The case has been much restored, Evidently the carving had suffered during its long life of some two and a half centuries. Unfortunately all the replaced work was executed in a style utterly alien to the original...This new Gothic detail is very well done, but it has none of the charm of such fragments of the original Renaissance work as have been preserved.'

Musical Opinion 56, no. 672 (Sept. 1933): 1044

Freeman's sketch of this organ is on p. viii.

Plate 128 — St John the Baptist, Paignton, Devon (c.1930)

Freeman/842, plate 1103

Plate 129 — St Mary the Virgin, Ottery St Mary, Devon (1930)

Freeman/843, plate 1104

Plate 130 — St Andrew, Chippenham, Wiltshire (1930)

Freeman/846, plate 1107

Plate 131 — St Peter's College, Radley, Berkshire (1931)

Freeman/849, plate 1110

Plate 132 — St Paul's Cathedral, North Case (1931)

Freeman/865; plate 1126

'There can hardly be two opinions as to the merits of this magnificent composition: designed by Wren, made by Hopson, carved by Gibbons, and re-arranged by Penrose, it is one of the most perfect Renaissance organ fronts in the world. Its proportions are admirable, while its wealth of carving is a delight to the eye, affording a happy instance of what can be achieved in this direction when a master-hand works in conjunction with a master-mind. The organ cases are certainly amongst the greatest treasures of St Paul's; and what is more, they are perfectly adapted to their purpose and their situation.'

The Organ 2, no. 5 (July 1922): 15

Plate 133 — Franziskaner-Kirche, Vienna (Chapel) (1932)

Freeman/869; plate 1130

'...we repaired to the church, where, after some palaver ...we were admitted into the chapel behind the altar. And there, to my great delight, under a lofty arch at the east end, stood, [an organ] in all its haunting loveliness. I found that the wood was dark oak with no gilding on it, and that its plain metal pipes were rather dull. The carving is both profuse and highly skilful, every bit of it perfectly adapted for its place and function. A figure of David stands atop the large central tower, and a trumpeting angel above each of the side towers....I started a photograph of the case, but a heavy thunderstorm came on and made the thing impossible. It was the only real failure amongst the eighty-two plates exposed on this holiday, – all organs!'

The Organ 13, no.50 (Oct. 1933): 92–3

Plate 134 — Mondsee, Stiftskirche, Salzkammergut, Austria (1932)

Freeman/871; plate 1132

'There are, in truth, three distinct and easily recognisable organ cases [within the larger case]... and yet they form a single and harmonious whole. One would like to know the name of the artist who designed such a masterpiece.'

The Organ 17, no. 66 (Oct. 1937): 67

Plate 135 — Finnish Chapel, Hannah Street, Cardiff (1931)

Freeman/872; plate 1133

'Although the organ bears the nameplate of George Parsons [fl. c.1810–30], it has no date on it, and I confess I am puzzled about the case. George may have made it, but I think it more likely that he used up one that had come into his possession in the course of business. It looks more like 1780 than (say) 1825, but I would not like to rob its maker of the credit due to him for so pleasing a piece of work.'

The Organ 24, no. 96 (April 1945): 158

Plate 136 — St Michel, Louvain, Belgium (1932)

Freeman/879; plate 1140

'St Michel's was in festive array for the Feast of Corpus Christi. Huge drapes of blue and white hung down from the ceiling close to the west end, making it impossible to take a complete view of the case without tipping the camera more than could be counteracted by the rising front...The case, one of the finest in Belgium, is dark brown in colour. There is no gilt on it except for the trumpet held by the angel on the extreme left-hand tower, and the flute in the hands of the small angel on the small tower to the left of the centre. The other small angel holds a lute, but the large one on the extreme right has lost his instrument.'

Musical Opinion 56, no. 662 (Nov. 1932): 146–7

Plate 137 — St Agatha, Aschaffenburg, Germany (1932)

Freeman/890; plate 1151

'...a very charming case, excellently placed in the west gallery and simply begging to be photographed.'

Musical Opinion 57, no. 682 (July 1934): 889–90

The church was destroyed in World War II.

Plate 138 — Spitalkirche (also known as Heiliggeistkirche), Nürnberg, Germany (1932)

Freeman/891; plate 1152

'[The organ] is quite modern, of a somewhat mixed style but quite effective. The groupings of pipes is pleasing, and the use of colours for the case and gold for the pipe-shades gives good effect.'

Musical Opinion 59 (Oct. 1935): 53

Freeman's sketch of this organ is on p.61.
The church was destroyed in World War II.

Plate 139 — St Sebald, Nürnberg, Germany (1932)

Freeman/892; plate 1153

'The organ stands above the entrance to the south aisle of the nave. Its case puzzles me. I feel that it cannot be older than 1870, but I was distinctly told that it was quite ancient. I should have said that it was the work of a modern architect who had studied the best old examples and nearly caught the ancient spirit. In spite of excellent features, it is not quite up to the standard of the best of Bodley's work, which it somewhat resembles. I feel sure it has suffered a certain amount of "corrective" restoration at the hands of a nineteenth century purist.'

Musical Opinion 59 (Oct. 1935): 52

The organ was destroyed in World War II.

Plate 140 — Stiftskirche (Abbey Church), Melk, Austria (1932_

Freeman/901; plate 1162

'[Its organ is] one of the loveliest imaginable.'

The Organ 13, no. 49(July 1933): 7

Plate 141 — Stephansdom (St Stephan) (1932)

Freeman/906; plate 1167

'As there are no clerestory windows to the nave, it is always twilight within, even when the sun is shining at its brightest – very impressive, but not conducive to photography. For this reason I made no attempt to photograph the fine case at the west end, but rested content with the smaller instrument in the quire. And even that had an exposure of a full hour on a sunny day. The instrument was made by Messrs. Rieger Bros., apparently a few years before the war. But the old case, dating I should say ca. 1709, was utilised. This...is a pleasing and original composition of five towers, two of them placed angle-wise. It is the treatment of the four rounded towers that gives it its distinctive character. These are separated from the double-storied tiers by double pilasters, which are carried up to widely spreading cornices that had been extended for the purpose...The carving is lavish and for the most part gilt, so the effect is very fine.'

The Organ 15, no.57 (July 1935): 41

Plate 142 — St Martin, Klosterneuburg, Austria (1932)

Freeman/917; plate 1179

'The word "gorgeous" would not be out of place in estimating [the organ's] effect, both at first sight and upon reflection.'

The Organ 15, no. 58 (Oct. 1935): 72

Plate 143 — Stiftskirche, Klosterneuburg (1932)

Freeman/918, plate 1180

'Surely no one can look critically at the composition and fail to be impressed by its beauty, but attention may be drawn to a few points. In the first place, the main case has no projecting towers: all its pipes stand in the same vertical plane. Then all its front pipes, seemingly without exception, are of natural speaking length, whilst the carving has been designed to display their natural inequalities of length, not to hide them. The engrailing of the pipe shapes is worth studying, since, with the exception of that in the large middle tower, the "edging" of the outer half of the shade of each compartment is more squarely cut than the inner. I think this is very unusual. The shade of the middle tower differs from all the rest in design: it may have led the architect to the decision that his new shades should harmonize with it without too strict a conformity. Certainly the newer ones suggest that their creator looked forward to greater freedom as well as backward to a tradition of respectable antiquity. The three broken pediments above the towers, one curved and two triangular, as well as the five pear-shaped ornaments that stand above the cornice, and the elaborate brackets (terminating in cherubs with widespread wings), are worthy of attention.'

The Organ 15, no. 58 (Oct. 1935): 76

Plate 144 — St Cajetan, Salzburg (1932)

Freeman/937, plate 1200

'The organ stands along the whole front of the west gallery: indeed, its case forms the front of the gallery, though I fancy that the two flats on either side contain only dummy pipes. It should be noticed that the pipes in the three projecting divisions are not symmetrically trimmed, but are left their natural length. The tone is quite delightful. There is nothing shrill about it: rather is there a fullness and a sparkle that all the all-8ft-and-4ft. organs entirely lack.'

The Organ 16, no. 63, (Jan. 1937): 130

Plate 145 — Annenkirche, Augsburg, Germany (1932)

Freeman/944; plate 1208

'The organ case is said to date from 1512. This case is a unique and noble piece of work, and one that can hold its own with any of the resplendent Baroque cases I came across in Austria...Nearly all its pipes stand clear under the case,...and that both great case and positiv have painted shutters. The overhanging of the sides is very marked: they are supported by elaborately carved brackets. The intricate carving of the pipe shades and impost is masterly alike in design and execution.'

Musical Opinion 58, no.688 (Jan. 1935), 340–1

Plate 146 — St Columba, Cologne, Germany (c.1932)

Freeman/949, plate 1213

The church was destroyed in World War II.

Plate 147 — St George, Littleport, Cambridgeshire (1933)

Freeman/970, plate 1235

[The case] is a fine bit of work, and certainly closely modelled on [Great St Mary's (Cambridge)], but its carving is not comparable with that of Father Smith's craftsmen, neither is its joinery. That is especially noticeable in the moulding of the tower caps, which are also less lofty at Littleport...'

Musical Opinion 59, no. 707 (Aug. 1936): 948

Plate 148 — St John the Baptist, Epping, Essex (1933)

Freeman/972, plate 1237

Plate 149 — All Saints, Santon, Norfolk (1930)

Freeman/974, plate 1239

'On the south side of the chancel stands a little organ with black keys and a painted case, which has a lattice work front of the type favoured by advocates of total enclosure. I cannot bring myself to believe that this lattice work is an original feature. It was probably put in by a Gothic revivalist, who was offended by a disposition of pipes and carving of a Renaissance character. Or, possibly, the original front had been badly damaged, and the criss-cross idea seemed the most economical way of getting out of a difficulty.'

The Organ 19, no. 74 (Oct. 1939): 108

Plate 150 — Mold Parish Church, Flintshire, chancel (1934)

Freeman/982, plate 1247

Plate 151 — St Mary B V, Ecclestone, Cheshire (1934)

Freeman/983, plate 1248

Plate 152 — St Michael, Winforton on Wye, Herefordshire (1934)

Freeman/991, plate 1256

Plate 153 — St Lawrence, Evesham, Worcestershire (1934)

Freeman/993, plate 1258

Plate 154 — St Peter & St Paul, Shepton Mallett, Somerset (1934)

Freeman/994, plate 1259

Plate 157 — St Margaret, Barking, Essex (c.1934)

Freeman/1009, plate 1274

The case is by Green/Byfield. 'The case, which dates from 1770, is a good one of its period. There is not a great amount of carving on it, but what there is of it is quite good, and it is effectively distributed. The most noticeable thing about the design is the flatness of the side towers. In these the pipes stand almost in a line, and only a very little in advance of those in the flats. Actually the roundness is observable only in the caps and in the little platforms on which the pipes stand. The absence of a similar platform from the centre tower makes one wonder whether the case was not made in the first place with flat towers, which the authorities did not approve, and whether the slightly rounded caps were not in the nature of a compromise, and the least expensive way of rectifying a mistake....They are certainly a curious feature.'

Musical Opinion 61, no. 721 (Oct. 1937): 57

Plate 158 — St Mary's Church, Haverfordwest, Pembrokeshire (c.1934)

Freeman/1012; plate 1281

Plate 159 — St James', Kinnersley, Herefordshire (c.1934)

Freeman/1014; plate 1285

This case was designed by Bodley. Freeman's sketch can be seen on p.21.

Plate 160 — Harlton Church, Cambridgeshire (1935)

Freeman/1015; plate 1286

'I am quite certain that the architect, whoever he was, took the case at St Germain's, Tirlemont, which is the oldest case in Belgium as his model. It has a character of its own, and a pleasing one at that.'

The Organ 18, no. 71 (Jan. 1939): 145

Plate 161 — Protestant Basilica, Trier (Germany) (1935)

Freeman/1021; plate 1293

The basilica was destroyed during an air raid in 1944.

Plate 162 — St Emmeran, Mainz (1935)

Freeman/1023; plate 1295

This church, along with its organ, was destroyed in an air raid in 1945.

Plate 163 — St Wolfgang Church, Salzkammergut, Austria (1935)

Freeman/1046; plate 1318

'What a delightful case it is! ...The main case was made in 1629, – that date is inscribed on the caps of the two end towers – and a very fine case it is. The elaborate brackets supporting the overhanging sides are a fine feature of the design. ...The Positiv –possibly older, possibly a little later – -would look much better if it were placed in front of the gallery instead of being perched on top of the middle tower of the Hauptwerk, where it spoils the balance of the design. This is a pity, for in itself it is a case of singular charm.'

The Organ 17, no. 67 (Jan 1938): 166

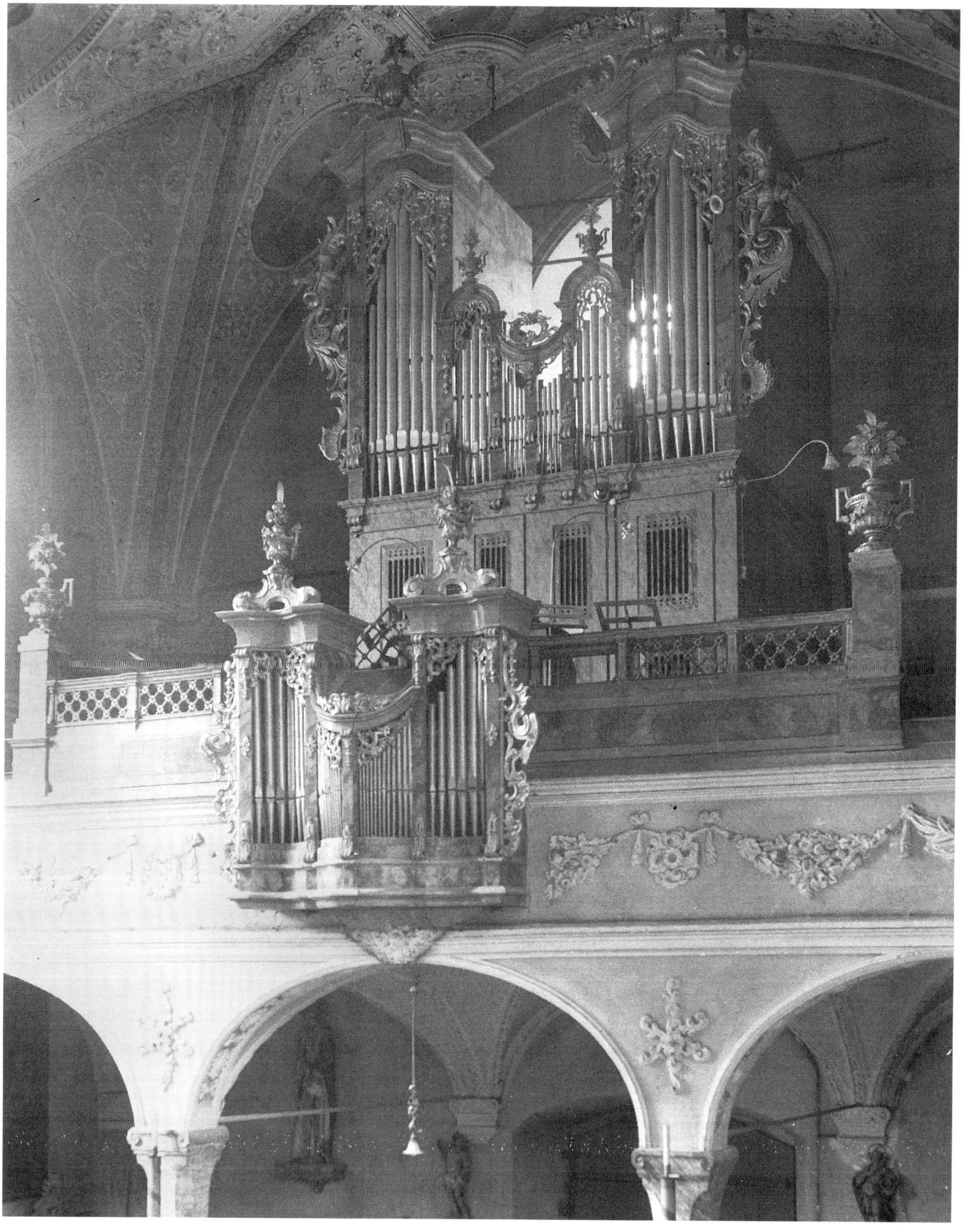

Plate 164 — Pfarrkirche, Jenbach (Tirol), Austria (1935)

Freeman/1050, plate 1322

'...delightful organ case. The appearance of this organ is extremely good, but it is a pity that the window behind it had not been screened. It gives no light to the church...but it shines through the pipes in a most annoying fashion.'

The Organ 18, 72 (April 1939): 231

Plate 165 — St Jakob, Stadtpfarrkirche, Innsbruck, Austria (1935)

Freeman/1056, plate 1329

'The organ was built by Kaspar Humpel, of Meran, in 1725. The splendid case was probably designed by Andrea del Pozzo, the architect responsible for the church. It stands in the west gallery, where it presents a very fine appearance in perfect accord with its surroundings. The pipes of its central compartment are cunningly arranged, so that they seem to be recessed, whereas they are all in the same vertical plane as the large ones in the towers on either hand. This feature is characteristic of other parts of the church; the altar piece, for instance, consists of a series of arches in perspective intended to give the effect of distance, and a feeling of loftiness is obtained by painting a cupola on the ceiling. These things should be seen before being miscalled shams. They appeal to something deeper down than do the disgruntled remarks of self-styled purists...A brilliant sun shining through the window behind the organ augured ill for the photograph I had taken on Saturday afternoon, so I returned on Monday morning to make another exposure under more favourable conditions. When I had set my camera in position and begun the exposure, I found to my horror that a congregation had silently assembled, and that a Mass was already in progress. I went hot and cold all over, but as the camera was well on one side of the chancel and no one seemed disturbed, I decided that it was better to let the camera continue its silent work than to dismantle it, for to do this would certainly have caused some slight commotion.'

The Organ 26, no. 101 (July 1846): 5

Note the ghostly congregation.

Plate 166 — Pfarrkirche, Bregenz, Austria (1935)

Freeman/1069; plate 1342

Joseph Gabler organ, c.1750. 'It is worth spending a few moments on noticing the skill with which the designer of the case has surmounted a real difficulty forced on him by the position chosen for the organ. With the upper gallery so close to the roof, many architects might have produced a case that looked cramped, besides having the demerits of bottling up the tone of the instrument. Not so did this man. By a careful choice of five well-proportioned towers, so arranged that the strong line made by their own cornices fell in graceful loops from the tallest at the sides to quite a small one in the centre, he almost makes one feel that he had been set no problem at all. Like Mozart, he could "dance in chains." But he also wanted to fly, and this he did by poising a light frame of pipes over the middle of the case so that there is rise in it as well as fall, and also a satisfying centre. The charming Positiv case seems to grow out of the lower gallery...This case at Bregenz is both beautiful and a masterpiece.'

The Organ 26, no. 103 (Jan. 1947): 127

Plate 167 — St Lawrence, Bishopstone, Herefordshire (c.1935)

Freeman/1078; plate 1351

Plate 168 — St Bartholomew, Holmer, Herefordshire (1935)

Freeman/1079; plate 1352

'Organ by Bevington: originally built for Carbery Evans, Esq., of Hatley Park, Gamlingay, Beds. It then had 2 manuals and was blown by a "Hot air engine". Date 1883. Removed to Olton Hall (Mr G. E. Wright) when it was "altered" by Halmshaw. This was in 1899. In 1912 the Choir organ was added by Hill. This, presumably, was when Mr. Wright removed it to Puddleton Court, Herefs. In 1934 Mr. Wright presented it to Holmer Church, when it was set up in a lift at the west end. The case is very good indeed, though obviously designed for a music room in a private house. It is of light oak with gilding on it. The front pipes are of type metal [*sic*], with leaf lips, lightly decorated. Broken curved pediment over central portion (3 flats), with cherub between 2 halves of cornice and a carytide [*sic*] at either end...The whole case, except for the pediment, stands under a horizontal cornice – same height, but bent in plan.'

From Freeman's hand-written notes in the British Organ Archive: Box 083, 'Notebooks (organ visited)', vol. 12: 2, 128–30

Plate 169 — All Saints, Cottenham, Cambridgeshire (1935)

Freeman/1080; plate 1353

Plate 170 — Franziskaner Hofkirche, Innsbruck, Austria (c. 1935)

Freeman/1085; plate 1358

'Probably very few amongst the innumerable visitors to the Franziskaner Hofkirche, or Franciscan Court Church, at Innsbruck, have eyes for anything except the world-famous cenotaph to the Emperor Maximilian and its remarkable surroundings. Yet the church contains one of the loveliest and most perfect organ cases in the whole world...[It has a] calm yet intricate beauty...Both cases have shutters that are painted within and without... There is a lavish amount of fine carving, – below as well as above the various groups of pipes, in between the towers of the larger case as well as above their cornices, and also under the impost. The brackets that support the overhanging sides should not be passed over, nor should the simple but elegant little loft, which makes with the two cases so perfect a whole. The man who designed this case knew his business and loved his task – of that there can be no possible doubt – while the men who made it must have shared to the full its creator's delight...'

Organ 8, no. 32 (April 1929): 225

Plate 171 — St Andrew, Ombersley, Worcestershire (1935)

Freeman/1088; plate 1361

'My theme at this moment is...to say a good word for some [cases] that cannot be called beautiful, yet are not without merit, or even a certain air of distinction and fitness. These all belong to the class dubbed (rather unfairly as well as uncritically) "Churchwarden Gothic"...[This case] is admirably in keeping with its surroundings, and is certainly far superior to the ungainly gallery front. Six pipes are framed in six attenuated windows. It has a fidgety effect, but it was done, and that's an end of it. The middle compartment is not at all original in conception, but it looks exactly right here.'

The Organ 18, no. 69 (July 1938): 41

Plate 172 — Nettlecombe Court, Somerset (1936)

Freeman/1097; plate 1370

Plate 173 — St Mary's Parish Church, Dunsford, Devon (1936)

Freeman/1107; plate 1380

'… a west gallery organ that looks extremely well.'

The Organ 18, no. 69 (July 1938): 42

Plate 174 — Beaminster Congregational schoolroom, Dorset (c. 1936)

Freeman/1111; plate 1384

Plate 175 — St Mary's Church, Brent Pelham, Hertfordshire (c.1936)

Freeman/1128; plate 1401

'...an unassuming case that could easily be made most attractive.... By raising the pipes in the flats somewhat, the designer of this front secured two compartments of smaller pipes which act as a foil to the larger ones in the towers. It is a pity that all the front pipes are dummies, for their proportions are about right and an octave-and-a-half of speaking pipes could have stood in their places without any undue lengthening of their bodies. But the voracious stomach of "general swell" claimed every available pipe, and it was either dummies to the front or nothing...I think this front could be improved by putting a shield of some kind (wood, preferably, though canvas would do) behind the tracery in order that the tops of the pipes might be hidden. Nothing is more exasperating than the sight of odd bits of pipes showing between the openings in tracery that is obviously not fulfilling its proper function. The carving would be gilded with advantage, and the background coloured. Gilding would also improve the rather heavy battlemented cresting at the top; while plain gilding for the pipes and a bold colour scheme would make this case one of considerable charm.

The Organ 18, no 70 (Oct. 1938): 91

Plate 176 — All Saints Church, Horseheath, Cambridgeshire (1936)

Freeman/1129; plate 1402

'Notwithstanding a certain coarseness in its detail, there is an air of distinction about the case that can hardly be overlooked.'

The Organ 18, no. 70 (Oct. 1938): 91

Plate 177 — Christ Church, Coleford, Gloucestershire (1936)

Freeman/1131; plate 1404

Plate 178 — St James, Cowley, Oxford, Oxfordshire (1936)

Freeman/1132; plate 1405

'One feels that the architect called upon the builder to supply a number of pipes of equal length (mostly dummies) to fill in the openings, whereas his proper course was to take speaking pipes offered by the builder, not unduly lengthened, and to make his framework accordingly.'

The Organ 18, no. 69 (July 1938): 42

Plate 179 — St Mary's Church, Whaddon, Buckinghamshire (1936)

Freeman/1139; plate 1412

Plate 180 — St James Church, Great Packington, Warwickshire (1936)

Freeman/1144; plate 1417

'The case is cast in a severe mould…[It] is well-proportioned, but its chief characteristic is its air of restraint and dignity.'

Musical Opinion 60, no. 710 (Nov. 1936): 149

Plate 181 — St Margaret's Crick, Northamptonshire (1936)

Freeman/1145; plate 1418

Plate 182 — St Mary the Virgin, Welford, Northamptonshire (1936)

Freeman/1147; plate 1420

Plate 183 — St Mary & St Michael, Great Malvern, Worcestershire (1936)

Freeman/1149; plate 1422

Plate 184 — St Peter's, Bromyard, Herefordshire (c. 1936)

Freeman/1151; plate 1424

'Its appearance is quite satisfactory. The projecting towers may be passed as satisfactory: they would have looked rather better with traceried shades, provided that these had been shaped to come down lower over the shorter pipes than over the tall middle one.'

The Organ 18, No. 70 (Oct. 1938): 92

Plate 185 — St Mary's, Bampton Proper, Oxfordshire (c. 1936)

Freeman/1153; plate 1426

Gray & Davison organ (1870) in an older case. 'This case would appear to be somewhat earlier than that at Ombersley [Plate 171, p. 241]: it is coarser in its detail, and one has to admit the ogee gable together with its suspended cuspings, is clumsy in execution as well as in design. Yet it came as a feast for weary eyes that had found nothing but "ugly pipe-stalks, mere concatenations of zinc chimney-cans" (fn.: Somers Clarke's expressive epithet in Micklethwaite's *Modern Parish Churches*, 1874) in the churches of a dozen neighbouring villages, and its gilt pipes had a friendly look.'

The Organ 18, no. 69 (July 1938): 42

Plate 186 — St Lawrence Parish Church, Towcester, Northamptonshire (1936)

Freeman/1157; plate 1430

'The style of the case is totally unlike the work of any of our native craftsmen with which I am acquainted, though I should not be greatly surprised to learn that it had been designed by one of the Adam brothers, or (perhaps less likely) by one of the Chippendales. A glance at the photograph should show that its creator was strongly influenced by French architecture of the eighteenth century. So much so, indeed, that I cannot help wondering if it were not actually designed and made in France.'

Musical Opinion 60, no. 717 (June 1937): 818

Plate 187 — All Saints, High Street, Oxford, Oxfordshire (1936)

Freeman/1160; plate 1433

Plate 188 — St Denys Parish Church, Warminster, Wiltshire (1937)

Freeman/1184; plate 1457

'...one of [organbuilder George Pike] England's best examples... It has an air of distinction that marked the very best furniture of the period, and it would not be surprising to discover that it was designed by some quite noted person in the furniture world.'

The Organ 21, no. 82 (Oct. 1941): 44

Plate 189 — Micheldever Primitive Methodist, Hampshire (1937)

Freeman/1193; plate 1466

Plate 190 — St Michael & All Angels, Colehill, Dorset (1937)

Freeman/1194; plate 1467

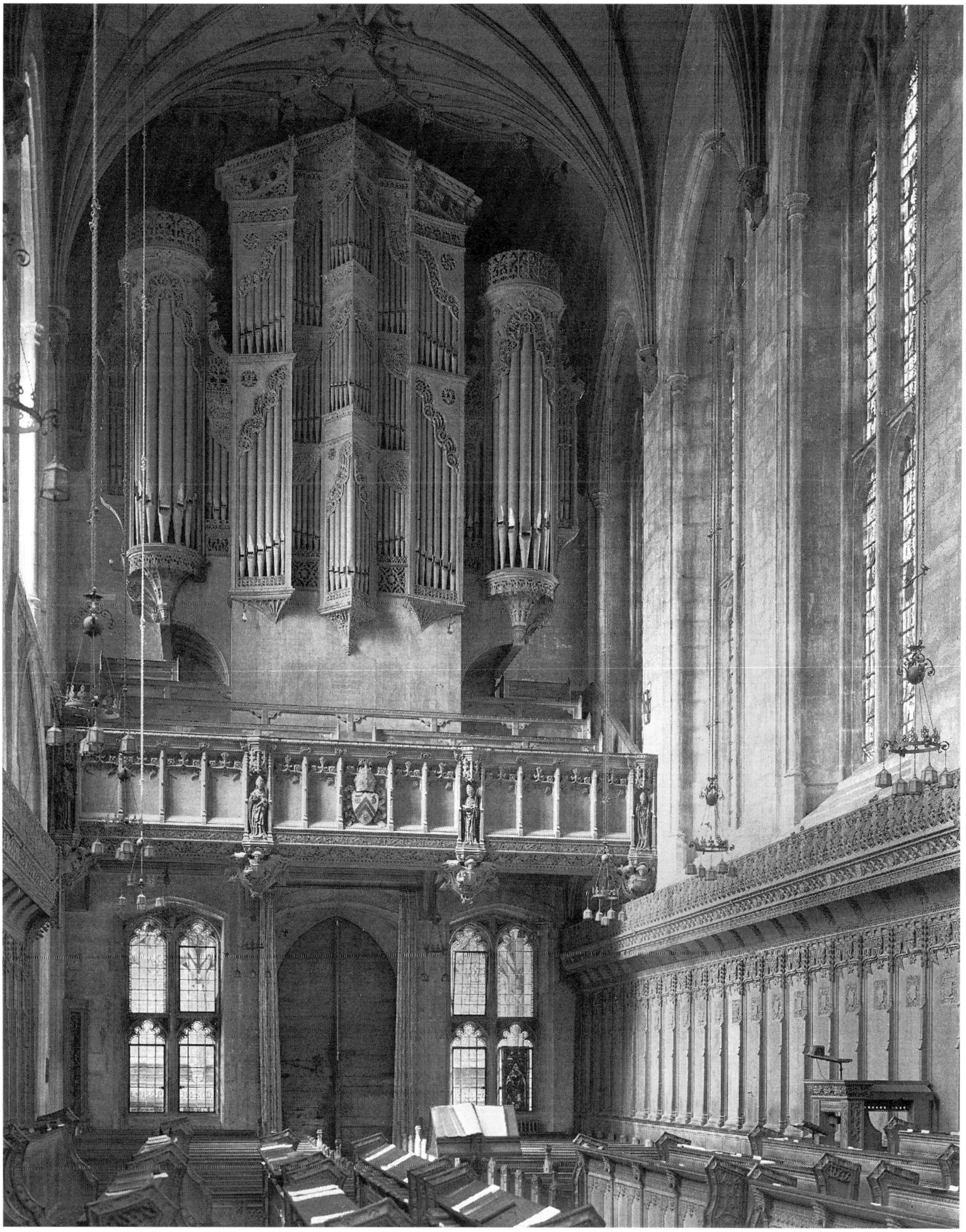

Plate 191 — St Mary College Chapel, Winchester, Hampshire (1937)

Freeman/1197; plate 1470

Plate 192 — Christian Science Church, Cambridge, Cambridgeshire (1937)

Freeman/1205; plate 1478

Plate 193 — St Mary the Virgin, Wotton under Edge, Gloucestershire (1937)

Freeman/1208; plate 1481

Freeman sketched a detail from this case, which is on p.28.

Plate 194 — St Julian, Shrewsbury, Shropshire (1937)

Freeman/1214; plate 1487

Plate 195 — St Mary the Virgin, Hartpury, Gloucestershire (1937)

Freeman/1216; plate 1489

'...whilst talking of towers, what shall we say of the two that flank the rather charming arch-shaped compartment at Hartpury Church, Gloucestershire? Nothing good, I fear. They look sturdy and strong where neither quality needs such emphasis, and they are indisputedly clumsy. The twelve pipes separately set in them are an example of the thing that should never be done, for the veriest tyro could see at once they are a sorry sham... Yet I would not scrap this case, if it were mine though I would consider the effect of three pipes standing under each of the spirettes, The case has a character of its own, and that is to its credit, so I should probably decide not to spoil it.'

The Organ 18, No. 70 (Oct. 1938): 92

Plate 196 — St Michael, Great Witley, Worcestershire (1938)

Freeman/1225; plate 1498

Plate 197 — All Saints, Carshalton, Surrey (1938)

Freeman/1230; plate 1503

Plate 198 — St Peter & St Paul, Appleford, Berkshire (c. 1938)

Freeman/1233; plate 1506

'In a chamber on the north side of the chancel is a pleasing little chamber organ, made by Samuel Green in 1777 and presented to the church by Theobald Theobald, Esq., of Sutton Courtenay, in 1855. It has a mahogany case, with dummy gilt pipes, [and] a sliding keyboard...'

The Organ 19, no. 74 (Oct. 1939): 109

Plate 199 — St Alphege, Solihull, Warwickshire (1938)

Freeman/1235; plate 1508

Plate 200 — St John the Baptist, Coventry, Warwickshire (1938)

Freeman/1236; plate 1509

Plate 201 — St Mary Magdalene, Castle Ashby, Northamptonshire (1938)

Freeman/1237; plate 1510

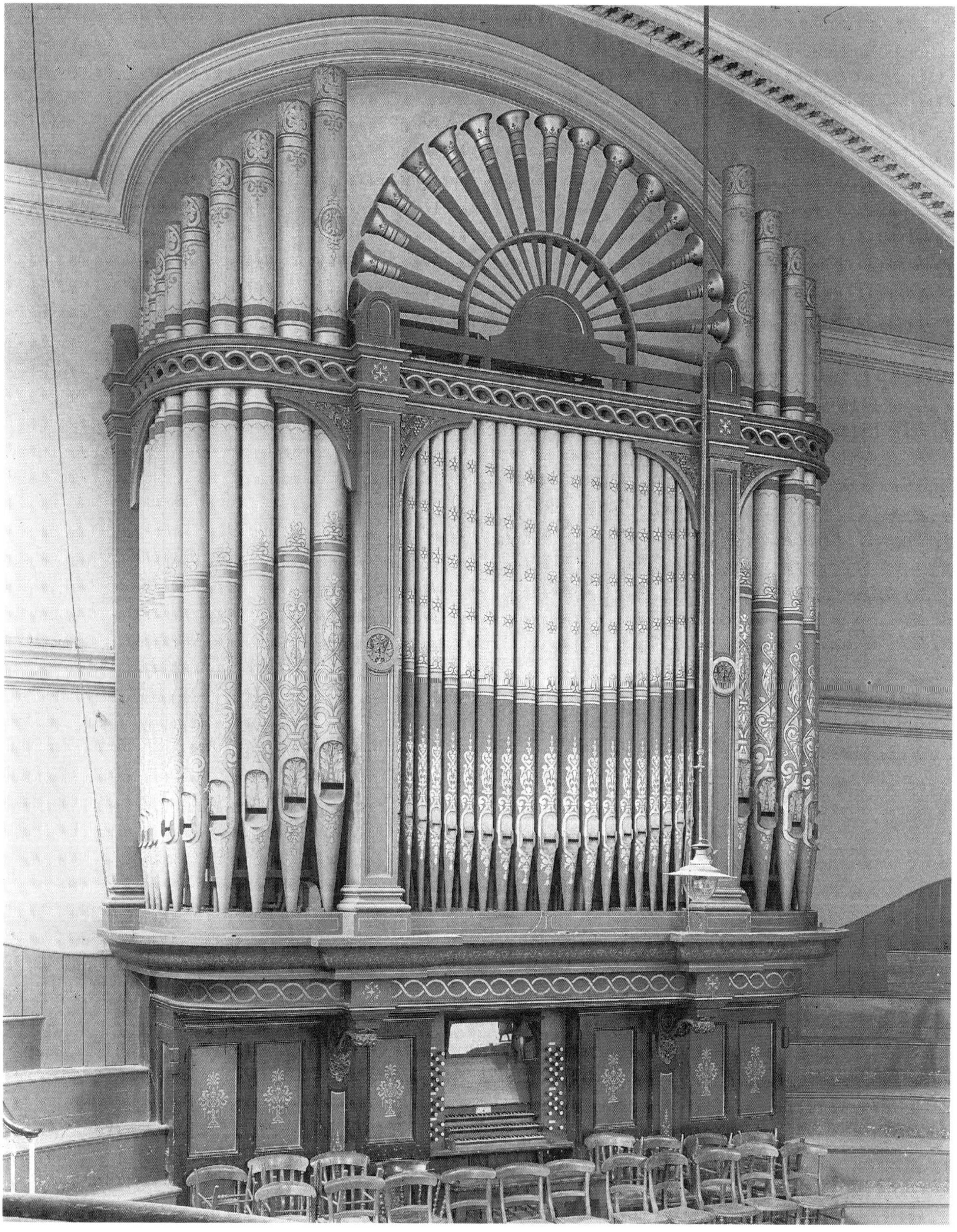

Plate 202 — St John's Hall, Penzance, Cornwall (1938)

Freeman/1245; plate 1518

Plate 203 — St Chrysostum, Hockley, Birmingham (c.1938)

Freeman/1246; plate 1519

Plate 204 — St Thomas, Old Swinford, Stourbridge, Worcestershire (1938)

Freeman/1248; plate 1521

George Pike England organ case, c.1811.

Plate 205 — All Saints, North Cerney, Gloucestershire (1938)

Freeman/1253; plate 1526

Plate 206 — St Catherine, Wormington, Gloucestershire (1938)

Freeman/1255; plate 1528

'In a chapel, on the north side of the chancel, is a quaint looking Gothic organ, made about 1820. It has a mahogany case with five flats of gilt pipes, – all dummies except seven in the middle compartment...'

The Organ 19, no. 74 (Oct. 1939): 109

Plate 207 — Astwood Bank Church, Worcestershire (c. 1938)

Freeman/1256; plate 1529

Plate 208 — Countess of Huntingdon's Chapel, Worcester, Worcestershire (1938)

Freeman/1257; plate 1530

Plate 209 — St Mary the Virgin, Cleobury Mortimer, Shropshire (1938)

Freeman/1267; plate 1540

Plate 210 — Quendon Church, Essex (1939)

Freeman/1275; plate 1548

See also Plate 34, p.104.

Plate 211 — Hilborough Church, Norfolk (c.1939)

Freeman/1277; plate 1550

Plate 212 — St Mary & All Saints, Sculthorpe, Norfolk (1939)

Freeman/1278; plate 1551

Plate 213 — St Swithin, Great Chishill, Cambridgeshire (1939)

Freeman/1280; plate 1553

Plate 214 — St Mary, Westcott, Buckinghamshire (1939)

Freeman/1284; plate 1557

'Of the case little need be said. It is clearly of amateur construction, and was probably added by a former owner who was also responsible for enclosing the whole of the pipes in a swell box. It has a front of blue and gold dummy pipes, whose chief offence is that fifteen of them are of exactly the same length.'

The Organ 19, no.74 (Oct. 1939): 107

Plate 215 — Sigriswil, (near Oberhofen), Pfarrkirche, Switzerland (1939)

Freeman/1289; plate 1562

'In thorough keeping with the [attractive] interior is the jolly little organ case, which stands on the floor facing the people. It is painted brown, and has gilded carving and bright tin pipes in front....It was after 6p.m. and raining, and most of what light there was seemed to come through the windows at the back of the organ. I hardly expected a good photograph under such conditions, but the result was highly satisfactory. The exposure completed (twelve minutes with an *f8* stop), we set off down hill to catch the boat for Gunten...'

The Organ 19, no.76 (April 1940): 206

Freeman's sketch of this organ can be seen on p.65.

Plate 216 — Ringgenberg Pfarrkirche, Switzerland (1939)

Freeman/1294; plate 1567

'...an entrancing little organ. As the colour of the case is brown, the carving gilt, and the front pipes (which have rounded lips) are of bright tin, the general effect is most pleasing: it is a well-designed composition, entirely in harmony with the setting...On [the case] I found an inscription to the effect that Mendelssohn had played on the organ in 1847.'

The Organ 20, no. 77 (July 1940): 30

Plate 217 — Jesuit Church, Lucerne, Switzerland (1939)

Freeman/1297; plate 1570

'a fine case with bright tin pipes and much gilded carving.'

The Organ 19, no. 75 (Jan. 1940): 140

Plate 218 — Franciscan Church, Lucerne, Switzerland, chororgel (1939)

Freeman/1300; plate 1573

'Herr Imahorn, the Chor-direktor of the Franciscan church, took me into the Quire of the church where, from an unused loft above the stalls on the north side, I contrived, not without difficulty, to take a photograph of the fascinating old Chor-orgel opposite. This was constructed by R. Amstalden in 1733, and last used in 1893; all its pipes, except those belonging to the principal, have been stolen by boys.'

The Organ 19, no. 75 (Jan. 1940): 142

Plate 219 — Benedictine Abbey, Einsiedeln, Switzerland, Psallier Choir organ (1939): 1751 Bossart (Zug, Switzerland) organ.

Freeman 1304; plate 1577

'He who designed [the case] was a genius, and a happy one at that; and he was well served by those who shaped the wood and metal in accordance with his fancy.'

The Organ 22, no. 85 (July 1942): 2

Plate 220 — Abbey Church, Muri, Switzerland, North-east case (1939)

Freeman/1319; plate 1592

'Notice how the tops [of the pipes] rake down from the tallest pipe in the centre to the smallest at the two sides, and then notice how the case maker has framed the three sections, fitting his carving most carefully to each of the pipes so that he does not spoil their proportions but rather sets them off. There was perfect collaboration here between pipe-maker and carver: surely those concerned must have had a common mind as well as a common purpose to have achieved such delightful harmony. What we miss in England – what we have missed for nearly a century – through treating the organ almost solely for its appeal to the ear of the listener, and forgetting that if it be made beautiful to the eye its capacity to please is enhanced, and, moreover, does not cease during its many long silences! ...We must not forget the two little compartments at either side: these hold eleven pipes apiece, and form, together with the delicately carved wings, the overhangs that were at one time the sine qua non of all proper fronts, and add grace to those of any period...Surely we have here a perfect case in a perfect setting. Of course it costs money, and now-a-days its expense would be considered prohibitive. But why? Has not the money expended upon it borne a sort of spiritual interest every year of its existence?'

The Organ 22, no. 87 (Jan. 1943): 97–98

Plate 221 — St Martin, Schwyz, Switzerland (1939)

Freeman/1320; plate 1593

'Note the engrailing of the central pipe-shade to fit the unsymmetrical pipe tops. The whole effect is rich and pleasing. The way in which the large and small pipes have been grouped is quite masterly: those responsible for inflicting canister-like fronts on good English organs in lovely English churches could learn a lot from contemplating such a case as this one at Schwyz.'

The Organ 20, No. 78 (Oct. 1940): 68

Plate 222 — Pfarrkirche, Steinen, Switzerland (1939)

Freeman/1325; plate 1598

'...an organ case of outstanding merit. This is one of the brilliantly decorated cases, – red, blue and black on the main structure, and much gold and red on the carved work...Hinged shutters add greatly to the effect. Originally it appears to have had overhanging sides, but the base is now as wide as the upper portion. It is a lovely thing, and one that is entitled to be described as gorgeous.'

The Organ 20, No. 78 (Oct. 1940): 72

Plate 223 — Thornbury Baptist Church, Gloucestershire (1939)

Freeman/1349; plate 1622

Plate 224 — Convent Church of Montorge, Fribourg, Switzerland (1939)

Freeman/1341; plate 1614

'In this church the organ has a really beautiful case. As it is light brown in colour with a profusion of gilded carving and bright tin pipes, it presents quite a brilliant appearance. Perhaps I ought to reserve superlatives for such cases as those at Muri (Chor-orgeln), Quenast, King's College, Cambridge, and a hundred others of greater size and intricacy and of equal workmanship, but this one at Montorge seems to me to be a flawless example of its kind. The proportion of large pipes to small ones, and of the metal and wood displayed in the front, seems absolutely right, and the massing is both skilful and pleasing.'

The Organ 23, no. 90 (Oct. 1943): 75

Plate 225 — St Peter's Parish Church, Pilning, Gloucestershire (1939)

Freeman/1350; plate 1623

Plate 226 — St Swithin, Brookthorpe, Gloucestershire (c.1939)

Freeman/1351; plate 1624

Plate 227 — East Hagbourne Church, Hagbourne, Berkshire (1940)

Freeman/1352; plate 1625

Plate 228 — St Bridget, Skenfrith, Monmouthshire (1940)

Freeman/1355; plate 1628

Plate 229 — Wanstead, London E., Father Smith organ belonging to Captain Lane (1944)

Freeman/1371; plate 1644

Plate 230 — Wanstead, London E., Snetzler organ belonging to Captain Lane (1944)

Freeman/1372; plate 1645

Plate 231 — St Peter & St Paul, Great Bowden, Leicestershire (1944)

Freeman/1375, plate 1648

Plate 232 — St Mary Magdalene, Holloway Rd., Islington, London N (1944)

Freeman/1377, plate 1650

Plate 233 — St John the Baptist, Hoxton, Shoreditch, London E (1944)

Freeman/1379, plate 1652

Plate 234 — St George, King Stanley, Gloucestershire (1945)

Freeman/1386, plate 1659

See also St Rose's Convent, Stroud: Plate 92, p.162.

The Plates – Geographical Index

The county place-names below are given as they were when Freeman would have known them. London is treated separately.

United Kingdom

Bedfordshire

Berkshire

Bristol

Buckinghamshire

Cambridgeshire

Cardiff (Glamorgan)

Cheshire

Cornwall

Devon

Dorset

Essex

Flintshire

Glamorgan

Gloucestershire

Hampshire

Herefordshire

Hertfordshire

Huntingdonshire

Kent

Leicestershire

London

France

Belgium

Austria

Germany

Switzerland